THE HISTORY AND VARIETIES OF JEWISH MEDITATION

The HISTORY AND VARIETIES OF JEWISH MEDITATION

MARK VERMAN

JASON ARONSON INC.
Northvale, New Jersey
London

For credits, see page 225.

This book was set in 12 pt. Antiqua.

Library of Congress Cataloging-in-Publication Data
Verman, Mark, 1949–
    The history and varieties of Jewish meditation / Mark Verman.
      p. cm.
    Includes bibliographical references and index.
    ISBN 1-56821-522-3 (alk. paper)
    1. Meditation—Judaism. 2. Spiritual life—Judaism. 3. Judaism—
Customs and practices. I. Title.
BM723.V427 1996
296.7'2—dc20
                                  95-51819
                                        CIP

Manufactured in the United States of America. Jason Aronson Inc. offers books and cassettes. For information and catalog write to Jason Aronson Inc., 230 Livingston Street, Northvale, New Jersey 07647.

Dedicated to my father,

Samuel Verman, of blessed memory,

and father-in-law,

Cantor Nathan T. Adler, of blessed memory

—you are always in our thoughts.

CONTENTS

PREFACE

There is no one dominant form of traditional Jewish meditation. Rather, there are dozens, if not hundreds, of disparate techniques, ranging from visualizations of Divine Names to candle gazing and chanting. It is not the goal of this book to be comprehensive—merely expansive. This entails an examination of a wide variety of meditative practices, spanning many centuries. Unless otherwise indicated, I have translated all of the primary sources. My goal has been to offer faithful and intelligible readings, as well as to provide sufficient background information, such that the sources become lucid and replicable. This will allow you, the reader, the opportunity to explore various techniques. Hopefully you will incorporate some of these resources into your personal spiritual repetoire.

Several steps have been taken to ensure that the book is user-friendly. Standard abbreviations are delineated immediately after this Preface. Footnotes have been kept to a minimum and usually provide suggestions for further reading. The end of the book includes a Glossary and Selected Bibliography, as well as an Index.

The presentation seeks to combine the academic virtue of methodical study with the creativity and spontaneity of Divine discovery. Some sections, such as Chapter 1, "The Ancient Roots of Jewish Meditation," are more historical in orientation. Others, like Chapter 6, "Breathing" are more experientially focused. It has been my observation that different approaches and techniques resonate with different people. The richness of the Jewish meditative tradition is highly adaptable to promoting widespread spirituality. This variety is one of its greatest assets. The paths to God are diverse; let us begin the journey.

Acknowledgments

"You are the source of life; through Your light we become enlightened" (Psalms 36:10). I render heartfelt gratitude to *Ha-Shem*, Creator of the universe—without whose continuous sustenance nothing could exist.

This project began more than fifteen years ago. While pursuing graduate studies in Jewish mystical literature at Harvard, I started to collect texts that advocated specific meditative practices. Eventually, I amassed a book's worth of selections and tried without success to have it published. Some of these sources formed the basis of a series of articles that appeared a decade ago in *Four Worlds Journal*, a spiritually progressive periodical edited by Edward Hoffman. This material has now been greatly expanded and recast herein.

Modern publications on Jewish meditation are fairly recent and not very numerous. One can start with Gershom Scholem's scholarly article, "Meditation," first published in the *Encyclopedia Judaica* (1972) and reprinted in his collection of essays entitled *Kabbalah* (1978), wherein he offered a pioneering overview of the topic, noting a number of important kabbalistic writers who discussed this issue. A more experiential approach was advocated by Rabbi Zalman Schachter in *A First Step,* published by R. Siegel in *The Jewish Catalogue* (1973). Reb Zalman's *Fragments of Future Scroll: Hassidism For the Aquarian Age* (1975) likewise offered significant hasidic material promoting spiritual awareness. The erudite chapters on mystical activities in sixteenth-century Tzefat (Safed) by R. Werblowsky, *Joseph Karo: Lawyer and Mystic* (1977) are very worthwhile.

It was at this time that the prodigious literary activity of Aryeh Kaplan began. Two of his books on Jewish meditation: *Meditation and the Bible* (1978) and *Meditation and Kabbalah* (1982) have recently been issued by Jason Aronson. The third book in his series *Jewish Meditation: A Practical Guide* (1985) is the most accessible, constituting a wonderful introduction to the topic. Kaplan's translation of Rabbi Nachman of Breslov's *Outpouring of the Soul* is also highly recommended. Two other monographs that are very informative are Moshe Idel's *The Mystical Experience in Abraham Abulafia* (1988) and Yitzhak Buxbaum's monumental sourcebook, *Jewish Spiritual Practices* (Aronson 1990).

I have greatly benefited from all of the above, as will be evident. My appreciation for the dynamics of Jewish meditative practices was enhanced by collaborating with Dr. Deane Shapiro on a major essay, "Jewish Meditation: Context and Content," written for an international colloquium whose proceedings are to be published under the title *Comparative and Psychological Study of Meditation* (Waseda University Press).

Although my exploration of traditional Jewish meditation has entailed much research and study, it has been complemented by the private practice of these sources. I have also been fortunate to share some of this material with students in various courses that I have taught over the years. The experiential element is ultimately what is most important about this enterprise. This book is your personal invitation to participate in traditional Jewish spirituality.

I am truly grateful to Dean Elizabeth McKinsey and Carleton College for their generous assistance with publication expenses. I would also like to thank the staff at Aronson, specifically Arthur Kurzweil, vice-president, Pamela Roth, associate publisher, and Janet Warner, production editor, for their supportiveness. Finally, as the last mentioned is the most beloved—thanks to my beautiful and talented wife, Dr. Shulamit Adler.

ABBREVIATIONS

B. = *Babylonian Talmud*
b. = *ben*, i.e. son of
M. = *Mishnah*
M.T. = Maimonides, *Mishneh Torah*
n.d. = no date
R. = Rabbi
R.M. = *Raaya Mehemna*
T. = *Tosefta*
T.Z. = *Tikkunei Zohar*
Y. = *Jerusalem Talmud*

1

THE ANCIENT ROOTS OF JEWISH MEDITATION

I sought Your nearness;
  with all my heart I called out to You.
When I went out to greet You,
  I discovered You coming to greet me.
            —R. Yehudah Halevi, *Shirim Nivcharim*, 8

We are all seekers, our souls longing to ascend and embrace the Merciful One. How beautifully this is expressed in the *Song of Glory,* attributed to the late 12th century figure R. Yehudah Hasid and traditionally recited at the end of the *Shabbat* morning service. "My soul covets the shade of Your hand, to know the entire mystery of Your secret" (*Shir ha-Kavod,* in *Siddur Rinnat Yisrael,* 295).

According to Rabbi Joseph B. Soloveitchik, of blessed memory—the revered leader of modern Jewish orthodoxy in this country—there is an extralegal requirement, stemming from the original covenant that God established with Abraham. It is the obligation "to strive for religious experiences, in which God is encountered."[1]

Meditation is a path to God, entailing deep reflection and concentration. It is both a preparation for further spiritual activity, by promoting a proper mind-set, and in itself a medium for encountering God. Meditation inhibits the constant flow of everyday thoughts by replacing random, mundane musings with focused contemplation of the Infinite. Through meditation we can become attentative to the Divine imprint upon our lives.

What, then, is Jewish meditation? Virtually all of the material that we shall discuss comes from Hebrew sources. Accordingly, the English word "meditation" does not appear in any of these texts.[2] In fact, seldom are any technical terms utilized, though *hitbodedut* (literally self-isolation/seclusion) appears with some frequency. It seems appropriate, nonetheless, to characterize certain spiritual exercises developed by authoritative Jewish teachers over the last two millenia, as Jewish meditation, insofar as these practices fit the general characterization of meditation.

What is the purpose of Jewish meditation? The fundamental aim is clear—to increase an individual's understanding and experience of the Divine. We generally assume that there exists a chasm separating us from God. Though we may pray to God and hope that our petitions are heard, God often seems remote, transcendent. Meditation is a bridge that enables us to approach the Ultimate.

---

1. W. Wurzburger, *Ethics of Responsibility* (Philadelphia 1994), 15; see p. 117 n. 34 for the circumstances in which this unpublished discourse was delivered.

2. "The English word meditate comes from the Latin *meditari. Meditari* connotes deep, continued reflection, a concentrated dwelling in thought." *The Encyclopedia of Religion* 9:325.

Judaism is the traditional religious experience of the Jewish nation. Holidays and rituals are generally observed in a communal or family setting. Jewish meditation can likewise be practiced in groups. Some of the particular techniques that we shall explore were developed specifically for public prayers; nevertheless, *hitbodedut* usually implies a private act. Rabbi Nahum Schulman cautioned me recently, when I informed him that I was working on a book on Jewish meditation. He encouraged me to emphasize that even when an individual is engaged in private spiritual pursuits, he or she must be aware of, and connected to, the larger community. We shall revisit this important issue at the start of the next chapter.

In the next few pages, after a discussion of the Name of God, we shall offer a brief historical overview of ancient Jewish meditation, starting with the biblical period and continuing until early rabbinic times. Pertinent later commentaries will also be cited to elucidate these sources. This background discussion will provide us with a basic orientation to the tradition of Jewish meditation.

For almost 4,000 years, since the time of Abraham and Sarah, the focus of Judaism has been God—as designated by the four Hebrew letters that can be transliterated *YHVH*. This epithet connotes eternal existence; however, it is commonly rendered in English translations of the Hebrew Scriptures as "Lord."[3] Owing to the absolute sanctity of the Four-Letter Name, which in

---

3. Whereas "Lord" is an appropriate translation of *Adonay*, the standard Hebrew substitution for the Tetragrammaton (i.e., the Four-Letter Name), it does not at all convey the original meaning of *YHVH*, namely, existing eternally.

The substitution of *Adonay* for *YHVH* is based on Exodus 3:15, "this is My Name *le-[o]lam* (perpetually/to hide) and this is My appellation for future generations"; see Rashi's comments thereon, as well as *B. Kiddushin* 71a for a different interpretation.

later Temple times was only vocalized by the High Priest on Yom Kippur (the Day of Atonement), it has become traditional to refer to God as *Ha-Shem*, (literally "The Name," i.e., the ineffable and sacrosanct Name of God, which is unpronounceable and inscrutable). This practice will also be followed in this book.

The High Priest would vocalize the Name while confessing, in preparation for entering the Holy of Holies (see *M. Yoma* 6:2). When he pronounced the Ineffable Name, the entire congregation would prostrate themselves on the ground. This dramatic event has been preserved in the Yom Kippur prayer service, wherein it is reenacted.[4] After the destruction of the Temple, the proper pronunciation of the Name was lost and forgotten. According to R. Nachman b. Yitzhak, in the World to Come it will be restored (see *B. Pesachim* 50a).

In the Temple, there were twenty-six steps from the Holy of Holies to the Ark.[5] Similarly, the numerical value of the Four-Letter Name (*YHVH*) is twenty-six. On Yom Kippur, the High Priest would only climb up to the fifteenth step, lest he be unworthy and punished. The number 15 corresponds to the initial two letters of the Name (i.e., *YH*), which is found in the Torah as the condensed version of the Name of God. The connection between the number 15 and the Israelite priesthood is reinforced owing to the fifteen Hebrew words that constitute the priestly blessing (see Numbers 6:24–26).

This symbolism occured in another aspect of Temple practice. There were fifteen steps from the Court of the Israelites to the Women's Court. The levites would stand on these steps and sing. This is the significance

---

4. For example, *The Complete ArtScroll Machzor* (New York, 1990), 560.

5. This description is based on the text *Brit Menuchah*; cf. L. Jacobs, *Jewish Mystical Testimonies* (New York, 1977), 96. Interestingly, there were twenty-six generations from Adam to Moses.

of the fifteen consecutive Psalms (120–134), which all bear the title, "A Song of Steps" (*shir ha-maalot*).

Great is the power of the Name, even unvocalized. The following is a meditative prayer, *migdal oz* (Tower of Strength), which is recited on Rosh Hashanah and Yom Kippur, while the cantor intones *Alenu*:

> The Name of *Ha-Shem* is a tower of strength. By means of It the righteous can run and be exalted. Master of the universe, from the day the Temple was destroyed we have nothing that promotes atonement: no sacrifices, priestly garments, grain offerings, slaughtering and no altar—only Your great Name sustains us. (*Machazor Rabba*, 207)

Let us now begin our overview. The Hebrew Scriptures are replete with spiritual directives, which form the basis of Jewish meditation. "For you, who adhere (*ha-devekim*) to *Ha-Shem* your God, are all alive today" (Deuteronomy 4:4). From this verse the Rabbis deduced that *devekut* (attachment) to God is life-sustaining and will ultimately result in resurrection (cf. *B. Sanhedrin* 90b). The Psalms contain countless verses of great spiritual power such as, "In God alone is my soul quiet; from Him comes my salvation" (Psalms 62:2), or, "Seek out *Ha-Shem* and His mighty deeds; demand His presence always" (Psalms 105:3).

The seminal formulation for achieving *devekut* is ascribed to King David, "I have continuously placed (*shiviti*) *Ha-Shem* before me; He is at my right hand so that I shall not falter" (Psalms 16:8). The ancient Rabbis cited this verse as indicating that "one who prays should perceive the Divine Presence before him" (*B. Sanhedrin* 22a). This verse also gave rise to various meditative techniques in which the Divine Name is visualized, as will be illustrated in subsequent chapters. Starting in the Middle Ages and continuing until today, domestic amulets bearing this verse and referred to as a *shiviti* have been popular in certain Jewish cultures.[6]

The above-cited psalm encourages constant mindfulness of the Divine Being (see also Isaiah 62:6). It was incorporated into mainstream *halachah* (standard Jewish practice), in the opening comments of R. Moshe Isserles (Rama) in his notations on the *Shulhan Aruch*.[7]

> "I have continuously placed *Ha-Shem* before me" (Psalms 16:8)—this is the cardinal principle of the Torah and the ideal of the righteous who walk before God. For an individual would not sit or move or act alone in their house, as they would sit or move or act in the presence of a great king[;] ... how much more so when one realizes that the great King, the Holy One, blessed be He, whose Glory fills the world, is always present and watching one's activities. . . . Immediately, one would be overcome by fear and humility in awe of *Ha-Shem*. . . . When an individual awakens from sleep, he should arise quickly to serve his Creator. (*Orah Hayyim* 1:1)

In addition to the spiritual directives that are found in the Hebrew Scriptures, there are indications that specific biblical figures engaged in meditation. Admittedly, this material is very sketchy. In examining this issue, we shall first consider references to two of the biblical Patriarchs, Isaac and Jacob, and then continue with a discussion of biblical prophecy. To aid in our understanding of this material and its connection with meditation, we shall cite the explanations of medieval rabbinic commentators.

According to the account in Genesis 24:63, Isaac would venture out into the fields at sunset *la-suach*, "to

---

6. This is well documented in T. Schrire, *Hebrew Magic Amulets* (New York, 1982), 87–90, 147–149.

7. As R. Moshe clarifies in his *Darkei Moshe, Tur Orah Hayyim* 1:1, he based his formulation upon Maimonides's *Guide of the Perplexed*, trans. S. Pines (Chicago, 1963), 3:52 (not 3:32), as is listed therein.

commune/meditate." During one such excursion, he was encountered by his bride-to-be, Rebekah, who was so overpowered by Isaac's intensity that she fell off her camel. Although the biblical text does not provide any details of Isaac's meditative method, biblical exegetes have probed this passage for hints. For example, R. Avraham Saba, a Spanish exile writing around 1500, commented:

> "Isaac went into the field to commune" to isolate himself (le-hitboded) and pray with concentration. . . . "He lifted his eyes and saw camels approaching" (Genesis 24:64). Evidently, until that time he had lowered his eyes and closed them, in order to concentrate. . . . For the Shechinah (Divine Presence) is opposite someone who is reciting the Amidah (Standing) prayer; therefore, [while praying] it is forbidden to open one's eyes and gaze at the wall. (Tzeror ha-Mor, 53)

Nor do we know what technique Isaac's son, Jacob, utilized. R. Avraham b. Maimonides, a twelfth-century sage, asserted in his commentary on the verse, "Jacob was left alone" (Genesis 32:25):

> Jacob isolated himself (hitboded) physically: no servants nor objects remained with him. He ascended from physical self-isolation into a spiritual self-isolation. Finally, he perceived in a prophetic vision that it seemed as if a man was wrestling with him. This actually was an angel, as it is written concerning Gabriel, "And the man Gabriel . . . " (Daniel 9:21). (Perush ha-Torah le-Rabbenu Avraham ben ha-Rambam, 108).

In this brief discussion of seclusion as a preparation for spiritual elevation, R. Avraham reflects the teachings of his illustrious father, Maimonides. In the Mishneh Torah, Maimonides examined the nature of biblical prophecy and, in so doing, makes explicit the connection between biblical prophecy and meditation.

> The biblical prophets did not prophesize whenever they wanted. Rather, they directed their minds and sat joyfully

and contentedly in a state of self-isolation—for prophecy does not occur in sadness or lassitude, but only in joyousness. (*M.T., Yesodei ha-Torah* 7:4)

In the preceding citations, the term *self-isolation* (*hitbodedot*) is utilized by these writers in a twofold manner. It simultaneously refers to physical withdrawal from social interactions, as well as a synonym for the act of meditation itself.

The connection between prophecy and meditation is complex. Few biblical accounts provide sufficient information to arrive at firm conclusions. Whereas some prophetic visions were spontaneous, others were self-induced, as noted by Maimonides. (In Chapter 7, we shall consider the role of music in promoting a mind-set conducive to meditation and even prophecy.)

In the postbiblical period, beginning around 200 B.C.E. and continuing for a number of centuries, we find evidence of various Jewish groups that developed an intense form of spirituality, which included meditation. We shall consider three distinct movements: the *Hasidim Rishonim*, the Therapeutae, and finally, the *Hechalot* mystics.

The *Hasidim Rishonim* (early pietists), referred to by scholars as Hasideans, are first mentioned in historical documents from the second century B.C.E. According to a later rabbinic tradition, they incorporated meditation into their daily prayers.

The Hasideans would be still (*shohin*) one hour prior to each of the [three] prayer services, then pray for one hour and afterwards be still again for one hour. Since they were still and prayed nine hours each day, how was their Torah knowledge preserved and their work accomplished? Because they were pietists, their Torah knowledge was preserved and their work was Divinely blessed. (*B. Berachot* 32b)

Although the specifics of their practice have not been preserved, Maimonides, the great twelfth-century rabbinic authority, notes the following in his commentary to the *Mishnah, Berachot 5:1*:

> The explanation of *shohin* is they restrained themselves: that is to say, they restrained themselves for one hour prior to praying in order to settle their minds and quiet their thoughts. Only then would they pray.

Two thousand years ago, a second group of Jewish contemplatives built a community around the Mareotic Lake near Alexandria, Egypt. The only historical account of their activities is by Philo of Alexandria, a seminal Jewish philosopher and statesman. Philo labels them Therapeutae, healers; namely, "therapists of the spirit." For six days of the week the Therapeutae would reside separately, each in his or her own dwelling. Their days were devoted entirely to spiritual pursuits, in fulfillment of the biblical directives to be continuously mindful of God. Then, on *Shabbat* they would gather together for communal prayer, study, and meals.

It should be noted that both men and women were members of the Therapeutae. This deserves special mention, insofar as the involvement of women in ancient Jewish religious praxis and especially spirituality is severely underrecorded.[8] Note that the Therapeutae were so successful at being ever mindful of God that this impacted their dreams, as well.

> In each house there is a sacred chamber, which is called a sanctuary or closet, in which in isolation they are initiated into the mysteries of the holy life. They take nothing into it, neither drink, nor food, nor anything else necessary for bodily needs, but laws and oracles delivered through the prophets, and psalms and the other books through which

---

8. It is revealing that the recent anthology, *Four Centuries of Jewish Women's Spirituality*, ed. E. Umansky and D. Ashton (Boston, 1992), begins with seventeenth-century sources; moreover, even this period is sparsely represented.

knowledge and piety are increased and perfected. They always remember God and never forget Him, so that even in their dreams no images are formed other than the loveliness of divine excellences and powers. Thus many of them, dreaming in their sleep, divulge the glorious teachings of their holy philosophy.

Twice daily they pray, at dawn and at eventide; at sunrise they pray for a joyful day, joyful in the true sense that their minds may be filled with celestial light. At sunset, they pray that the soul may be fully relieved from the disturbance of the senses and the objects of sense, and that retired to its own consistory and council chamber it may search out the truth. The entire interval between early morning and evening is devoted to spiritual exercise. They read the Holy Scriptures and apply themselves to their ancestral philosophy by means of allegory, since they believe that the words of the literal text are symbols of a hidden nature, revealed through its underlying meanings. . . . And so they not only apply themselves to contemplation, but also compose chants and hymns to God in all kinds of meters and melodies. (D. Winston, trans., *Philo of Alexandria*, 46)

Scholars speculate that the work known as the *Wisdom of Solomon* was either composed by the Therapeutae or influenced them. This text portrays Wisdom as a feminine entity and the Divine companion at the beginning of time. This theme is adumbrated in Proverbs 8:22–30, wherein Wisdom asserts: "The Lord fashioned me at the beginning of His enterprise—the first of His primordial works. . . . I was nurtured by Him, a daily delight, continuously playing in His presence."

Undoubtedly, these verses influenced the following description in *Wisdom of Solomon* (7:22–8:1).

For in wisdom there is a spirit intelligent and holy, unique in its kind. . . . For wisdom moves more easily than motion itself, she pervades and permeates all things because she is so pure. Like a fine mist she rises from the power of God, a pure effluence from the glory of the Almighty; so nothing defiled can enter into her by stealth. She is the brightness that streams from everlasting light, the flawless mirror of the active power of God and the image of His goodness. She is but one, yet can do everything; herself unchanging, she makes all things new; age after age she enters into holy souls, and makes them God's friends and prophets, for nothing is acceptable to God but the man who makes his home with wisdom. . . . She spans the world in power from end to end, and orders all things benignly. (*The New English Bible with the Apocrypha*, 104–105)

Beginning with a text from the second century B.C.E., known as 1 Enoch, there is an extensive collection of Jewish writings that describe celestial journeys to the seven Heavens. Most of these works can be classified as pseudepigraphic, in that they are attributed to legendary figures. In 1 Enoch 14:8–9 we read,

And behold I saw the clouds: And they were calling me in a vision; and the fogs were calling me; and the course of the stars and the lightnings were rushing me and causing me to desire, and in the vision, the winds were causing me to fly and rushing me high up into heaven. And I kept coming [into heaven] until I approached a wall which was built of white marble and surrounded by tongues of fire. (J. Charlesworth, ed., *The Old Testament Pseudepigrapha* 1:20)

The narrator continues by describing the power and majesty of the heavens, the angelic hosts and the Divine Glory, in somewhat similar terms to Ezekiel's vision, as recorded in the initial chapter of the Book of Ezekiel.

Before proceeding, let me add a few words about the intriguing biblical figure, Enoch, to whom the preceding material was attributed. The narrative in Genesis is short and suggestive. Unlike Enoch's ancestors and immediate descendants, who lived for almost a thousand years—for example, Enoch's son, Methuselah lived 969 years—Enoch *only* lived for 365 years. The entire biblical account states: "Enoch walked with God 300 years after the birth of Methuselah, and he generated sons and daughters. All of Enoch's days were 365 years. Enoch walked with God and he was no more, for God had taken him" (Genesis 5:22–24).

This last verse was interpreted by the ancients as an example of someone who was physically elevated to Heaven. It is, therefore, related to the story of Elijah being taken to Heaven in a fiery chariot (see 2 Kings 2:11). Although the classical narratives focus on Enoch's celestial sojourn and his transformation into the supernal angel Metatron, there is a medieval tradition that is also worth noting. In it Enoch became the paradigm for someone who is able to transform a mundane task into a spiritual activity.

The earliest version of this popular motif was recorded by R. Yitzhak of Acco around 1300:

> I asked my teacher, R. Yehudah, the Ashkenazic biblical expositor, "Why was Enoch so deserving of all of this?" . . . He answered that he had received a tradition that Enoch was a shoemaker, that is he sewed shoes. With each and every hole that he made in the leather with an awl, he would recite a blessing with a complete heart and with complete concentration for *Ha-Shem's* sake, may He be blessed. . . . He never forgot to recite a blessing for even one hole. He always did this until his love [for *Ha-Shem*] was so intense that "he was no more, for God had taken him" (Genesis 5:24). He merited being called Metatron and his status is exceedingly elevated. (*Meirat Aynayim*, ed. A. Goldreich, 47)[9]

Several centuries later, R. Yosef Karo expanded upon this theme by connecting Metatron, the angelic manifestation of Enoch, with the kabbalistic doctrine of the ten intraDivine states known as *Sefirot*. In this context, Enoch was associated with the lowest of the *Sefirot*, which is referred to by various names, including

---

9. Thanks to Professor Goldreich for pointing out this source, as well as the erudite references on p. 398 of his edition of *Meirat Aynayim* (Jerusalem, 1981).

Malchut (Sovereignty) and *Shechinah,* the feminine manifestation of the Divine Presence.

> As they said about Enoch who was a shoemaker, each time he threaded his needle into the sandal he would praise the Holy One, blessed be He. The secret of this matter is that he is Metatron, who is the shoe of the Matron (i.e. *Malchut/ Shechinah*). He joins Her with the King, by means of the actions of the righteous ones, which he elevates Above to Them and draws down from Above the abundance of Their blessings to feed the worlds. Accordingly, he (i.e. Enoch) is His shoe and since he was righteous, the Holy One, blessed be He, elevated him from this world, prior to his sinning, and he became a fire amidst the torches of fire. Hence Metatron was transformed from flesh in fire, which is the meaning of 'and he was no more, for God had taken him' (Genesis 5:24). (R. Yosef Karo, *Maggid Mesharim,* 42)[10]

This narrative was subsequently crystallized in hasidic literature: "As our Sages, of blessed memory, said about Enoch, who sewed leather shoes and with each stitch he said, 'For the sake of the unity of the Holy One, blessed be He and His *Shechinah*'" (R. Dov Baer of Mezeritch, *Maggid Devarav le-Yaakov,* 164).

Beginning with the ethical writings of the sixteenth-century Kabbalists, this expression, which is here-

---

10. *Maggid Mesharim* (Jerusalem, 1970) is one of the most fascinating Jewish texts. It is the mystical diary of R. Yosef Karo, the seminal rabbinic authority and author of the *Shulhan Aruch. Maggid Mesharim* is a journal of the secret Torah instruction that Karo received nightly, over a forty-year span, from his angelic mentor. This book is the subject of R. Werblowsky's superb study, *Joseph Karo: Lawyer and Mystic.*

The kabbalistic legend of Enoch, the shoemaker, was developed by R. Menachem Azariah of Fano. He contended that with each stitch Enoch would recite the liturgical formula: "Blessed is the Name of His glorious kingdom forever." Fano's version was included in *Yalkut Reuveni* (Warsaw, 1892), 1:120, an important mid-seventeenth-century collection of *Midrashim* and kabbalistic interpretations.

in attributed to Enoch, became a standard formula that is recited prior to the performance of any commandment.[11]

Returning to the classical period and the theme of celestial journeying, one of the few autobiographical accounts is Paul's first-century (C.E.) report, found in 2 Corinthians 12:2-4.[12] He is undoubtedly referring to himself, though modestly, in the third person.

> I know a man . . . who fourteen years ago was caught up to the third heaven. Whether it was in the body or out of the body I do not know—God knows. And I know that this man—whether in the body or apart from the body I do not know, but God knows—was caught up to paradise. He heard inexpressible things, things that man is not permitted to tell.

It is quite interesting that Paul himself is uncertain if this event was an out-of-body experience or physical teleportation.

An early mystical text from the rabbinic period is a commentary on the opening chapter of Ezekiel, entitled *The Visions of Ezekiel*. The anonymous author was intrigued by a seemingly mundane detail in the opening verse of Ezekiel, which reads, "And it was in the thirtieth year, on the fifth day of the fourth month that I was in the diaspora on the Chebar river when the heavens opened and I saw visions of God." He explained the phrase "*on* the Kebar river" as follows:

> Thus Ezekiel stood on the Chebar river and was gazing in the water when the seven heavens opened up for him and he saw the holy Glory and the Creatures and ministering angels and the celestial hordes and the fiery angels and the winged beings attached to the Chariot. They were travers-

---

11. An excellent study of the evolution of this saying and its incorporation into the liturgy is found in L. Jacobs, *Hasidic Prayer* (New York, 1978), 140–153.

12. New International Version.

ing Heaven and Ezekiel saw them in the water. That is why it states "*on* the Chebar river." (I. Gruenwald, "Reuyyot Yehezkel," *Temirin* 1 [1972]: 113–114)

The rabbinic period also produced a collection of texts known as *Hechalot* (Celestial Palaces/Temples) literature. The central figures in these writings were the prominent second-century Rabbis Akiva, Yishmael, and their colleagues, who ascended to the Heavens and gazed upon the Divine Chariot. An example of the praxis advocated by these texts is the following: "R. Akiva said, Anyone who wishes to master this authoritative teaching and fully explicate the Divine Name shall sit and fast for forty days. He shall place his head between his knees until the fast has conquered him. Then he shall whisper to the earth and not heaven, for the earth shall hear him, but not heaven" (*Hechalot Zutarti*, R. Elior, ed., 36).

Ostensibly, this text offers specific directives on how to become a *Hechalot* mystic. The requirement for fasting forty days, however, is presumably symbolic. It alludes to Moses' forty-day sojourn on Mount Sinai, after the revelation of the Ten Commandments (cf. Exodus 24:18).

In general, the *Hechalot* writings are complex and difficult to understand; nevertheless, their goal is to have the practitioner focus on the Divine realm. As a first step on the arduous path advocated by *Hechalot* mystics, we shall conclude this chapter with two basic meditations that promote this process of visionary focusing. The first is from a sixteenth-century manual by R. Eleazar Azikri.

At special times you should go off to a secluded place, where no one can see you. Lift your eyes upwards to the unique King, the First Cause and Prime Mover, like a bull's-eye for an arrow, "like water reflects a face, so to the human heart reflects another person" (Proverbs 27:19). In this manner, when you direct your face to God, He will turn to you—then you will adhere together. Thus I have heard directly from my teacher and Rabbi, the holy *hasid*, the honorable Rabbi Yosef Sagis, may he be remembered for eternity. This is what he would do. (*Sefer Haredim*, 309)

A similar, though somewhat more involved, meditative technique was suggested by one of the last hasidic rebbes to be active in the Warsaw ghetto, prior to its destruction in 1943. R. Kalonymus Kalmish Peasetzna suggested that if someone is having trouble visualizing that he or she is standing in the Divine Presence, he or she should go outside.

Look to Heaven and contemplate. Concentrate your mind and think, I am standing [here] beyond the heavens and beyond that is another Heaven, a totally different realm. The angels and the fiery angels and all of the souls of the ancestors, prophets and righteous are there and in their midst is the Throne of Glory. *Ha-Shem*, the great, holy and awesome, is seated upon it. The hidden God is also present in this realm. There the splendor of His Glory is likewise revealed.

Concentrate, look and reflect: I am standing here beyond Heaven, praying to Him, who is blessed, "Blessed are You, *Ha-Shem*. . . ." I bless You, to whom my eyes are upraised. Whether I can see You or not, I concentrate my vision and gaze upon You—blessing and conversing with You, *Ha-Shem*. (*Hovat ha-Talmidim*, 27b)

This concludes our historical overview of ancient Jewish references to meditation and related spiritual activities, including prophecy. The earliest sources concerned specific individuals, such as Isaac, who meditated in private. In the postbiblical period, groups like the Hasideans and Therapeutae emerged, indicating that entire communities were devoted to this pursuit. In general, we lack information about the specifics of their meditative praxis, though medieval and modern practitioners afford us some insight. Additionally, in Chapter 8, we shall offer a detailed presentation of an ancient Jewish meditation.

What we have already seen, and will become even clearer throughout this book, is that unlike in some Eastern religions, there has not been regulated meditation in Judaism—rather, individuals and small groups developed an array of spiritual exercises. Accordingly, it is difficult, and perhaps even unnecessary, to try and characterize Jewish meditation. Owing to the personalization of Jewish spirituality, meditation has remained quite flexible and open-ended. In the following chapters, we shall explore dozens of different techniques. Hopefully, some of this material will resonate with each of you.

2

ORIENTATION AND PREPARATION

For the first few months of life, all newborns have an innate ability to swim and can thereby survive being thrown into water. As an infant grows older, however, it loses this skill and needs to be taught how to swim— so, too, it is with *devekut* (attachment to God). We are all able to connect with *Ha-Shem* and yet, when we try to intellectualize and verbalize this process, we become tongue-tied and insecure. Learning how to meditate is like learning how to swim. On a fundamental level, it is very natural; nevertheless, there is much to discover and master.

We will start this chapter, which focuses on background issues and preparatory steps, with a cautionary note involving an explanation of the traditional restriction of teaching Jewish mysticism only to mature individuals. This will be followed by a discourse on the communal imperative in Jewish spirituality and its rootedness in the revelation of the Torah. In the latter half of the chapter, we will consider appropriate preparations for fruitful meditation.

Many of the sources in this book are derived from the mystical tradition known as the *Kabbalah*. There is a commonplace notion that one must be at least forty years old in order to study such esoteric material. It stems from a mid-eighteenth-century decree by the Rabbinical Council of Brody in response to the Sabbatean and Frankist heresies. This rabbinical body advocated restricting the study of the *Zohar* and R. Moshe Cordovero's writings to age thirty and Lurianic texts to forty.[1] This concern about the spread of Sabbatean heresy is no longer relevant. A more appropriate approach was advocated by the kabbalists themselves, as expressed by R. Moshe Cordovero:

> Also, [the student] has to have reached at least [his] twentieth year in order to have achieved at least half the age of "understanding"; (see *M. Avot* 5:25). Though some have stated [that this study should not be undertaken] until he reaches his fortieth year, we disagree. Many have acted in accordance with our opinion and succeeded. (I. Robinson, *Moses Cordovero's Introduction to Kabbalah: An Annotated Translation of His Or Neerav*, 56)

Using Cordovero's criterion as a basis, an individual should be a responsible adult before engaging in serious mystical studies, in order to appreciate the value of this challenging material. It seems that, in general, the Sephardim have followed this advice and the Ashkenazim have ignored it. For example, the Ashkenazi savant, the Vilna Gaon (1720–1797) studied

---

1. On this issue, see R. Elior, "Natan Adler . . . ," *Tzion* 59:1 (1994): 57 n. 85, and the sources cited therein. Moshe Idel has demonstrated that the original impetus for applying age limits came from the Islamic philosopher and medical authority Ibn Sina, who asserted that a person's intellectual capacity was not fully developed until forty; see M. Idel, "Le-Toldot . . . ," *A.J.S. Review* 5 (1980): 1–20.

complex kabbalistic works at age nine. When he was twelve, he set out to create a *golem* (humanoid), by means of *Sefer Yetzirah*; however, he received a heavenly sign to desist.[2]

We have previously mentioned that there is a dialectical tension that exists between an individual who wishes to achieve spiritual elevation in isolation and the centripetal force of Judaism, which requires Jews to function as members of a national community. Ruth's declaration to Naomi can be seen as paradigmatic: "your people shall be my people and your God, my God" (Ruth 1:16). If taken literally, the lesson of this verse is that one must first self-actualize within the national context, before intimacy with *Ha-Shem* is possible.

The opposing tendencies of isolation versus communal connectedness are succinctly expressed in the paradoxical dictum of the hasidic master, R. Moshe Leib of Sassov, "It is good to practice separation (*prishut*) in the company of others" (*Tzevvaot Ve-Hanhagot*, 101). A classical formulation of this notion is: "it is good to practice *hitbodedut* by acquiring a partner" (*Reshit Hochmah ha-Shalem, Shaar ha-Kedushah*, 6:19). Insofar as this dialectic is such a basic issue, it is worthwhile to consider it at some length.

In order to better appreciate the communal imperative of Judaism and its role in Jewish spirituality, we shall examine a series of sources that discuss various aspects of this topic. Let us start by considering an exposition by the hasidic master, R. Kalonymus Kalman Epstein. He commented on the pivotal biblical verse, "Speak to the entire Israelite community and

---

2. See the sources cited by G. Scholem, *Sabbatai Sevi* (Princeton, NJ, 1973), 203 n. 14, and R. Werblowsky, *Joseph Karo: Lawyer and Mystic* (Philadelphia, 1977), 313; see also Elie Wiesel's reminiscences of studying *Kabbalah* as a boy, in *Night* (Toronto, 1986), 1–5.

say to them: 'You shall be holy, for I, *Ha-Shem*, your God, am holy'" (Leviticus 19:2). He began his discourse by mentioning that Rashi, the medieval biblical commentator par excellence, noted that the ethical directive of imitating *Ha-Shem* was conveyed in a national assembly.

A person might mistakenly think that the interpretation of "you shall be holy" is achieved by isolating oneself (*yitboded atzmo*) and separating oneself from the community and in that way he will achieve holiness. It is for this reason that Rashi informed us that [these instructions] were proclaimed during a national gathering. That is to say that a person cannot achieve holiness unless he joins the community of seekers of *Ha-Shem*; however, concerning those issues that are obstacles to serving *Ha-Shem*, from them it is good to isolate oneself. . . .

Behold, there are people who think that the path to service of *Ha-Shem*, may He be blessed, and to achieve *devekut* (attachment) is through *hitbodedut*—that a person would isolate himself within a room and study there and not speak to or be seen by anyone and that this is the essential service that will lead to *devekut*. This, however, is not completely true; a person can isolate himself for many years and not speak to anyone else and still not arive at the truth.

I once heard from my master and teacher, the famous Rabbi Elimelech of Lizhensk, may the memory of the righteous and saintly be for a blessing, the explanation of "Can a person hide in a hiding-place and I shall not see him, says *Ha-Shem*?" (Jeremiah 23:24). A person may isolate himself in a special, private room and think that this is the essential service [of God], but the Holy One, blessed be He said, "and I shall not see him"—that is to say that even I [i.e., God], as it were, will not see him.

Rather, the essential service is when a person joins with righteous and proper Jews and in this way he can come to serving *Ha-Shem* in truth through studying their good deeds— for the quintessence is to isolate thought by constantly thinking about the exaltedness of his God, may He be blessed, even when he is in the midst of a large crowd, he should attach his thought constantly to the Creator, may He be blessed. (Kalonymus Kalman Epstein, *Meor va-Shemesh* 1:360)

Some people feel that the Jewish demand for communal involvement is merely burdensome and lacks any substantial theoretical basis. In fact, it reflects the ethical underpinnings of Judaism. Its core is the moral imperative, "You shall love your friend as yourself" (Leviticus 19:18). R. Akiva, the pivotal talmudic sage, commented, "This is the great principle of the entire Torah." Akiva's colleague, Ben Azzai, extended it even further by claiming, "'This is the Book of the Generations of Adam' (Genesis 5:1). This principle is even greater than that one" (*Sifra, Kedoshim,* 19:18.). In other words, Ben Azzai felt that R. Akiva's statement might imply that ethics only involves Jews, by referring to Adam, Ben Azzai sought to include all human beings—in that we are all equally created "in the image of God" (Genesis 1:27).

R. Eliyahu de Vidas, in his monumental *Reshit Hochmah,* explains the spiritual mechanics of love in a very interesting fashion:

> The love of one person for another is by means of the soul (*nefesh*), for love is the desire of the soul. Even though bodies are distinct and separate from each other, souls are spiritual. Spirituality is not predicated on separation but on unique and absolute unity. When the soul of someone awakens her desire to love another, the soul of this person likewise awakens to love. Then the two souls become one, as it is written in connection with David and Jonathan "The soul of Jonathan was bound up with David's soul and Jonathan loved him, like himself" (lit., like his soul) (1 Samuel 18:1). (*Reshit Hochmah Ha-Shalem, Shaar ha-Ahavah,* 1:25, 361)

Love and compassion for another within the context of spiritual pursuits have been implemented in many different ways. What follows are several examples. The first is from a discussion by Rabbi Walter Wurzburger concerning the talmudic sage R. Eleazar.

> Ethical conduct, especially to the extent that it involves imitation of the ways of God, is an avenue to Him. The

widely copied practice of R. Eleazar, who gave charity *before* the recital of prayers, illustrates this point (*B. Baba Batra* 10a). He did not treat prayer as a prelude to ethical living. Instead, basing his practice on the biblical verse, "I shall behold Thy face with righteousness" (Psalms 17:15), he looked upon ethical conduct as a prerequisite for proper communion with God. (*Ethics of Responsibility*, 112f.)

Consider also the directive by R. Yitzhak Luria, the revolutionary mystic from sixteenth-century Tzefat, to his disciples.

Furthermore, my teacher, of blessed memory, admonished me and all the *haverim* (colleagues) that belonged to his *hevrah* (group), that before the morning prayer we should accept upon ourselves the positive commandment "and you shall love your friend as yourself" (Leviticus 19:18). A person should intend to love every Jew like oneself, for by this means his prayer will ascend, included with all of Israel. It will be able to ascend and to bring about the restoration above. Especially important is the love of all our *haverim* [towards each other]. Each and every one must include himself, such that he is one of the limbs of these *haverim*. My teacher, of blessed memory, especially admonished me concerning this matter. If, God forbid, any *haver* is plagued by anguish or his wife or children are sick, then one should join in his pain and pray for him. Thus, in every matter one should join together with his *haverim*. (R. Hayyim Vital, *Shaar ha-Gilgulim* no. 38, 333)

What emerges from an involvement in the well-being of others is the realization of mutual interdependence. It is best summarized by the maxim, "All Jews are responsible for each other" (*B. Shevuot* 39a). The Hebrew word for "responsible," *arevim*, connotes mixed or comingled—a very graphic way of depicting interdependence. Another meaning of this word is "sweet," which can be interpreted as referring to the benefits of the relationship.

This sense of responsibility is illustrated in an interesting anecdote, concerning the Besht, the founder of

Hasidism, and his brother-in-law, R. Gershon Kutover, who was likewise a prominent kabbalist. Once, R. Gershon visited the Besht. It was a Friday afternoon and they recited *minchah* (the afternoon prayer) together.

The Besht stood and prolonged the afternoon prayer until nightfall. R. Gershon had likewise used the *Siddur* (prayer book) of the Ari, of blessed memory.[3] Then he reviewed the weekly Torah recitation three times and had pillows delivered so that he could rest.

At the Sabbath nighttime meal R. Gershon asked his brother-in-law, the Besht, why he had excessively prolonged his prayers and gestured vigorously. . . . At first the Besht laughed and did not reply. Upon further questioning the Besht responded, "When I reach the expression 'He resurrects the dead' and I undertake the *yichudim* (unifications) [see Chapter Eleven], tens of thousands of souls from deceased individuals approach me and I must speak to each one as to why that person was excluded from His realm [i.e. Heaven]. Then I perform a *tikkun* [rectification] and pray for that person in order to elevate him. The most important take precedence. There are so many that if I wanted to elevate them all, I would have to stand in prayer for three years. It is only when I hear the proclamation that the Sabbath is being sanctified and it is no longer possible to elevate the souls that I cease praying." (*Shivhei ha-Besht*, A. Rubinstein, ed., 97f.)

R. Avraham Kalisker, a hasidic master, wrote extensively on the social aspect of *devekut*. Therein, he addressed the issue of the benefits of being involved in a spiritual community.

It is a wonderful boon for the individual to continuously have the advantage of Divine Providence through his associates who are attached in *devekut* with God, and to be eligible for all good things and success in the uplift of body and soul. . . . Now if some misfortune befall him . . . all he needs to do

---

3. R. Yittzhak Luria's more meditative version of the liturgy.

is to make his misfortune known to the many with whom he is in a relationship of *devekut* and who are themselves protected by Divine Providence from suffering and distress by the abundance of their *devekut* with God. Thus those who are in trouble live under the Divine protection which shields them. In order that the perfect ones might suffer neither pain nor grief, he too, will have Divine Providence extended to him when they become aware of his grief. (Cited by J. Weiss, *Studies in Eastern European Jewish Mysticism*, 162)

From the next source by R. Pinchas of Koretz, we see that the issue goes beyond mutual responsibility. Our lives overlap and are interconnected.

He responded in answer to someone who asked how it is possible to pray that someone else will repent, when "everything is in Heaven's hands, [except for the fear of Heaven]?" (*B. Berachot* 33b). He explained that *Ha-Shem*, may He be blessed, is the sum of all souls. Everything that pertains to the whole is also found in a part. Consequently, what is related to one soul pertains to all the souls and therefore when you yourself return [to *Ha-Shem*], as a result of this even your friend returns [to *Ha-Shem*]—for he is included in his colleague and his colleague is included in him. (*Midrash Pinchas*, no. 21, 13b)

Thus, each of us is not only responsible for directly helping our neighbor, but our private acts of *teshuvah* (returning to *Ha-Shem*), have an indirect impact on that person. This theory can obviously be extended to meditation, as well. The bond that an individual forges with God is not confined to that moment or that particular relationship. By connecting with *Ha-Shem* during meditation, you are involving *Ha-Shem* in a communion with all humanity.

Let us probe deeper. We have been circumambulating the issue of national cohesiveness and therefore it is appropriate to consider the origination of Jewish peoplehood. According to the census taken of the Israelites after the Exodus, approximately 600,000 individuals were numbered.[4] This statistic has served as the basis for some interesting reflections on the relationship between the sum of the Israelites, the number of their souls, and the letters of the Torah.

R. Hayyim Vital wrote:

> Know that the sum of all of the souls is 600,000—no more. Behold, the Torah is the root of the souls of Israel, for from it they were hewn and in it are they rooted. Accordingly, there are 600,000 approaches [lit. interpretations] to the Torah. . . . Therefore, from each of these approaches a Jewish soul was created. In the future each Jew will achieve knowledge of the entire Torah according to the approach which is aligned with the root of his soul. (*Shaar ha-Gilgulim*, no. 17, 128f.)

Since the Jewish nation is comprised of 600,000 souls and all participated in the revelation of the Ten Commandments at Mount Sinai, an obvious inference is that we were all spiritually present at this epochal event. There is a scriptural basis for this assertion, as well.

At the end of his life, Moses summoned the nation and proclaimed: "Not with you alone, do I establish this covenant, with its sanctions, but both with those who are standing here with us this day before *Ha-Shem*, our God, and with those who are not with us here this day" (Deuteronomy 29:13–14). These verses were interpreted in midrashic literature as follows: "R. Yitzhak said that everything that the prophets would prophesize in the future, all of them received it at Mount Sinai. From whence [is this notion]?—as is written . . . 'and with those who are not with us here this day' . . . these are the souls that will be created in the future" (*Midrash*

---

4. See Numbers 2:32. Although it is beyond this discussion, the numerical relationship between the 600,000 who were counted at the Exodus and the 6,000,000 who perished in the *Shoah* is startling.

Tanchuma, Yitro, 89a). This theory was taken quite seriously.

> It is well-known that all the souls were present at Mount Sinai. I heard directly from our master and teacher, our Rabbi, the holy torch, [Naftali] from Ropshitz, whose domicile is Eden, in the name of the Rabbi, the famous and holy *tzaddik*, our teacher and Rabbi, Rabbi Elimelech, eternally blessed, who said the following: "Not only do I remember the event at Mount Sinai, but I even remember who was standing next to me." (Cited by R. Avraham Sperling, *Taamei ha-Minhagim*, 279)

Another hasidic master, the Maggid of Mezeritch, developed this doctrine and came to a fascinating conclusion.

> It is well known that within every speech and every letter [uttered] are included all 600,000 letters of the Torah, which corresponds to the 600,000 Jewish souls. . . . Consequently, when a person learns and is dedicated to Heaven, even if he does not learn all of the Torah at once; nevertheless, he can still awaken and connect all of the worlds . . . for all 600,000 letters of the Torah are included within each other; therefore, whatever he learns, whether a little or a lot, all of the Torah and all of the Jewish souls are included therein. (*Maggid Devarav le-Yaakov*, 305)

In actuality, the letters of the Torah are considerably less—304,805 according to the Masoretic reckoning.[5] This discrepancy is well known and there are at least two ways of reconciling the theory of 600,000 letters in the Torah, with the fact that the number is only about half that. One approach is to note that some letters are composed of other letters. For example, in the

---

5. See R. Yaakov Kamenetzky's *Emet le-Yaakov* (New York, 1991), 546, for a learned discourse on the significance of this traditional calculation. According to a modern computation it is actually 400,945; see *Torah, Neviim u-Chetuvim* (Jerusalem, 1975), 360.

Zohar we read that the *alef* is a composite of three letters: a *yod* on top and bottom and a diagonal *vav*.[6] R. Moshe Cordovero expanded upon this insight by linking this to the *gematria* of the Ineffable Name, *YHVH* (=26): "It is worth knowing that all of the letters are dependent upon the Four-Letter Name, even to the extent that some of the letters acquire their existential quality from It. For example, the *alef* has the form of two *yodin* and a *vav*. The numerical value yields 26, which is the value of the Name."[7]

A second solution to the riddle of the missing letters is found in *Shoshan Sodot*, an anthology of mystical arcana: "This is the secret of the 600,000. . . . Customarily, the Israelite nation recites 'Blessed is the Sage of the mysteries.' The reason for the blessing of mysteries is that some letters have been absorbed into other ones. For example *b, g, d* yields *ba gad* (fortune has come). Similarly, here *razim* (mysteries) yields *arazim* (cedars)" (*Shoshan Sodot*, 44b). The author continues by relating the image of the cedars of Lebanon to the Israelites, as well as the lower levels of the *Sefirot*.

According to this source, certain syllables preserve unwritten letters. Presumably, adding up all of these secret letters would yield 600,000. This still leaves us with the puzzle of why one would develop a rather widespread teaching that does not correspond to a verifiable reality. Perhaps the source for the hypothesis of the 600,000 letters is a discussion in the *Zohar* concerning the priestly blessing, which consists of three verses (Numbers 6:24–26) totaling fifteen words (the numerical value of the Divine Name *Yah*) and sixty letters.

---

6. *Zohar* 3:223b.

7. M. Cordovero, *Pardes Rimmonim* (Jerusalem, 1962), 21:1, 97a. It is quite appropriate that the first letter of the alphabet alludes to the Creator of the universe.

> At the time when this blessing leaves the mouth of the priest, these sixty letters depart and fly in the heavens. Sixty princes are assigned to each letter. Each offers thanks for these blessings. What is the reason for the sixty letters in these blessings? Since Israel numbers 600,000, the mystery of the 600,000 perpetually exists in the world—every one of them [i.e. the sixty letters of the priestly blessing] constitutes 10,000. (*Zohar* 3:145a)

The above-cited text, *Shoshan Sodot*, mentioned an unusual blessing that requires some elucidation. By tracing the sources of this practice, we will eventually arrive at the pivotal theory that *Ha-Shem*, the Torah and Israel are one.

The talmudic source for the blessing of "mysteries" is the following:

> Our Rabbis taught: When one sees myriads of Jews, recite: "Blessed [are You, King of the Universe,] the Sage of the mysteries"—for neither are their minds the same, nor are their faces the same. . . . [R. Hanina b. R. Ika] said to them . . . you reminded me of 600,000 Jews . . . [so I recited] "Blessed . . . the sage of mysteries." (*B. Berachot* 58a–b)

Rashi commented that *Ha-Shem* is the "Sage of the mysteries" for "He knows what is in the heart of each of them." Ramban expounded upon this topic:

> Our Sages transmitted that there are only 600,000 different facial types and that this number includes all of the mind-sets. It was for this reason that the Torah was revealed to this number and they said that it was only appropriate for the Torah to be transmitted if it would be received by all of the mind-sets. Since the Creator, may He be blessed, knows the minds and thought processes of all creatures, the blessing "Sage of the mysteries" is recited [upon seeing] myriads. (*Kitvei Ramban, Torat Ha-Shem Temimah* 1:162)

Ramban continued by explaining R. Hanina b. R. Ika's unexpected action in that he recited the blessing after encountering just two fellow Rabbis. Ramban stated, "There are truly exceptional individuals that know and understand all of the wisdoms and have mastered all of the mind-sets." Accordingly, if one were to encounter such a person, it would be appropriate to recite the "Sage of the mysteries" blessing.

There is a further step to this line of reasoning, which entails the identification of *Ha-Shem* and the Torah. It is predicated upon Maimonides's formulation that *Ha-Shem* and His knowledge are indivisible.

> The Holy One, blessed be He, recognizes truth and knows it as it is. He does not ascertain knowledge by a means that is outside of Himself, in the way that we acquire knowledge. For we and our knowledge are not one, but the Creator, may He be blessed, and His Knowledge and His life are identical from every aspect, perspective and manner of unity. . . . You can therefore conclude that He is the Knower, the Knowing and the Known all in one. (*M. T., Yesodei ha-Torah* 2:10)

Since the Torah represents the treasure-house of Divine wisdom, the *Zohar* plausibly identifies the Torah and God. "And the Torah is the Holy One, blessed be He" (*Zohar* 1:24a). Later Jewish sources reformulated and extended this doctrine in an Aramaic expression that sounds zoharic: "The Holy One, blessed be He, the Torah and Israel are one." The closest that the *Zohar* comes to this is: "There are three levels that are connected one with the other—the Holy One, blessed be He, the Torah and Israel" (*Zohar* 3:73a). Professor Berachah Zak, in a study on the evolution of this saying, concluded that the popular reformulation was ultimately dependent upon a statement by R. Moshe Cordovero in his commentary on the *Zohar*, "The Torah, and the souls and the *Sefirot* are all one thing" "*Ve-Od . . . ,*" *Kiryat Sefer*, 57:179).

An interesting rationale for the identification of *Ha-Shem* and the Torah is found in the writings of Ramban. "We have received a true *Kabbalah* [i.e., tradition] that the entire Torah consists of Names of the Holy One, blessed be He—for the words can be divided into various Names" (*Introduction to Torah Commentary*; see also *Kitvei Ramban*, 1:167).

He continues by giving an example from the first verse of Genesis, by realigning the letters of the initial words. Instead of the standard reading—"In the beginning God created . . ." —a radically different version emerges: "From the beginning God is created. . . ." The kabbalists took this to mean that God, namely, *Binah* (Understanding), was emanated from "the beginning," namely, *Hochmah* (Wisdom).[8]

A talmudic source can also be cited in this connection. R. Yohanan contended that the homiletical practice of *notarikon* (i.e., interpreting a single word as an entire statement by expanding each letter of the word into a complete word in itself) is authenticated in the Torah itself. His source is the word *anochi*, "I," which *Ha-Shem* proclaimed at the start of the Ten Commandments (Exodus 20:2). According to R. Yohanan the individual letters of the word *anochi* can be rendered: *ana nafshi ketevat yehavet* (*B. Kiddushin* 31a). This phrase is ambiguous. It can either be translated: "I, Myself, have written and transmitted [it]" (i.e., the Torah) or, "I have written and transmitted Myself."

Owing to the ultimate significance of the Torah, if a scroll has any words misspelled, then it should not be used until checked and fixed—even if only one letter is defective (see *M. Soferim 3:9*). The importance of every single letter is illustrated in the following anecdote. R. Meir, one of the principal sages of the *Mishnah*, recounted: "When I visited R. Yishmael he said to me, 'My son, what is your profession?' I said to him, 'I am a scribe.' He said to me, 'My son, be extremely careful

---

8. See *Zohar* 1:15a, and D. Matt, *Zohar: The Book of Enlightenment* (New York, 1983), 49.

in your craft, for your craft is Heaven's work. If you omit a letter or add an extra one, you may cause the destruction of the entire universe'" (*B. Eruvin* 13a).

The previous associations of souls, letters, and Divine Names are brought together in an intriguing anecdote transmitted by R. Pinchas of Koretz.

> After death a *tzaddik* (righteous master) ascends from level to level until he is transformed into a letter or a thought or one of the Divine Holy Names. The Rabbi, the great *tzaddik*, our teacher, Tzvi, the son of the Rivash [Baal Shem Tov], was travelling to Bender and had to sleep in a field. It was a place of danger. His father appeared to him in a dream and told him, "Concentrate on the Forty-two-Letter Name, for I myself am that Name." And it helped him. (*Midrash Pinchas*, no. 39, 11a)

The potent Forty-two-Letter Name has been incorporated into the liturgical prayer *Ana Be-Choah* and is found in the daily morning service and the Friday evening service. One of the phrases therein reads: "Please, [Divine] Hero . . . guard them like the apple of [Your] eye."

One can also note that Numbers, chapter 33, enumerates forty-two encampments that constituted the various stages of the journey of the Israelites when they left Egypt. The Spanish exile R. Avraham Saba, in his Torah commentary, associated this with the Forty-two-Letter Name. He explained that the Forty-two-Letter Name consists of seven sequences of six letters each. He derives this from the seven primal days, the first six of which were devoted to the creation of the universe. Thus, the number 42 is connected both with the inception of the universe and the Jewish people.[9]

Interestingly, the Besht asserted that this national itinerary is repeated by all of us. Each person traverses forty-

---

9. R. Avraham Saba, *Tzeror ha-Mor* (Brooklyn, NY, 1961), 4:45.

two stages in life. For example, "the day of one's birth, when one exits their mother's womb, is like the exodus from Egypt" (*Degel Machaneh Ephraim, Masei*, 65b).

Another comment on the interrelationship between God, Israel, and the Torah is by R. Nachman of Bratzlav. He developed the theme that truth is absolute and does not vary; hence, it is appropriate to characterize it as one. He continues: "Therefore, The Holy One, blessed be He, the Torah and Israel are all one. *Ha-Shem*, may He be blessed is truth, His Torah is truth, and Israel is truth. Since they are all truth, they are all one, for truth is not variable" (*Likkutei Moharan*, no. 251:270).

We shall conclude this section with a potent assertion by R. Pinchas of Koretz, which extends our notion of God even further: "Everyone thinks that they are praying to the Holy One, blessed be He. This is not the case—prayer is truly the Divine essence, as is written 'He is your praise; He is your God' (Deuteronomy 10:21). Moreover, 'prayer' is one of the Divine epithets" (*Midrash Pinchas*, no. 52, 7b). From this we see that our spiritual activities are not simply directed to *Ha-Shem*; they are in themselves Divine.

PREPARATIONS AND SETTING

Now that we have a clearer sense of the spiritual enterprise and what is at stake, we shall consider how to prepare to meditate. R. Yitzhak of Acco, an early fourteenth-century mystic, offered the following three suggestions for anyone who desires to meditate successfully: "Be content with your life; enjoy meditating alone; flee public office and acclaim."[10] From this ad-

---

10. Cited by R. Hayyim Vital, "Shaarei Kedushah," 4:1, in *Ketavim Hadashim le-Rabbenu Hayyim Vital* (Jerusalem, 1988), 4.

vice we see that productive meditation involves self-perception and basic life-style choices.

There is a general awareness that whereas any time or place offers infinite possibilities for spiritual elevation, nevertheless, some circumstances are more conducive than others. There are even situations that are quite constraining. The texts that follow are concerned with issues involving the physical environment, orientation, and time frame.

It is traditional to refrain from spiritual activities such as prayer, Torah study, and meditation in places that are physically contaminated. Maimonides begins his codification of improper settings as follows: "One should not recite [the *Shema*] in a bathhouse or bathroom, even if it is void of excrement, nor in a cemetery, nor in the vicinity of a corpse" (*M.T., Hilchot Keriat Shema* 3:2).[11] The scriptural basis for such restrictions is the verse, "For *Ha-Shem*, your God, walks in your camp to protect you and to deliver your enemies to you—your camp must be holy. Let Him not see anything unseemly in your midst that He would turn away from you" (Deuteronomy 23:15).

An intriguing extension of this principle was formulated by the Maggid of Mezeritch.

It is forbidden to vocalize the Divine Name according to its letters—(see *M. Sanhedrin* 11:1)—because the general atmosphere is not suitable clothing for these holy letters. The exception is the Temple mount for there the atmosphere stems from the *Shechinah*, as is written, "And *Ha-Shem* is in His holy sanctuary" (Habakkuk 2:20). For this reason it is forbidden to concentrate on Torah matters in a defiled place, except to prevent someone from transgressing. This is the secret meaning of "[*Ha-Shem* prepared His throne in Heaven] and His kingdom reigns over everything" (Psalms 103:19)—

---

11. The talmudic sources that Maimonides utilized include *B. Berachot* 25b and *B. Shabbat* 150a.

one can mention Torah matters there between the husks (*kelippot*) in order to constrain them. (*Maggid Devarav le-Yaakov,* no. 139, 238)

Thus it is necessary to ensure that one's general environment is conducive to spiritual activity. Some also recommend that a person select a special locale for prayer and meditation. R. Eliahu de Vidas offered a detailed discussion of the importance of securing "a holy place" in order to advance spiritually. He contended that an individual should either choose a location that already has intrinsic sanctity, such as a *beit midrash* (study hall) or a synagogue, or "a holy place that is separate and apart from other people—a place that is isolated from people is a great preparation for achieving *devekut*" (*Reshit Hochmah Ha-Shalem, Shaar Ha-Kedushah* 6:16, 89).

The following advice was transmitted by R. Nachman of Bratzlav's disciple.

> It is very beneficial for a person to have a special room for serving *Ha-Shem* through Torah study and prayer. This is particularly important for meditation and communing with one's Master. For this [pursuit] an individual definitely needs a special room. And our Rabbi, of blessed memory said that even sitting alone in one's special room is very beneficial. Nevertheless, even if a person does not merit having a special room, one can still meditate in seclusion with one's Master. And our Rabbi, of blessed memory said that being covered by a *tallit* [prayer shawl] is also like having a special room . . . or one can meditate while lying in bed by covering oneself with a blanket, as King David used to do. (*Sichot Ha-Ran,* nos. 274–275:167–168)

Creating a proper environment for meditation goes beyond locating a space within which to practice. As we shall see in the following sources, orientation is also a fundamental issue. The term *orientation* is used here both in its literal sense of facing east towards Jerusalem as well as, figuratively, becoming in tune with one's surroundings. The Book of Daniel offers an important description of personal piety, which serves as a prooftext for several liturgical practices: "When Daniel learned that it [i.e., the ban on praying to *Ha-Shem*] had been written down, he went to his house, in whose attic he had windows constructed that faced Jerusalem, and three times a day he knelt on his knees, prayed, and confessed to his God, as he had always done" (Daniel 6:11).

This verse is the oldest source for the Jewish custom of praying three times daily. It also underscores that one should pray facing Jerusalem. This would naturally pertain to meditation, as well. Finally, it indicates that it is beneficial to pray in a room that has windows. Accordingly, this verse served as a source for synagogue architecture and the requirement that synagogues have windows (typically twelve, corresponding to the tribes of Israel).

Consider also R. Elimelech's comments on orientation during prayer.

> It is stated in the *Gemera*, "One who is standing in the Diaspora and wishes to pray should direct his heart towards the land of Israel. One who is standing in the land of Israel should face Jerusalem" (*B. Berachot* 30a). Accordingly, all Jewish prayers pass through the same gate. Therefore, if a person wants his prayers to be heard he should imagine that he is praying in the land of Israel and that the Temple is standing and the altar and inner chamber are operational and behold he is presently living in the land of Israel. By means of this [visualization] he will achieve illumination and complete *devekut* in order to pray with utmost concentration with fear and love, as if he were standing in the Holy of Holies. (*Noam Elimelech*, "Lech Lecha," 7a)

Here is another of R. Elimelech's general comments on prayer, which is quite beautiful. He explained the instructions that God gave Noah for constructing the ark. God required that Noah install a skylight in the ark. Note that the Hebrew word *tevah* has two distinct meanings: "ark" and "word." "'You shall make a sky-light (*tzohar*) for the ark' (Genesis 6:16). Rashi interpreted [*tzohar*] to mean a precious stone. One can say that this hints at the connection between ark and word. A person should ensure that each word that he utters shines like a precious stone" (*Noam Elimelech* 3b).

Finally, it can be helpful to indicate that the place that you have chosen in which to meditate is special, by graphically designating it in some way. Some people create a sacral space by inscribing a circle around themselves. There is a famous narrative in the Talmud about the miracle worker, Honi the Circle Drawer, who lived in the first century B.C.E.

> It once happened that the people said to Honi the Circle Drawer, "Pray that rain should fall." . . . He prayed, but no rain fell. What did he do? He drew a circle and stood within it and exclaimed, "Master of the Universe, Your children have turned to me because I am like a member of Your household. I swear by Your great Name that I will not move from here until You have mercy upon Your children." A few raindrops began to fall. He responded, "This is not what I requested." Thereupon it became a torrential downpouring. Honi, however, chastized God for not providing benevolent rain; the deluge was transformed into life-sustaining precipitation. (*M. Taanit* 3:8)

Circles are a common element of Jewish magical texts. An example is the medieval Aramaic work published by Scholem and entitled *The Smaller and Larger Praxis*. In *The Smaller Praxis* one reads about a ceremony for overcoming demonic forces on Yom Kippur.

> On the eve of Yom Kippur, a circle is made: five cubits [i.e., 8½ feet] in length by five cubits in width. . . . Three or four wise elders [participate], at least 50 years old,—who had fasted for fifteen days and nights, eating only during three of the nights: at the end of seven days, the end of ten days and at the end of thirteen days,—three or four elders, meri-

torious and wise Torah scholars, who had separated from their wives for thirty days. On the night of Yom Kippur, the oldest and accomplished one, stands in the middle of the circle, wearing a wool *tallit*. The other elders circumambulate, wearing cotton *tallitot*. (Scholem, *"Sidrei de-Shimusha Rabba,"* 200)

Having considered issues pertaining to environment and orientation, we shall conclude with a discussion of other aspects of preparation. Insofar as meditation is considered to be a significant religious activity within the Jewish tradition, certain preliminary steps are encouraged. The following, detailed discussion of lifestyle changes prerequisite to meditation was formulated by the sixteenth-century mystic, R. Yehudah al-Botini, who was a rabbinic authority living in Jerusalem.

Chapter Ten: An explanation of the paths of meditation (*hitbodedut*) and *devekut* (attachment), as well as the preparations that the meditator should undertake, in order to arrive at the goal of contemplation, by attaching his soul to the Active Intellect and thereby becoming embued with the Holy Spirit.

Know that the necessary preparations that a meditator must undertake in order to accomplish his desire involves abstraction, by removing his intellect from coarse matter on many levels. First, related to the body, he must minimize physical desires—in relation to eating, he should constantly accustom himself to eat small quantities of high quality food. He should limit his intake of cooked meat dishes and wine, as our Sages have formulated: "This is the path of the Torah . . . (*M. Avot* 4:4)." The intention is not that one should live a life of deprivation and pain, on the contrary overindulgence itself distances one from the achievement of perfection. Rather, the intention is that even if he possesses great wealth and sustenance, it is appropriate that he not pleasure himself but merely sustain his soul in his body. He should restrict his animal urges and not give them what they desire, for in the diminution of their power, his soul will dominate and his intellect will escape the prison of his animal urges in order to actualize and adhere to His Owner. ("Sulam ha-Aliyah," in *Kitvei Yad ba-Kabbalah*, ed. Scholem, 225)

Thus, al-Botini emphasized that spiritual elevation requires a concerted effort on the physical level. For example, a person should minimize his intake of meat and wine. The other aspects of physical self-control that al-Botini recommended include limiting sexual intercourse and purifying one's body through immersion in a *mikvah* (ritual bath). All of these physical preparations should be followed, "for a long time, not merely a day or two days or even a month, but a long time, until one arrives at the point where one's physical urges do not bother him" (226).

In addition to physical preparations, al-Botini also insisted on emotional and intellectual prerequisites.

> Especially removing the characteristics of anger, worry, and excessive petitioning, for these attributes prevent him from ascending to the attribute of equanimity ... for realignment (*tikkun*) of the body, namely asceticism, leads to the purification of one's powers and cleansing of attributes. [This leads to] equanimity, which leads to the Holy Spirit, which leads to prophecy, which is the highest level. (226)

Next, al-Botini described the immediate preparations that should be undertaken prior to meditating. By way of background, it should be noted that al-Botini utilized standard, medieval psychology in discussing the various levels of the soul: vegetative, animal, and rational. This tripartite construct was based upon Aristotle's biological theory of the soul, namely, that the more complex an organism's functioning, the more sophisticated the soul necessary to actualize such activities. Al-Botini embellished upon this theory and contended that meditation could only succeed once the lower souls, namely the vegetative and animal, had been satisfied.

> When he continuously strives to acquire this behavior, [namely, equanimity, which is the starting point for *hit-*

bodedut], he will choose for himself a house where he can sit completely by himself. If he has a house wherein his voice cannot be heard outside that is even better. At the outset it is necessary to adorn the house with one's nicest and most important possessions, as well as various spices and other pleasant smelling objects. If the house has trees and lush bushes, it is very beneficial that his vegetable soul should take pleasure in all of these things when he meditates, for it is a partner with the animal soul. Also, he should try to play on all types of musical instruments, if he has them and knows how to play them. If not, he should sing verses from Psalms and the Torah, in order to please the animal soul, which is a partner with the rational soul and intelligence. If he undertakes this during the day it is fine, but it is necessary that the house be slightly dark. It is better, however, if he does this at night and he should have many candles burning in the house. Also, he should wear proper, clean clothes. It is preferable that they are white, for all of this promotes concentration on Divine fear and love.

After accomplishing all of these preparations, at the time you are readying yourself to speak to your Creator, take care to empty your thoughts from all worldly vanities. Wrap yourself in your *tallit* and place your *tefillin* on your hand and head, if you are able to—in order that you are in awe and quake in the presence of the *Shechinah*, for She is with you at that moment. ("Sulam ha-Aliyah," 226–227)

The particular method of meditation that al-Botini advocated was originally formulated by one of the major proponents of ecstatic mysticism, R. Abraham Abulafia. Abulafia was born in Saragossa, Spain, in 1240, and he traveled widely throughout the Mediterranean region, studying philosophy and *Kabbalah*. Eventually, he developed his own intense spiritual regime, which entailed chanting and letter permutations. We shall explore some of this material in Chapter 7, on chanting.

Al-Botini's concluding comment on the preferability of wearing white while meditating is echoed by another of Abulafia's students, the anonymous author of *Shaarei Tzedek*, who advised, "And cleanse yourself and your garments, and if possible let them all be white, for all this greatly assists the intention of fear and love" (Idel, *Mystical Experience*, 39). Additionally, Abulafia encouraged wearing a *tallit* (prayer-shawl) and *tefillin* (phylacteries) while meditating. Similarly, in *Shaarei Tzedek* we read, "And wrap yourself in *tallit* and place your *tefillin* on your head and your arm, so that you may be fearful and in awe of the *Shechinah*" (Idel, *Mystical Experience*, 39).

In the traditional *Siddur*, there are numerous biblical verses that are recited prior to and immediately upon donning *tallit* and *tefillin*, as well as specific meditations that are recited in conjunction with each article.[12] Among the verses associated with the *tallit* is, "And humans seek refuge in the shadow of Your wings" (Psalms 36:8). This evokes the image of the *Shechinah* as a mother bird protecting her young. Similarly, prior to the revelation at Mount Sinai, *Ha-Shem* commented upon the exodus from Egypt: "How I bore you upon eagles' wings and brought you to Me" (Exodus 19:4). R. Yosef Hayyim pointed out that the Hebrew term for *eagles—nesharim—*has the numerical value of 600, which is identical to that of *tzitzit* (i.e., the fringed *tallit*).

Finally, the basic issue of how often one should meditate is ultimately left up to the individual. R. Eleazar Azikri recommended one day a week or at least one day a month (see Chapter 9). Several hasidic masters formulated a daily regime for their followers. R. Mordechai from Chernobyl encouraged his disciples to meditate for one or two hours daily in a specially designated room, (*Tzevvaot Ve-Hanhagot*, 151). R. Nachman of Bratzlav likewise encouraged his fol-

---

12. For a translation of this material, see *The Complete ArtScroll Siddur* (Brooklyn, NY, 1986), 3–9.

lowers to practice his particular form of *hitbodedut* daily: "*Hitbodedut* is the supreme level and the greatest [undertaking] of all. Accordingly, one should set aside an hour or more [daily] to meditate alone in a room or field" (*Likkutei Moharan* 2:25).

3

THE ROLE OF NATURE
IN JEWISH SPIRITUALITY
AND MEDITATION

Up to this point, most of the sources that we considered have portrayed Jewish meditation as an indoor activity. There is, however, extensive material that discusses the relationship between nature and spiritual growth. As noted in Chapter 1, the earliest biblical passage connected with meditation is Genesis 24:63, which describes Isaac going out into the field at evening to meditate (*la-suach*). As Isaac and other biblical figures consciously chose to commune with *Ha-Shem* by going outdoors, it is certainly appropriate to explore the role of nature in Jewish spirituality. We will take a leisurely, roundabout path through the fields and forests of this theme, pausing to digress and reflect before resuming our journey.

It is noteworthy that the verbal infinitive *la-suach* in Genesis 24:63 is ambiguous. In fact, this is the only occurrence of this particular root form in *Tanach*. All grammarians agree that *suah* is related to *siach*. The latter, however, has two distinct connotations: conversing and vegetation.[1] *La-suach* was rendered by the Sages as talking with God (i.e., praying). This also resulted in the standard translation, "meditate." The medieval commentator R. Abraham ibn Ezra and, following him, the modern Jewish Publication Society *Tanach* chose the second connotation and therefore rendered the word as "walking outdoors." Whatever translation one adopts, it is significant that communing with God and walking outdoors are interwoven in this one word.

If you are interested in the number technique of *gematria*, consider the following. Metatron, the Prince of the Divine Countenance and cosmic scribe, is an extremely important angel in rabbinic and *Hechalot* literature. The numerical value of Metatron is 314, the same as the Divine Name, *Shaddai*. In an early medieval Ashkenazic manuscript it states, "Metatron . . . in *gematria* is *suach* (meditate) for he was designated to receive prayers. This is also the *gematria* of *ha-sadeh* [the field], for there is no prayer except in the field, as it is stated, 'And Isaac went out to *la-suach* in the field' and *sihah* connotes prayer."[2]

Another *gematria* germane to our discussion was recorded by R. Moshe Cordovero. He noted that the name for God that appears at the start of the book of Genesis is *Elohim*, which has the numerical value 86. The definite noun *ha-teva* (i.e., Nature) likewise possesses this numerical value, "for Nature exhibits the Divine will" (*Pardes Rimmonim*, Shaar 12, ch. 2, f. 66a.

---

1. For an elaborate discussion of righteous individuals depicted metaphorically as shrubs/trees, see *B. Baba Batra* 78b, "the righteous are *sichin* (shrubs)" and Rashi's extensive comments, providing numerous biblical references.

2. Cited by M. Idel, *Tarbitz* 62:2 (1993) 270. Incidentally, *va-yetze yitzhak* ("and Isaac went out") has the numerical value of 315, one more than *Shaddai*. On the significance of this Divine Name, see Chapter 4.

R. Shneur Zalman of Liadi also commented on this association. He offered a somewhat different interpretation, stressing the hidden aspect of mundane life. "It [i.e., the Name, *Elohim*] is also equal to *ha-teva* [Nature], because *Elohim* hides the Supernal Light that causes the world to come into existence and gives it life. Rather, it appears that the world exists and functions naturally. The name *Elohim* is a shield and a sheath for the name of *Ha-Shem*" (*Tanya, Shaar ha-Yichud*, ch. 6).

As anthropocentric beings, we tend to assume that only humans are spiritual creatures. Our tradition teaches us otherwise. The *Tanach* is replete with assertions that the entire world and its component elements praise and glorify *Ha-Shem*. We read in Psalms:

> Praise *Ha-Shem*, O you who are on earth, all sea monsters and ocean depths, fire and hail, snow and smoke, storm wind that executes His command, all mountains and hills, all fruit trees and cedars, all wild and tamed beasts, creeping things and winged birds, all kings and peoples of the earth, all princes of the earth and its judges, youths and maidens alike, old and young together. (Psalms 148:7–12)

This universal theme reaches its climax in the last verse of Psalms, "Let all that breathes, praise *Ha-Shem*. Halleluyah!" (Psalms 150:6).

Nor is this process confined to earthbound creatures. Maimonides contended that the stars and planets are sentient beings, consciously involved in Divine service. "All the celestial bodies and spheres possess souls, knowledge, and intellect. They live, thrive, and recognize the Creator of the universe. Each according to its size and rank praises and glorifies their Creator, just as the angels do" (*M.T., Yesodei ha-Torah* 3:9).

This echoes an idea forwarded by Philo of Alexandria: "Heaven is ever making music, producing in accordance with its celestial motions the perfect harmony" (Winston, *Philo of Alexandria*, 115).

One of the most intriguing Jewish compositions that discusses nonhuman service of *Ha-Shem* is *Perek Shirah* (A Chapter of Song). Mentioned in the tenth century by Shlomoh B. Yeruham and found in numerous *Genizah* fragments, it is undoubtedly a very old work. It is printed in traditional prayer books, prior to the morning service. *Perek Shirah* lists dozens of creatures and objects and the corresponding song of praise that each offers *Ha-Shem*. For example, the frog is accredited with reciting the significant liturgical formula, "Blessed is the Name of His glorious kingdom for all eternity."

The prologue to *Perek Shirah* offers an interesting narrative. When King David completed the Book of Psalms, he was excessively prideful and boasted that no one had composed as many songs to *Ha-Shem* as he had. Thereupon, he was confronted by a frog, who rebuked him by asserting that it sang more songs of praise to *Ha-Shem* than King David.

King David's son, Solomon, was credited by the Rabbis with having the ability to converse with all of nature.[3] They based this assertion upon the biblical statement: "He was the wisest of all humans. . . . He spoke about trees, from the cedars of Lebanon to the hyssop that sprouted from the wall; he also spoke about the domesticated animals, birds, reptiles and fish" (1 Kings 5:11–14).

A comparable involvement of the ancient Rabbis with nature is exemplified by the great sage Hillel. It was said of Hillel that he had mastered all types of speech, "even the speech of mountains, hills and valleys, the speech of trees and grasses, the speech of wild

---

3. See the sources discussed by L. Ginzberg, *The Legends of the Jews* 6:287–289, especially nos. 34, 38. For source material on R. Yitzhak Luria's ability to communicate with birds, see the recent discussion by G. Bos, "Hayyim Vital's Practical Kabbalah and Alchemy," *Journal of Jewish Thought and Philosophy* 4 (1994) 73.

beasts and domesticated animals, the speech of spirits" (*M. Soferim* 16:9).

Hillel's special knowledge was carried on by his successor, Rabban Yohanan b. Zakkai, who preserved the rabbinic enterprise after the destruction of the Second Temple. Rabban Yohanan was characterized as the "least" (youngest?) of Hillel's disciples. He is credited with having mastered all of the traditional subjects, as well as "the speech of the ministering angels, the spirits and the palm trees" (*B. Sukkot* 28a). Not surprisingly, Rashi, writes that he does not know what is meant by the speech of the palm trees.

Many hasidic masters were also involved in communing with nature. The Baal Shem Tov (the Besht) spent many years of contemplation in the Carpathian Mountains. After marrying, he and his bride moved to a remote village. The Besht wandered through the mountains, and every two or three weeks his wife would bring him basic provisions. His activities during this period were as follows:

> He constantly engaged in protracted fasts and when he wanted to eat he would dig a pit in the earth and place therein some flour and water. Eventually it would be baked by the heat of the sun. This was his entire meal after fasting. All of his days he would be meditating.
>
> Behold, the mountains were exceedingly large. Between them were steep cliffs and valleys. . . . Once he was engrossed in profound meditation, while walking in the mountains. . . . Thieves saw him walking to the edge of the mountain engrossed in thought. They said that certainly he would fall into the valley and break his bones. As he came upon the valley, the opposing mountain shifted towards him, forming a plain. He walked some distance and the mountains split apart as they had been originally. (*Shivhei ha-Besht*, A. Rubinstein, ed., 51; cf. *In Praise of the Baal Shem Tov*, D. Ben-Amos and J. Mintz, trans., 22)

During this period, the Baal Shem Tov learned much about the mechanics of nature. This is evident in a subsequent encounter between the Besht and R. Aryeh (Yehudah) Leib of Polonnoye. The latter had come to the Besht with a unique request. He wanted to learn the language of the animals and birds, as he was a *maggid* (i.e., a preacher/storyteller). R. Aryeh felt that this special knowledge would help him communicate his ideas better.

While traveling together the Besht explained that the key is to contemplate the faces of the four Holy Creatures, human, lion, ox, and eagle, which constitute the core of Ezekiel's vision of the Divine Chariot (i.e., Ezekiel, ch. 1). The Besht then said:

> The choicest [image] in the Chariot is the human face, and from her [i.e., this face] the life force is emanated downward to earthbound humans. From the face of the upper ox, through the chain of stages, peregrinations and many contractions, the life force is emanated to all the lower animals. From the face of the lion the life force is emanated down to the lower beasts, and from the face of the eagle to all the lower birds. This is the secret of *Perek Shirah*. According to the speech of each type of creature in the Supernal Chariot, there is a devolution downwards to the lower animals, beasts and birds. One who is wise and perceptive can contemplate each thing according to its source in the Supernal Chariot. From the origin of each thing he will be able to comprehend all the details of the speech mannerisms of the animals, beasts, and birds. This is the general principle.
>
> Thereupon the Besht revealed the particulars of this mystery to R. Aryeh, who began to understand the chirping of birds and the howling of dogs. As they approached their destination the Besht passed his hands over R. Aryeh's face, erasing all of the esoteric knowledge that he had transmitted. The only thing that R. Aryeh remembered was the general introduction, as recorded above. [The rest, the Besht claimed, was not necessary for R. Aryeh to know.] "For this is not your task, rather 'simple [wholehearted] shall you be [with *Ha-Shem*]' (Deuteronomy 18:13)." (*Shivhei ha-Besht*, S. Horodezky, ed., 87; cf. *In Praise of the Baal Shem Tov*, 242)

Although R. Aryeh was made to forget much of what he learned from the Besht, the Maggid of Mezeritch, who was the Besht's disciple and successor, was more fortunate. One of the Maggid's students noted, "Once I heard directly from his holy mouth [i.e., from the Maggid] that the Besht, may he be remembered eternally, taught him the speech of birds and palm trees" (R. Shlomoh of Lutzk, in his introduction to *Maggid Devarav le-Yaakov*, R. Shatz, ed., 2).

This is substantiated in the following story.

> After the death of Rebbe Ber of Mezeritch, his students sat together and talked about his deeds. When it was the turn of R. Shneur Zalman [of Liadi], he asked: "Do any of you know why our Rebbe would go each morning to a nearby pond and tarry there for a while, before returning home?" No one knew why. [R. Shneur Zalman] responded, "He was studying the song of the frogs who were giving glory to the Creator. Many days must pass until this song can be learned." (M. Buber, *Or Ha-Ganuz*, 117, based on *Kerem Yisrael*)

In reflecting upon our relationship with nature, it is noteworthy that for the first two thousand years of our national existence, we were primarily an agrarian people and our religion was intimately connected with the land. For the last two millenia, however, Judaism evolved as a diaspora phenomenon. In the diaspora, we were alienated and estranged from both land and nature; accordingly, Judaism became an indoor religion.

Very few Jewish liturgical events are choreographed outside. Some notable exceptions to this generalization that come to mind are: *Sukkot, Kiddush Levanah* (the monthly sanctification of the New Moon), *Tashlich*, and weddings. All of these rituals are relatively infrequent. *Kiddush Levanah*, which is the most frequent, is the least observed of all of them.[4]

---

4. Consider the following talmudic statement concerning the significance of sanctifying the New Moon: "R. Yohanan said, 'Anyone who blesses the month at the appropriate time, it is as if they have welcomed the *Shechinah*'" (*B. Sanhedrin* 42a).

In the sixteenth century, the situation changed. The expulsion of Jews from Western Europe resulted in their migration eastward to the Ottoman Empire and, eventually, Israel. A reconnection with the land was thereby forged. Not surprisingly, it was at this time that nature became reintegrated into the Jewish liturgy. It is well known that the *Kabbalat Shabbat* service, inaugurating the Sabbath, was developed in mid-sixteenth-century Tzefat.[5]

The *Shulhan Aruch* of the Ari prescribes: "At *Kabbalat Shabbat* go into a field, according to the secret of the *hakal tapuchin kadishin* [the field of the holy apples], since the Aramaic for field is *hakal*. Behold, during *Kabbalat Shabbat* it is necessary to stand and face west. It is preferable if [one is on] an elevated place" (*Shulhan Aruch ha-Ari*, 54.)

Similarly, R. Moshe ibn Machir, who was the head of a *yeshivah* in the town of Ein Zeitun (on the outskirts of Tzefat), wrote a spiritual manual, *Seder ha-Yom*. In describing the practice of *Kabbalat Shabbat*, he commented: "The ancient sages used to say to each other or to their students, 'let us go out to greet the Bride.' This implies that they would go out somewhere, namely out of their houses and into the fresh air—to the garden or the open space of the yard" (*Seder ha-Yom*, 42).

An amazing discussion of this practice is found in the early eighteenth-century homiletical work, *Hemdat Yamim*. It describes groups of people going out to welcome the Sabbath, playing musical instruments, as if they were musicians at the wedding of the Sabbath Bride.

Since the *Shabbat* represents the enveloping of the *Shechinah* upon us, therefore it is appropriate to welcome the *Shabbat*

---

5. For a discussion of the evolution of these prayers, see G. Scholem, *On the Kabbalah and Its Symbolism* (New York, 1969), 141–146.

with joy and singing. In a number of locales in Europe during *Kabbalat Shabbat* they play musical instruments, lutes
and lyres, just like a wedding party for the groom and bride.
This is because the *Shabbat* represents the welcome presence
of the *Shechinah* and the *Shechinah* is manifest only in joy.
(*Hemdat Yamim* 38b)

This is a wonderful precursor to the creative energy
of the *havurah* movement. It should be pointed out that
since the Sabbath does not formally start until after the
Kabbalat Shabbat service has been concluded, playing
musical instruments was not halachically problematic.

Before proceeding, let us consider the rabbinic
source of the symbolism incorporated into the *Kabbalat
Shabbat* service. First, there is apple imagery. In the
Talmud, Israelites are compared to apple trees: "In the
same way that apple trees produce fruit before sprout-
ing leaves, so too Israel put *naaseh* (we shall perform)
[the Divine commandments] before *nishma* (we understand) [them]" (*B. Shabbat* 88a). The Rabbis also focused
on specific biblical accounts. Of significance was
Isaac's blessing of Jacob: "And he [i.e., Jacob] drew near
and kissed him [i.e., Isaac] and he smelled the aroma
of his clothes and he said, 'See, the aroma of my son is
like the aroma of the field that *Ha-Shem* has blessed'"
(Genesis 27:27).

On this verse, "R. Yehudah in the name of Rav stated,
'[The aroma was] like a field of apples'" (*B. Taanit* 29b).
Further, one finds in *Bereshit Rabbah* 65:18: "When
Jacob, our forefather, entered his father's room, [the
aroma of] the Garden of Eden entered with him." The
association of the fragrance of apples and the Garden
of Eden is also brought out in the Song of Songs. The
description of the beautiful Shulamite in Songs 7:9
includes a reference to "your breath, like the aroma of
apples," to which the *Targum* adds "of the Garden of
Eden."

Although *tapuchim* are usually translated "apples,"

they are occasionally rendered as *etrogim* (citrons). Examples of this include the *Targum* on Songs 2:3 and *Tosafot* on *B. Taanit* 29b. This association with *etrogim* may also have significance for our discussion. It might be the basis for the custom to use an *etrog*, embedded with cloves, during *havdalah*, at the conclusion of *Shabbat*. This may also be connected with a comment in *Tikkunei Zohar* (143b), which recommends smelling *tapuchim* during *havdalah*, as this corresponds to the fragrance of the dual Messiahs.

Another extension of this imagery is the identification of the field of apples as the domain of mystical experience. In classical rabbinic mysticism the locus of visionary ascent is referred to as *pardes*, the celestial orchard. *Pardes* and its cognate, *paradise*, evoke the primal Garden of Eden. This association is made explicit in *Tikkunei Zohar* 88b.

The directive to face west during the *Shabbat* eve service is also highly unusual and deserves consideration. It is based on a talmudic statement in *B. Baba Batra* (25a) that the *Shechinah* (Divine In-Dwelling) is located in the west.[6] Since the *Shechinah* is synonymous with the Sabbath Bride—in order to welcome the Bride, it is appropriate to face west. Nowadays, this custom has been preserved, in a much abbreviated fashion. At the end of hymn *Lecha Dodi*, the congregation turns and faces west and bows to the Sabbath Bride as she enters.

Few of us think about the act of turning. We just do it when necessary. Maimonides discusses this issue, while considering the procedure followed by the

---

6. In his Torah commentary on Exodus 33, Rashi equates east with the Divine front and west with the Divine back.

In order to underscore that the *Kabbalat Shabbat* service was an innovation, in traditional synogogues the *shaliach tzibbur* will lead services from the *bimah* and only move to the *amud* for *Maariv*, proper.

kohanim (priests) when they bless the people. "When the *kohanim* turn to face the congregation to bless them and also when they turn from the congregation after blessing them, they should always turn to the right. Similarly, every time a person turns, he should only turn to the right" (*M.T., Hilchot Tefillah* 14:13). This ruling follows Rabbi Yehudah's assertion in *B. Zevachim* 62b. Interestingly, R. Yehudah adds that turning to the right entails moving eastwards.

From all of the discussion above, we see that there is a matrix of kabbalistic symbols, connected with *Kabbalat Shabbat*. There is the association of *Malchut*, the lowest of the *Sefirot*, with the *Shechinah*, the Sabbath Bride and the sexual energy of marriage. This is further combined with the direction of west, sunset, Friday evening, fields, and the outdoors. All of these motifs are illustrated in the *Shabbat zemirot* of R. Yitzhak Luria. The following is his Friday night song:

> I shall sing praises
>   to enter the doorways
> of the field of apples
>   that are holy.
>
> Let us invite Her now
>   to this new table,
> decorated with a fine candelabrum
>   that casts light on our heads.
>
> Standing to the right and left,
>   the Bride walks between us.
> She passes by bedecked in jewels
>   and regal garments.
>
> Her Husband will embrace Her
>   in Her *Yesod* [Foundation].
> Giving Her pleasure
>   as they are squeezed together.
>
> Woes and even torments
>   are destroyed and nullified.

> Now there are new faces,
>   and spirits and souls.
> (*Zemirot Shabbat*, 13).

In addition to the special *Shabbat* service that they innovated, the mystics of Tzefat would also go out into the fields during the week to practice a form of meditation that they referred to as *gerushin* (literally, banishments or exiles).[7] A master would wander outside of the city with a group of disciples. They would randomly discuss biblical verses. Rather than engaging in a focused discourse, their wanderings would promote spontaneity, and they would perceive startling new insights. R. Moshe Cordovero described this process as follows: "For we would 'exile' ourselves to the field with the divine Rabbi Solomon ben Alkabetz the Levite, may God preserve him, to occupy ourselves with the verses of the Torah extemporaneously without study in depth. [Then] many times matters were innovated which no one could understand unless he saw or experienced the matter" (I. Robinson, *Moses Cordovero's Introduction*, 107).

The spirit of Tzefat eventually found a home in Eastern Europe. Undoubtedly, the hasidic master who responded to the call of nature in the most profound way was R. Nachman of Bratzlav. At the end of this chapter, we shall examine his approach more fully. Representative of R. Nachman's lifelong attachment to the outdoors as a stage for spiritual actualization is the following account, as recalled by Rabbi Shimon, one of R. Nachman's senior disciples. While visiting the home of R. Nachman's in-laws, where he lived after his marriage, R. Nachman and his disciple went walking in the fields.

---

7. See the excellent discussion of this practice in R. Werblowsky, *Joseph Karo: Lawyer and Mystic* (Philadelphia, 1977), 50–54.

Our Rabbi, of blessed memory, became very nostalgic. How wonderful this place was for him—"with each step I experienced the taste of the Garden of Eden." For there on those paths he used to meditate. . . . Another time he told me that in his youth he would meditate in the fields or forests. When he returned home, the entire world was new in his eyes and it seemed to him that the entire world was different and it seemed totally dissimilar to how it had been previously. (*Hayyei Moharan*, no. 107:105)

R. Nachman reflected intensely upon his meditative experiences and discoursed upon them. Consider his comments in *Likkutei Moharan*, the definitive collection of R. Nachman's homilies. Significantly, he discusses our biblical prooftext:

Know that when an individual prays in a field, all the plants enter the prayer. They help him and give him strength to pray. It is for this reason that prayer is called *sichah*, as in "*siah* (shrub) of the field" (Genesis 2:5)—for each shrub of the field gives him strength and assistance during his prayer. This is the significance of "And Isaac went out to pray (*la-suach*) in the field" (Genesis 24:63). His prayer was helped and strengthened by the field, since all the field's plants fortified and assisted his prayer. (*Likkutei Moharan* 2:11)

There is a wonderful anecdote told by one of R. Nachman's disciples. Once, when R. Nachman was visiting this individual, R. Nachman insisted that they go for a walk outside of the city, into fields of grasses. R. Nachman then said to his follower:

If only you merit hearing the sound of the songs and praises of the grasses: how each blade recites a song to *Ha-Shem*, without any deviation or foreign thought. Nor do they anticipate any reward. How beautiful and pleasant to hear their song. He concluded, "*Es is sehr gut, frum tzu zein, tzvishen zaya.*" (It is so good to be *frum* [pious] in their midst.) (*Sichot Ha-Ran*, no. 163)

Before tracing the influence of R. Nachman's thought upon various twentieth-century figures, there is another teaching of his that is pertinent. In it R. Nachman demonstrates how to integrate his love for nature with the very act of prayer itself—even indoors.

> Each and every utterance is an entire universe. When one stands in prayer [i.e., reciting the *Amidah*] and utters the words of the prayer, then he is gathering lovely blossoms, flowers and roses. It is like one who is walking in a field and gathering beautiful roses and flowers, one by one, until he has a bouquet. Then he gathers others, one by one, and makes a second bouquet and joins them together. So he continues gathering and collecting many beautiful and lovely bouquets.
>
> Similarly, one proceeds in prayer from letter to letter, until several letters are joined together thereby forming an utterance. In this way he makes whole words and then two words are joined together. He continues to collect more until he concludes one blessing. . . .
>
> Every utterance pleads and petitions the soul not to leave it. As soon as the first letter is uttered—for example, the letter *bet* from the word *baruch* [blessed]—it pleads and petitions the soul not to leave it: "How could you leave me owing to the great bond and love that there is between us?—for you see the preciousness of my beauty, my radiance, my splendor and my grandeur. How can you cut yourself off from me and leave me? It is true that you must proceed, in order to collect other precious treasures and magnificent acquisitions, but how can you leave and forget me? No matter what, take care that wherever you go, do not forget and leave me." . . .
>
> Accordingly, the basic principle is that it is necessary to make the entire prayer into a unity. In each utterance that is spoken there should be all of the utterances of the prayer. From the beginning of the prayer until the end, all should be one. When a person comes to the last utterance of the prayer, he should still have in mind the first word. (*Likkutei Moharan* 65:2,186)

This straightforward and elegant notion of transforming your prayers into bouquets for *Ha-Shem* requires much concentration and practice. It is an excellent idea to start out by working with a short passage.

As R. Nachman suggests, proceed from one word to another, always keeping in mind what you have recited up to that point. After you have practiced with this same text for several sessions and mastered the technique, you can gradually expand your bouquet.

Moving into the twentieth century, R. Nachman's involvement in nature exerted a profound influence on two seminal religious thinkers/philosophers, R. Hillel Zeitlin and Martin Buber. Zeitlin was a prolific writer and incisive theologian. His prose poem *Kavvanot ve-Yichudim* (Meditations and Unifications) offers a lovely description of the author praying in a forest.

> Behold I am praying and the trees are praying with me. I bend and they bend with me, bow and they bow with me.
>
> A large, magnificent tree stands opposite me. He nods his head, bends his torso, bends and straightens up, bends and straightens up.
>
> He bends—and the other trees bend after him, bows—and they bow after him; he is a *shaliah tzibbur* [leader of communal prayers].
>
> The congregation and the cantor are wrapped in prayer shawls, all embroidered in *techelet* (blue thread). Their fringes drag on the ground. . . .
>
> And we are all praying together with awe and love, with intense concentration and special *devekut* (attachment).
>
> Reciting "one" [i.e., from the *Shema*] we concentrate on one basic thought: the Holy One, blessed be He, is one and His Name is one—everything is one. All of the differences and distinctions, separations, opposites, oppositions, contradictions, substitutions and permutations are merely illusory.
>
> We do not multiply private reflections, rather we concentrate on one general idea, which is that not just the entire Torah, but the entire universe is composed of Names of the Holy One, blessed be He.[8] (*Sifran shel Yehidim*, 180)

---

8. This concluding concept is an embellishment of Ramban's theory that the entire Torah consists of a series of Divine Names; see the introduction to his Torah commentary.

Martin Buber popularized R. Nachman's stories and other hasidic tales. His existential philosophy was a direct outgrowth of his hasidic studies. In his classic meditation on relationships, *I and Thou*, Buber writes:

> In every sphere, through everything that becomes present to us, we gaze toward the train[9] of the eternal You; in each we perceive a breath of it; in every You we address the eternal You. . . .
>
> I contemplate a tree.
>
> I can accept it as a picture: a rigid pillar in a flood of light, or splashes of green traversed by the gentleness of the blue silver ground.
>
> I can feel it as movement: the flowing veins around the sturdy, striving core, the sucking of the roots, the breathing of the leaves, the infinite commerce with earth and air—and the growing itself in its darkness. . . .
>
> But it can also happen, if will and grace are joined, that as I contemplate the tree I am drawn into a relation, and the tree ceases to be an It. . . .
>
> The tree is no impression, no play of my imagination . . . it confronts me bodily and has to deal with me as I must deal with it—only differently. (*I and Thou*, W. Kaufmann, trans., 57–58)

In March 1920, the Zionist youth movement met in Prague. The Central European contingent was headed by Martin Buber. The Palestinian pioneers, known as *halutzim*, were represented by a middle-aged Aaron David Gordon. Gordon told the conference participants: "What is happening here is not that we speak to you; it is our land that speaks to you. We are here merely to express what the land itself is saying. We say to you, to our entire people: *the land is waiting for you*" (S. Bergman, *Faith and Reason*, 98).

Gordon had immigrated to Israel some fifteen years earlier, and he reflected deeply upon the human situ-

---

9. This is an allusion to Isaiah 6:1, "and the hem of His robe filled the Temple."

ation. He characterized modern alienation from nature as follows: "You find that the more man takes from nature, the farther he moves away from it. The more wealth he acquires, the more industrious are his labors for building a thick barrier between himself and nature. He withdraws into his walled cities as a turtle within its shell" (*Selected Essays*, F. Burnce, trans., 175).

Gordon envisioned a radical transformation:

> And when, O Man, you will return to Nature, you will open your eyes on that day and you will gaze straight into the eyes of Nature; you will see therein your own image, and you will know that you have returned to yourself, that when you hide from Nature, you have hidden from yourself. . . . On that day you will feel with all the strength of your heart the weight with which the walls of the city houses, of the villages, too, press down upon you. You will feel every slight barrier that separates you from the universe, that divides you from universal life. Then it will happen that when you build a home for yourself, you will set your heart not on multiplying therein rooms and more rooms—but on this you will set your heart: that there be in your home nothing that will act as a barrier between you and the universal expanse, between you and universal life. Then, when you sit within your home, when you lie down, and when you rise up—at every moment and in every hour—your entire being will be surrounded by that expanse, by that life. (*Selected Essays*, 247–248)

The rabbinic leader of Gordon's generation was Rabbi Avraham Yitzhak Kook, the first Chief Rabbi of Israel. The universalistic thrust of Rav Kook's thinking is evident in much of his writings.

> Every plant and bush, every grain of sand and clod of earth, everything in which life is revealed or hidden, the smallest and the biggest in creation—all longs and yearns and reaches out toward its celestial source. And at every moment, all these cravings are gathered up and absorbed by man, who is himself lifted up by the longing for holiness within him. It is during prayer that all these pent-up desires and yearning are released. Through his prayer, man unites in himself

all being, and lifts all creation up to the fountainhead of blessing and life. (N. Glatzer, *The Judaic Tradition*, 558)

You may have noticed that, up to this point, all of the sources that we have discussed were originated by males. It has only been in the last century or so that Jewish women have found a literary voice to express their nature-rooted spirituality. Interestingly, their medium of expression has frequently been poetry. A fine example is the poem "The Moon Sings to the Stream" written in the 1940s by an Israeli poetess, Leah Goldberg.

> I am unity in heaven;
> I am multiplicity in the deep.
> My reflection gazes at me from the stream,
> My double.
>
> I am truth in heaven;
> I am fiction in the deep.
> My reflection gazes at me from the stream,
> In her deceptive fate.
>
> Above I am wrapped in silences,
> Murmuring and singing in the deep.
> I am the Deity in heaven;
> In the stream I am the prayer.
> (*Mukdam u-Meuchar*, 86)

At the same time that Leah Goldberg was writing in Israel, Etty Hillesum, a twenty-seven-year-old woman living in Amsterdam on the precipice of the Holocaust, recorded her spiritual growth in a diary. Here is the entry from August 26, 1941:

There is a really deep well inside me. And in it dwells God. Sometimes I am there too. But more often stones and grit block the well, and God is buried beneath. Then He must be dug out again. I imagine that there are people who pray with their eyes turned heavenwards. They seek God outside themselves. And there are those who bow their head and bury it in their hands. I think that these seek God inside. (*An Interrupted Life*, 44)

On August 18, 1943, Etty wrote a letter from Westerbork, a transit camp, prior to her final deportation to Auschwitz, where she would soon perish.

> You have made me so rich, oh God, please let me share Your beauty with open hands. My life has become an uninterrupted dialogue with You, oh God, one great dialogue. Sometimes when I stand in some corner of the camp, my feet planted on Your earth, my eyes raised towards Your Heaven, tears sometimes run down my face, tears of deep emotion and gratitude. . . . I may never become the great artist I would really like to be, but I am already secure in You, God. Sometimes I try my hand at turning out small profundities and uncertain short stories, but I always end up with just one single word: God. . . . [A]ll my creative powers are translated into inner dialogues with You; the beat of my heart has grown deeper, more active and yet more peaceful, and it is as if I were all the time storing up inner riches. (*An Interrupted Life*, 255)

We can draw at least four conclusions from this survey of richly variegated material: nature-rooted spirituality has not been confined to any particular historical period or locale. It finds expression in various genres, including halachic, philosophical, and literary compositions. Involvement in nature has enriched both religious observance as well as daily relations and living integrally in the world. And, finally, the land of Israel has often acted as a catalyst for this enterprise.

Having referred to R. Nachman of Bratzlav as the foremost proponent of meditating outdoors, it is appropriate to expand upon the spiritual path that he developed. In keeping with traditional terminology, R. Nachman referred to his technique as *hitbodedut*. The following selections outline the methods and goals of *hitbodedut*.

To one of his long-time disciples, R. Nachman gave the following advice: "Our Rebbe commanded him to practice *hitbodedut* for two hours a day. During the first hour he should go out and be silent and concentrate upon speaking [with *Ha-Shem*]. He should prepare his heart for this. Afterwards he should speak for an hour" (*Sichot*, no. 232).

Although R. Nachman lived in town and had a special, private room where he could practice his devotions; nevertheless, he preferred to journey into the fields and woods, secluding himself in prayer (see *Sichot*, no. 162). "He said that it is better to engage in *hitbodedut* outside of the city among the grasses, for the grasses promote arousal of the heart" (*Sichot*, no. 227).

R. Nachman especially encouraged his disciples to go outside in the spring.

> In the winter all of the grasses and plants are dead, for their strength has been nullified in the winter and they are in a state of death. As summer approaches all awaken and are alive. Then it is good and wonderful to go out "to commune (*la-suah*) in the field" (Genesis 24:63). This *sichah* (communing) is prayer and petition, desire and yearnings for *Ha-Shem*, may He be blessed. Then each and every shrub of the field begins to live and grow. All yearn and are included within his communing and prayer. (*Sichot*, no. 98)

On this theme, R. Natan recalled that he and several other disciples accompanied R. Nachman on daily walks outside of Lemberg. One day when it was time for *Minchah* (the afternoon service), they prayed in the field. Afterward, R. Nachman commented that in the same way that his disciples congregated around him during prayer, R. Nachman could see "how every one of grasses knocks against those standing [in prayer], so that they could ascend and enter within their prayer" (*Sichot*, no. 144).

For R. Nachman, the contents of private prayer are not nearly as important as sincerity and devotion.

He also said concerning *hitbodedut*, for it was his custom, may his memory be blessed, that he would greatly encourage everyone to regularly meditate and converse with *Ha-Shem* daily. He said that even if a person cannot speak at all—even if he is only able to utter one word, this too is very good. He said that if a person can only say one word, he should be mentally strong and recite that word repeatedly, countless times. Even if a person spends many days meditating on that one word, this too is very good. As long as he is strong and courageous and constantly repeats this same word, eventually *Ha-Shem*, may He be blessed, will have mercy on him and open his mouth, so that he will be able to fully express himself. (*Likkutei Moharan* 2:96)

Finally, R. Nachman offered a potent rationale for the value of personal, spontaneous prayer that forms the basis of *hitbodedut*.

I have also heard in his name, concerning the value of private communing with one's Master. He said in reference to the prayers, supplications, and petitions, which have been standardized [in the prayer book], that all the destructive spirits and prosecutorial angels already know them and await in ambush on the paths of these prayers because they are well known to them.

This is analogous to a well-travelled route that is known and publicized to all. Even murderers and robbers are there, for this road is well known. But when you travel along a new route or path that is not yet known, none [of the destructive powers] know how to ambush you there, at all. . . .

Private communing with one's Master is like a new path. It is a new prayer that one invents in his heart; therefore, prosecutorial angels do not lie in ambush so much. He nevertheless stressed that it was necessary to recite the rest of the [standard] supplications and prayers. (*Likkutei Moharan* 2:97)

Each of us communes and meditates differently— even if we work with the same technique. Our personal experiences constitute individual paths to *Ha-Shem*. How pleasant and pleasing to the Merciful One are all of our efforts!

4

THE BODY AND POSTURES IN PRAYER AND MEDITATION

We usually assume that spirituality is an intellectual pursuit, rooted in the mind. Too often we ignore the vital role that our bodies play. In fact, the body is an alchemical laboratory in which coarse matter and emotions are elevated and transformed into spiritual gold. Bodywork is underscored in the biblical tradition with statements such as, "From my flesh I shall see God" (Job 19:26). In the following discussion, we shall explore numerous biblical and rabbinic discussions on the body. Of special interest will be the significance of the spine. In the second half of this chapter we will consider body positions and postures, especially the role of sitting and prostration in prayer and meditation.

A good starting point is an encounter between the sage Hillel and his disciples. Hillel emphasized the importance of taking care of one's body. He reminded his students that their bodies constitute a heavenly gift, reflecting the Divine image.

Similarly it is stated, "One who cares for himself is a pious individual" (Proverbs 11:17). Thus Hillel the Elder, when he was about to depart from his disciples, persisted in walking with them. His disciples asked him, "Rabbi, where are you going?" He said to them, "To perform a *mitzvah*." They asked him, "What *mitzvah*?" He replied, "To cleanse [my body] in the bathhouse." They asked him, "Is this really a *mitzvah*?" He said to them, "Indeed. Consider the icons of the emperors that they [i.e., the Romans] erect in their theatres and circuses. The individual who is appointed to clean and wash them is provided with food and he is even glorified with the heroes of the realm. I have been created in the image and likeness [of God], 'for in the image of God did He fashion Adam' (Genesis 9:6). How much more so [must this Divine image be cared for]!" (*Va-Yikra Rabbah, Be-Har*, 34:3, 52b)

There is an interesting rabbinical commentary on Psalms 35:10, which compares the human body to the four species of plant-life that constitute the *lulav*.[1] In the same way that the four species are brought together and waved on Sukkot to celebrate Divine beneficence, so, too, can the human body glorify *Ha-Shem*. This interpretation is found in several different collections. Whereas in *Va-Yikra Rabbah* it is attributed to Rabbi Mani, it is formulated in *Midrash Tanchuma* as follows:

"You shall take for yourselves [on the first day a lovely tree fruit...]" (Leviticus 23:40). This is what Scripture states, "all my limbs shall proclaim, 'Ha-Shem, who is like You?'" (Psalms 35:10). David spoke beautifully when he composed this verse. You should know that the palm frond is like the human spine. The myrtle leaves are shaped like eyes. The willow leaves are shaped like lips and the *etrog* is like a heart. David affirmed that there are no organs more important than these which are equivalent to the entire body, hence "all of my limbs." (*Midrash Tanchuma, Emor*, 19:41a)

---

1. The *Bahir* expands upon this theme; see A. Kaplan, *The Bahir* (York Beach, 1979), 66.

The body not only mirrors the Divine image, it is imprinted with the name of God. In another passage from *Midrash Tanchuma*, there is the assertion that the anatomical shape of three appendages evokes the shape of the three letters that constitute the name *Shaddai* (commonly rendered "Almighty"), which sealed creation. "Every circumcised Jew shall come to the Garden of Eden, for the Holy One, blessed be He has imprinted His name upon each Jew, to enable them to enter the Garden of Eden. What is this name and seal that He placed upon them? It is *Shaddai*. He imprinted each nose with a *shin*, a *dalet* upon the hand and a *yod* upon the circumcision" (*Midrash Tanchuma, Tzav* 14:11a).[2]

The name *Shaddai* has been traditionally interpreted as *sh-dai*, that which is enough. This is explained in a midrashic statement attributed to R. Yitzhak: "'I am God Almighty (*Shaddai*)' (Genesis 17:1). I am He who said to My universe—to the heavens *dai* (enough) and to the earth *dai* (enough). If I had not said to them *dai*, they would have continued to expand until today" (*Bereshit Rabbah* 46:2).

The hasidic master R. Pinchas of Koretz expounded upon this further: "The name *Shaddai* connotes that there is *dai* (enough) in His Godliness for all of creation ... and therefore nothing else in the world is necessary. Understand this thoroughly. [R. Pinchas] was therefore adamantly opposed to patronizing apothecaries or Gentiles for medicinal cures" (*Midrash Pinchas*, no. 36, 14a).

Thus, *Shaddai* represents Divine power that has been harnessed for sacred purposes. One can therefore appreciate the custom of writing this Divine Name on the back of the parchment upon which a *mezuzah* is tran-

---

2. For an extended discussion of this and related passages, see E. Wolfson, "Circumcision and the Divine Name," *Jewish Quarterly Review* 78 (1987): 78.

scribed. Likewise, many covers for *mezuzot* have this Name inscribed upon them, or at least the initial letter, *shin*. *Mezuzot* are then positioned on all the doorways of a person's residence, thereby channeling creative Divine energy into one's domicile.

In the *Midrash Tanchuma*, cited above, we saw the association of the letters of *Shaddai* with different body parts. An interesting discussion of how the letter *shin* relates to the nose is found in the early thirteenth-century treatise, *Hochmat ha-Nefesh*, by R. Eleazar b. Judah, one of the major figures of the *Hasidei Ashkenaz* (German pietists). He notes that the two nostrils, divided by the septum, form an inverted *shin*. This text will be cited in Chapter 6, in conjunction with breathing techniques.

R. Abraham Abulafia formulated a detailed description of how the body is to be integrated into the practice of meditation. He focused on three parts of the body: the head, upper torso, and lower torso. Each of these in turn is divided into three sections: front, middle, and back.

The pertinent texts from Abulafia have been presented and analyzed by Professor Moshe Idel (*Mystical Experience*, 34–37). Idel posits that Abulafia derived his theory from studying *Sefer Yetzirah*. The pertinent passage therein is the following: "The three mother letters *alef, mem* and *shin* are found in each person, [corresponding to the primal elements] fire, water and air. The head is created from fire. The belly is from water. The torso is from air, which mediates between the other two" (*Sefer Yetzirah* 3:4).

Another text that may have influenced Abulafia is Maimonides's directive concerning the two straps of the *tefillin* worn on the head. Maimonides recommended that these straps extend from the head to the navel (*M.T., Hilchot Tefillin* 3:12).

Let us now turn to Abulafia's discussion as it appears in his major work on ecstatic contemplation, *Hayye ha-Olam ha-Ba*:

> There are so to speak three spots on your head: the front, which is the start of the head; the middle, which is the inside of the head; and the back, which is the end of the head. Likewise imagine that there are three points on your upper torso, which is where your heart is located. . . . Likewise imagine that there are three points in your belly: the front, which is the point of your navel[,] . . . the middle, which is the point of your entrails; and the back, which is the point of the end of your spine, which is the place of the kidneys where the spinal cord is completed, the end of the end. (Revised translation based upon Idel, *Mystical Experience*, 35)

A final selection on this topic is tangentially related to Abulafia's discussion of anatomy and is found in R. Hayyim of Volozhin's collected writings. It is based on the observation that there is a fundamental difference in the construction of the *tefillah shel rosh* (head phylactery) versus the *tefillah shel yad* (arm phylactery). Whereas the latter consists of a single compartment, housing four different passages from the Torah, the *tefillah shel rosh* is divided into four distinct compartments, each containing a different passage. R. Hayyim explains:

> The reason is that the head exhibits four senses: sight, hearing, smell and speech. All are separate—ears to hear, eyes to see, the tongue speaks and the nose smells. So it is with Him, may He be blessed; He, too, possesses these attributes according to the secret of the upper *Sefirot*. (*Nefesh Ha-Hayyim*, 370)

R. Hayyim is herein referring to the Kabbalistic doctrine of the *Sefirot*, which posits ten different characteristics or modalities within the Divine Being. On one level, this corresponds to human processes and therefore exemplifies our being created in the Divine image.

Symbolic of this parallelism between *Ha-Shem* and humans is the compartmentalized construction of the *tefillin.*

Let us now shift our focus from a discussion of anatomy to body position. R. Yaakov b. Asher in his religious law code explains that there are three distinct postures for praying: sitting, standing and prostration. In fact, the morning service incorporates all three in succession. He notes that the biblical precedent for each of these modes is Moses on Mt. Sinai, when he received the stone tablets. "I sat on the mountain" (Deuteronomy 9:9); "I stood on the mountain" (Deuteronomy 10:10), and finally "I prostrated myself before *Ha-Shem*" (Deuteronomy 9:18); (see *Tur Orach Hayyim,* 131). By considering these three basic postures, we will deepen our understanding of the role of the body in Jewish prayer and meditation.

SITTING

The initial segment of the morning service is characterized as *Pesukei de-Zimra,* verses from Psalms. The centerpiece is Psalms 145. "Rabbi Avina said, 'Anyone who recites "A Psalm of David" [i.e., Psalms 145] three times daily is assured of meriting the World to Come'" (*B. Berachot* 4b). Accordingly, this Psalm is repeated three times in the daily liturgy.

Each time that Psalms 145 is recited, it is preceded by the verse: "Happy (*ashrei*) are those who sit in Your house. May they eternally praise You. Selah!" (Psalms 84:5). As we shall see, this passage is at the crux of numerous rabbinic assertions. The verses that immediately precede this passage evocatively express the desire to dwell in *Ha-Shem's* earthly abode: "How lovely are Your residences, *Ha-Shem* of hosts. My soul yearns, even pines for *Ha-Shem*'s courtyards; my heart and body sing out to the living God" (Psalms 84:2–3).

According to Maimonides, Psalms 84:5 is the scriptural basis for the rabbinic assertion that spending time in a synagogue is in itself a meritorious act.[3] In this connection one can also mention the custom of sitting briefly in a synagogue before departing and reciting the verse: "Only the righteous will give thanks to Your Name; the upright will sit in Your Presence (Psalms 140:14)."

In his monumental *Guide of the Perplexed*, Maimonides described sitting as a Divine state of being. After quoting a series of verses, including: "You, *Ha-Shem*, sit for eternity; Your throne is perpetual" (Lamentations 5:19), he explained the significance of ascribing "sitting" to *Ha-Shem*: "That is, the stable One who undergoes no manner of change, neither a change in His essence—as He has no modes besides His essence with respect to which He might change—nor a change in His relation to what is other than Himself. . . . Consider every mention of sitting applied to God, and you will discover that it is used in this sense" (*Guide* 1:11, 37f). Thus, sitting represents Divine stability and permanence.

Additionally, we find that Psalms 84:5 was the scriptural basis for the *Hasidim Rishonim*, whom we discussed in Chapter 1. The core text reads: "The *Hasidim Rishonim* used to meditate for one hour prior to praying. What is the basis for this practice? Rabbi Yehoshua b. Levi said, Scripture states, 'Happy are those who sit in Your house' (Psalms 84:5)" (*B. Berachot* 32b).

A related statement by R. Yehoshua b. Levi is the following: "Anyone who enters a synagogue or study hall in this world will merit entering a synagogue or study hall in the world to come, as it says, 'Happy are

---

3. *M.T., Hilchot Tefillah* 11:9; cf. *B. Megillah* 28b.

those who sit in Your house' (Psalms 84:5)" (*Yalkut Shimoni, Tehillim,* no. 803, 938). This parallels a third statement attributed to the same Sage: "Rabbi Yehoshua b. Levi said, anyone who recites a song *shirah* in this world, will merit repeating it in the world to come, as is said, 'Happy are those who sit in Your house. May they eternally praise you. Selah'" (*B. Sanhedrin* 91b).

In general, Jewish sources are silent about how one should sit while praying. An exception to this are directives from R. Avraham, the son of Maimonides. In the early thirteenth-century in Cairo, R. Avraham spearheaded a liturgical reform movement that met with only limited success and much opposition. In an attempt to revitalize Jewish spirituality he advocated a number of innovations, which he contended were actually traditional Jewish practices that stemmed from the time of the prophets. According to R. Avraham, these techniques had long since been neglected and forgotten by Jews, but they had been preserved by Muslims. Three of the practices that he advocated were kneeling during prayers, frequent hand raising, and bowing. We will refer to the last two procedures later on in this chapter and revisit the Islamic connection in Chapter 10.

Concerning the necessity to kneel, rather than sit, during prayer, R. Avraham wrote:

> In the same way that the obligation to stand [during prayer] is standing in the manner that the Sages of blessed memory have explained "like a servant before his master" (*B. Shabbat* 10a)—so too is one obliged to sit during the performance of the prayers like a courteous servant before his master, who has granted him permission to sit. This was the way that the prophets sat during their supplications and prayers, as has been explained concerning Solomon and Daniel: they would petition on their knees [cf. 2 Chronicles 6:13 and Daniel 6:11]. This is an obligation from which one should not desist. (Cited in N. Wieder, *Islamic Influences on the Jewish Worship*, 65)

Whatever the actual body position that is adopted, it should be noted that regulated sitting was not confined to the synagogue. Prescribed sitting is important in the home as well, in connection with the recitation of the *birkat ha-mazon* (the blessings after a meal). The nineteenth-century rabbinic authority from Baghdad, R. Yosef Hayyim, in his Torah commentary, cites and expands upon an exposition by the eighteenth-century kabbalist R. Shalom Sharabi. Sharabi was head of the famous mystical academy in Jerusalem, Beit El. The following are his directives, with an addition in brackets from R. Yosef Hayyim. This material is especially interesting as it offers a precise description of the body posture that one should assume prior to reciting the blessings.

> Before *birkat ha-mazon* one should concentrate on preparing himself to fulfill the positive commandment of reciting *birkat ha-mazon* with awe and love, with forceful concentration, great joy and whole-heartedly, in order to channel Divine abundance (*shefa*), great blessings, wisdom, vitality and sustenance to the holy *Malchut* of *Atzilut*, (the World of Emanation). From her [it will flow] to us and all of the holy realms.
>
> He should close his eyes, fold his hands upon each other: the right over the left,[4] [placing them upon his chest], sit-

---

4. The importance of hand position was discussed by R. Yosef Hayyim in relationship to the recitation of Psalms 145:16, "You open Your hands and fulfill every creature's desire" during the daily liturgy. "The custom in our city is that when one recites the verse *potech* (open) one should turn one's palms heavenwards. It is a beautiful custom to do this symbolic act to receive the Divine abundance (*shefa*) from Above" *Ben Ish Hai*, "*Va-Yigash*," (Jerusalem, 1944), 65.

R. Yosef continues by disapproving of those who also raise their hands at this point. Basing himself upon a passage from the *Zohar*, he contends that there are only two occasions when it is appropriate to raise one's hands in prayer: following ritual hand washing and when the priests bless the congregation.

ting as if before a king—the King of the Universe, the holy *Malchut* of *Atzilut*. (*Ben Ish Hai, Hukkat*, 202)

Up to this point, we have seen discussed sitting within a liturgical context, be it in the synagogue or at home. Sitting is also recommended as a spiritual activity in itself. A biblical source for this is the following: "It is good to wait quietly for salvation from *Ha-Shem*. It is good for a man to bear the yoke [of Heaven] while he is young. Let him sit alone (*badad*) in silence, for He has placed it [i.e., the yoke] upon him" (Lamentations 3:26–28). Note that the word for sitting alone, *badad*, is the root of the technical term for meditation *hitbodedut*.

The spiritual guidebook, *Or Ha-Ganuz*, which is ascribed to the early hasidic master R. Aaron ha-Cohen of Zelichov and Apt, contains several beautiful discussions on the role of sitting in meditation.

> So it is with an individual, with each movement and especially with each act of walking, he should perform a *yichud* [i.e., unification]. When he sits alone and in silence, he becomes a chariot for the World of Thought—for he has taken it upon himself and he should greatly sanctify his thought. The moment that he awakens from thought, which is rest prior to movement, he should see to it that there be a *yichud*, that is a binding of movement and speech and walking and that all be done in sanctity, just like the thought. (*Or ha-Ganuz*, 46)

For a different perspective, see N. Wieder, *Islamic Influences on the Jewish Worship* (Oxford, UK, 1947), 79–82, who discusses R. Avraham b. Maimonides's advocacy of frequent hand raising during prayer; see M. Idel, *The Mystical Experience in Abraham Abulafia* (Albany, NY, 1988), 29, for Abulafia's mimicry of the priestly blessing during meditation; see also the hasidic sources cited by Yitzchak Buxbaum, *Jewish Spiritual Practices* (Northvale, NJ, 1990), 168.

Some forms of Divine service entail movement: these are the positive commandments and the study of Torah and prayer. To perform them entails doing unifications. There is also a type of service by means of resting: when one sits alone and is silent and contemplates upon His exaltedness, may He be blessed. This alludes to the World of Thought, which is the World of Rest that he has taken upon himself. This he should do when he wants to become attached in Divine attachment (*devekut*), he should sit peacefully amidst holy thoughts, in awe and attachment. Thus we read in the verse "when the ark travelled [etc.]" (Numbers 10:35) "and when it rested [etc.]" (Numbers 10:36)—the mysteries of wisdom [are contained therein].[5] (*Or ha-Ganuz*, 72)

STANDING, BOWING AND THE ROLE OF THE SPINE

The key rabbinic prayer, recited thrice daily is the *Shemoneh Esreh*, the "eighteen [actually, nineteen] blessings." It is also referred to as the *Amidah*, "standing prayer," as it is recited while standing. Traditionally, one recites the *Amidah*, with feet pressed together, emulating the celestial beings, described in Ezekiel 1:7, "the legs of each were [fused into] a single rigid leg." Although one's feet are generally immobile during the *Amidah*, the body often sways. "R. Yehudah said, 'This was R. Akiva's practice. . . . [W]hen he was praying privately he would start in one corner of the room and end in the other, owing to all of his bowings and prostrations'" (*B. Berachot* 31a).

Swaying is very common among hasidic Jews and others during prayer.[6] There is a wonderful teaching of the Baal Shem Tov on this issue:

---

5. Cf. Y. Buxbaum, *Jewish Spiritual Practices*, 368.

6. For a discussion of the conflicting perspectives on this topic, see the sources cited by L. Jacobs, *Hasidic Prayer* (New York, 1978), 55.

R. Yisrael Baal Shem, peace be upon him, said, "When an individual is drowning in a river and he is gesturing to remove
himself from the water that is engulfing him, certainly no one
who sees him would ridicule his exertions. So it is during
prayer, when one gestures, do not ridicule this person, for he
is saving himself from the insolent waters, which are the shells
and strange thoughts that threaten to undermine his concentration during prayer." (*Keter Shem Tov*, no. 215, 28a)

Here is another hasidic statement on this issue:

[R. Pinchas] said that all of the winds that blow across the
world are a result of the swaying of Jews while preoccupied
in Torah. This is why it stated in the *Gemara* "Just as the
world cannot exist without the winds, so too the world needs
Jews" [*B. Taanit* 3b]. Why did he compare [Jews] to the winds,
unless the winds were caused by the Jews? The swayings
sustain the souls. This is the mystery of all of the meditations connected with the shaking [of the *lulav*] on *Sukkot*.
(*Midrash Pinchas*, no. 45:7a)

Another aspect of swaying and shaking during prayer explicitly associates spirituality and sexuality.

From the Besht, of blessed memory, "For from my flesh I
shall see [God]" (Job 19:26). Just like physical coupling is not
productive unless intercourse occurs with a vital organ and
desire and joy, so too with spiritual coupling, which is speaking Torah and praying, when it occurs with a vital organ and
joy and pleasure, then it is productive. (*Keter Shem Tov*,
no. 16:4a, based on *Ben Porat Yosef, Noah* 19d)

The Besht's successor, the Maggid of Mezeritch, also commented on this issue:

Prayer entails coupling with the *Shechinah*. Just as there is
movement at the start of sexual coupling, so too one must
sway at the start of prayer. Afterwards one should stand
motionless and adhere to the *Shechinah* with great *devekut*.
Propelled by the swaying, one can attain a state of great
exaltedness. (*Torat ha-Maggid*, Y. Klafholtz, ed., 1:38)

A source for this striking assertion is the classic ethical manifesto, *Reshit Hochmah*, by R. Eliahu de Vidas. "It is proper for a person's complete desire to [be devoted to] fulfilling a Divine commandment, since through its performance he couples with the King's daughter, that is the *Shechinah*" (*Reshit Hochmah ha-Shalem, Shaar ha-Ahavah*, 4:24, 421).

Within this context, we can appreciate a surprising directive by de Vidas' contemporary, R. Moshe ibn Machir in his spiritual manual, *Order of the Day*. As far as I am aware it is unparalleled in any other Jewish source. In describing Friday-afternoon preparations for *Shabbat*, ibn Machir writes about going to the *mikvah* (ritual bath): "And so we have found that the ancient *hasidim* would immerse themselves together with their wives in order to unite their souls in Divine service" (*Seder ha-Yom* 41).

This connection between sexuality and spirituality will be revisited and amplified in Chapter 11.

In addition to swaying, the *Amidah* entails regular bowing. Rigorous bowing finds expression in the *Tanach*. "Elijah ascended to the summit of Mt. Carmel, prostrated himself on the ground and placed his face between his knees" (1 Kings 18:42). Based on this biblical precedent, one finds references to placing one's "head between one's knees" in various postbiblical texts. For example, this practice was recommended in the ancient text, *Hechalot Zutarti*, in a passage that was quoted in Chapter 1. To be sure, in none of the texts is the posture sufficiently described so that we can precisely replicate it. In the above-cited passage, Elijah may have been kneeling on the ground when he placed his head between his knees. Other texts imply that this is done from a standing position.

The act of bowing during the *Amidah* is highly symbolic. There are four customary bowings—two at the start of the prayer and two during the latter stages.[7] These four motions are associated with the four letters of the Ineffable Name, which in turn are connected with the Four [Primal] Worlds. A further extension of this matrix of symbols was suggested by R. Hayyim of Volozhin, who related the letters of the Name to the four terms of endearment found in the Song of Songs (see *Nefesh Ha-Hayyim*, 410).

An exploration into the regulated bowing that accompanies the recitation of the *Amidah* leads into a much broader discussion of the importance of the spine. "The lifeforce of a person and the human structure is dependent upon the spine" (R. Eliahu de Vidas, *Reshit Hochmah ha-Shalem* 3:384).

The eighteen benedictions that form the basis of the thrice daily prayer service are symbolically linked to the spine. Note that once again it is R. Yehoshua b. Levi, the seminal early third-century sage cited near the start of the chapter, who is accredited with these insights. "R. Tanhum reported that R. Yehoshua b. Levi said, 'this corresponds to the eighteen vertebrae in the spine.' R. Tanhum also reported that R. Yehoshua b. Levi said, 'one who prays must bow such that all of the vertebrae of the spine are loosened'" (*B. Berachot* 28b).

During the Middle Ages, there was considerable interest in the significance of the spine. R. Eleazar b. Judah, one of the *Hasidei Ashkenaz* whom we quoted above, offers the following discussion.

---

7. As noted above, R. Avraham, the son of Maimonides, advocated frequent bowing during prayer. Specifically he prescribed four bowings during the *kaddish* and two during the *kedushah* and elsewhere; see Wieder, *Islamic Influences*, 51–54.

The soul, residing on the brain, irrigates the spinal column from the brain. It enters the eighteen vertebrae of the spine. Accordingly, it is the practice upon reciting *modim* [i.e., "we are grateful"] that when she [i.e., the soul] recites "we are grateful to you," she bows until "all of the vertebrae are loosened" (*B. Berachot* 28b); therefore vitality is *hai* (eighteen) . . . as is written, "the soul that sins shall die" (Ezekiel 18:4). Sin (*het*) has the numerical value eighteen, but if there will be repentance then you will merit [the Garden of] Eden, which is a distance of 18,000 centuries. (*Hochmat ha-Nefesh*, 146)

R. Eleazar continues by enumerating eighteen angelic entities that encircle the Divine throne.

Towards the start of our discussion of the body, we quoted a *midrash* that compared the spine to a *lulav*. In the mystical homilies of the *Tikkunei Zohar*, this metaphor is developed and connected to the *Amidah*. The eighteenth homily includes a rich and symbolic discussion of the bowings and the spine that incorporates all of these motifs and others, as well. This presentation begins with a reference to the "Masters of the *Komah*" (i.e., stature/anatomy). This term refers to those individuals who have studied the enigmatic, ancient mystical text, *Shiur Komah* (Measure of the Divine Stature), which is concerned with the astronomical dimensions of the Divine Anthropos. The following selection from *Tikkunei Zohar* is primarily concerned with the human body, which is implicitly associated with the Divine Stature.

When they [i.e., the Masters of the *Komah*] knock on the door [of the Celestial Palace] and recite, "Lord, open my lips," the door of the Palace is opened with many lights that are embroidered with all of the colors of the world. When they enter the Celestial Palace, the *Shechinah* bestows them with privileges. She proclaims, "Master of the universe, behold, the Masters of the *Komah* bow four times during the *Amidah*. Twice during the initial three [blessings] and twice during the latter three. This corresponds to the four letters of Your [Name], [i.e., *YHVH*]. They also straighten up four times, corresponding to its four letters, which are *ADoNaY*. This results in four occurrences of *ADoNaY* within *YHVH*."

One must bend the eighteen vertebrae each time, corresponding to the eighteen benedictions, which are included in the eighteen worlds.[8] This is what the Masters of the *Mishnah* decreed, "[one should bow] until all of the vertebrae are loosened (*B. Berachot* 28b). The spine is a *lulav*, for if it is split, it becomes defective.

Accordingly, one must not interrupt the eighteen blessings of the *Amidah* for they correspond to the eighteen wavings of the *lulav*.[9] Thus the Masters of the *Mishnah* established that even if a snake coils around your foot, you must not interrupt your recitation of the *Amidah* [cf. *B. Berachot* 30b]. This is on account of the eighteen worlds, which consist of the union of *YHVH* and *ADoNaY*, in this fashion *YAHDVNHY*.[10] Its sum is *AMeN* (91). Therefore even if a snake is coiled around your foot you must not interrupt, when you are bowing at [the word] *baruch* (blessed). Concerning what is also stated "but one should interrupt [praying when threatened] by a scorpion" (*B. Berachot* 33a), this is because it has been established that [the laws of the Torah] are to live by and not to die from them (cf. *B. Yoma* 85b). (*Tikkunei Zohar*, no. 18:37a)[11]

In a technical kabbalistic discussion, the author then asserts that when one bows during the recitation of the word *baruch* (blessed), a person should concentrate on

---

8. The expression *hay ha-olamim* (eighteen worlds/eternal) as an epithet for *Ha-Shem* who is eternal is found in *Y. Berachot 10:2*. This is the conclusion of the blessing "*borei nefashot*" recited upon consuming miscellaneous food items.

9. Shaking the *lulav* three times in each of the six directions, yields eighteen. See Chapter 8 for a further discussion of this issue.

10. This is the basic configuration of the *yichudim*; see Chapter 11.

11. See the discussion of this material in P. Giller, *The Enlightened Will Shine* (Albany, 1993), 103–105.

unifying the ten *Sefirot*; furthermore, the letters of the word *baruch* allude to the various *Sefirot*.

In another discourse in *Tikkunei Zohar* the theme of the *lulav* is also discussed.

> When all the other species are bundled together with the *lulav*, which is the spine, what is the appropriate biblical verse? "And I said, I will ascend (*aaleh*) the palm tree (Song of Songs 7:9). [The four letters of *aaleh* form an acrostic.] a=*etrog*; a=*aravah*; l=*lulav* and h=*hadas*. All are fashioned to correspond to the four creatures of the Divine chariot, upon whom *Ha-Shem* rides. (*Tikkunei Zohar*, no. 13:29a)

To summarize, we have seen that the spine is viewed as the centerpiece of the body. It is compared to a *lulav*, which likewise is the anchor of the four species. This is then extended to the four creatures of the Divine Chariot, described in Ezekiel, Chapter 1. Thus, the human body, like the *lulav* and the Chariot, can become a domicile for *Ha-Shem*.

The spine and bowing during the *Amidah* are also connected with the image of the snake. We read in the *Talmud*: "This is what your father [i.e., Rav] said, 'When you bow, bow at the word *baruch* (blessed) and when you straighten up, straighten up at the Divine Name.' When Rav Sheshet bowed, he bowed like a cane and when he straightened up, he straightened up like a snake" (*B. Berachot* 12a–b).

Commenting on "snake" Rashi wrote that one bows "slowly, his head first and afterwards his body, in order that his bowing should not seem like a burden." Additionally, in *B. Baba Kamma* 16a and *Zohar* 3:164a, it is asserted that after seven years the human spine will turn into a snake if a person has not bowed during the *modim* prayer.

Although it is admittedly tangential, we can pursue the spine/snake motif further. We are predisposed to think of the snake as a negative image, owing to the account in Genesis 3, wherein the snake seduced Eve into eating the prohibited fruit. This led to the expulsion from the Garden and mortality. Even in Genesis, however, the snake is introduced as being the shrewdest of all creatures of the field. Recall as well that when *Ha-Shem* commissioned Moses to act as his agent for the liberation of the Israelites, Moses wondered how he could convince the people that he was divinely selected. Thereupon *Ha-Shem* told Moses to throw his staff to the ground, and it became a snake. This was to be the Divine sign (cf. Exodus 4:1–5). During the subsequent competition between Moses and Aaron and Pharoah's magicians, Aaron's staff was transformed into a snake and devoured the Egyptian staves. One can also mention the copper snake that Moses was commanded by *Ha-Shem* to make, to ward off the plague of fiery snakes that had attacked the Israelites (cf. Numbers 21:4–9).

Owing to the snake motif that permeated stories about Moses, it is not surprising that according to the Sages, this imagery was incorporated into the *mishkan* (Tabernacle) that Moses erected. The middle beam of the *mishkan* was said to be wondrous (cf. *B. Shabbat* 98b). It levitated in place without being connected to anything. *Targum Yonatan* on Exodus 26:28 elaborated upon this, and in so doing refers to the snake simile.

> The middle beam, between the struts, extends from one end to the other and was derived from the tree that Abraham planted in Beer Sheva. When the Israelites crossed the sea, the angels chopped down the tree and threw it into the sea, where it floated on the surface of the water. Then the angels proclaimed: This is the tree that Abraham planted in Beer Sheva and he prayed there according to Divine decree. The Israelites took it and fashioned the middle beam [of the *mishkan*] from it—70 cubits in length. It was wondrous that when they set up the *mishkan*, it [i.e., the beam] would wrap itself like a snake around the struts of the *mishkan* and when they would disassemble it [the beam] would straighten out like a staff.

Having explored numerous texts that discuss the role of the spine during prayer, let us further investigate the significance of the spine. The importance of the spine is explicated in medieval mystical literature. *Sefer Bahir*, one of the earliest kabbalistic works—from around 1200—offers an anatomy lesson that pertains to humans, as well as the Divine Anthropos (i.e., God imaged in human form). "The brain is the root of the spinal cord. The body constantly draws sustenance from there. If not for the spinal cord, the brain could not exist and without the brain, the body would not exist . . . therefore the spinal cord dispenses to the entire body from the brain" (*Bahir*, no. 37:9a).

The spine is critical for spiritual as well as physical health. According to an interesting midrashic statement, the soul is chained to the spine. "The soul is like a butterfly (lit. winged grasshopper), and a chain is attached to one of its legs and is connected to the spine. When a person sleeps, his soul leaves [his body] and roams the world" (*Midrash Tehillim*, ch. 11:102). Owing to the attachment of the soul to the spine, upon awakening the soul returns to the body.

There are numerous references in midrashic writings to the concept of an extraordinary spinal vertebra that we each possess, commonly identified as the tail bone and referred to in Hebrew as *luz*.[12] Whereas in general, the human body was formed from the earth and after death it decomposes and returns to the earth, the *luz*, however, is ascribed heavenly origins. According to the Rabbis, this bone is indestructible and can survive any eventuality. As it is the only vestige after death of an individual's corporeality, the *luz* is destined to be the start of resurrection (cf. *Bereshit Rabbah* 28:3).

---

12. R. Margaliot, in *Zohar* 1:137a, no. 9, cites a minority opinion that the *luz* is actually the top of the spine, located opposite the *kesher shel tefillin*.

The anonymous author of the anthology of mystical insights, *Shoshan Sodot*, initially discussed the function of the *luz* as the basis for resurrection in terms of the biblical verse, "Everything goes to one place—everything is from dust and returns to dust" (Ecclesiastes 3:20). He then associated the origins of the *luz* with the *Sefirah* of *Binah* (Understanding), which is commonly referred to as the Supernal Mother and is associated with the process of *teshuvah*, return to *Ha-Shem*. Next, a rather graphic description of resurrection is provided:

> Behold when the propitious time for resurrection of the dead arrives, dew will descend from *Keter Elyon* [the highest of the *Sefirot*] to *Binah*. This corresponds to the *luz* in the lower realm. It [i.e., the celestial dew] functions like leavening in dough and stretches out, extending to all of the limbs, sinews, skin and flesh. [All those who are resurrected] are transported [lit. somersault] to the land of Israel. There they receive their souls in the holy and pure land, for then *Binah* opens her gates and bestows bounty upon the supernal land. (*Shoshan Sodot*, 57a)

An interesting extension of the theory of the *luz* is the assertion that it only receives nourishment from the post-*Shabbat*, Saturday-night meal, referred to as either *melaveh malkah* (the accompaniment of the Queen), or King David's meal. In the well-known story in Genesis 2, Adam was commanded to refrain from eating from two of the trees in the Garden of Eden. Adam and Eve transgressed by eating from the Tree of Knowledge and were punished by expulsion and eventual death. As they committed their sin prior to the Sabbath, the *luz* was uneffected by their transgression and it is for this reason that it is incorruptible.[13]

The *luz* is described as being nut-shaped. As there is also a tree from the almond family that is called *luz*, presumably this is the etymology of the name. There

---

13. R. Avraham Sperling, *Sefer Taamei ha-Minhagim* (Jerusalem, n.d.), 191, cites all of this in the name of *Eliahu Rabba*.

is a twofold connection between *luz* and the patriarch, Jacob. The only biblical reference to the *luz* tree is a narrative involving Jacob (Genesis 30:37). He also experienced a very significant event in a biblical town that was originally named Luz[14]—that is where Jacob had his famous night vision of the ladder to Heaven, with angels ascending and descending upon it. Upon awakening, he realized the spiritual significance of the locale and renamed the place Beit El (i.e., the house of God) (see.Genesis 28:12–19).

Given the association of *luz* with the foundation of the spine and Jacob's vision of a ladder from earth to Heaven at a place called Luz, it is not farfetched to associate Jacob's ladder with the human body. This notion has been expanded upon by numerous renaissance and early modern luminaries. An early formulation is found in the influential Torah commentary of R. Moshe Alshech. Alshech was an important rabbinic authority in sixteenth-century Tzefat. He interpreted Jacob's vision as a message from *Ha-Shem*, confirming Jacob's spiritual superiority over other righteous individuals: "you are elevated over all of them for you are 'a ladder set on the ground'" (Genesis 28:12). Alshech continued by explaining the analogy with the ladder as follows. Owing to Jacob's physicality, he is grounded; nevertheless, his soul ascends to Heaven; (see *Torat Moshe*, 43b).

A fascinating and complex discussion on this topic was formulated by the seventeenth-century Moroccan kabbalist R. Avraham Azulai. He relates the human body to the topography of the land of Israel, as well as Jacob's ladder and the hordes of angels that accompanied the patriarch.

---

14. Interestingly, there was another city in the Near East that bore the name Luz. According to the Rabbis, *tachelet*, the special blue thread for the *tzitzit*, was manufactured there (see *B. Sotah* 46b, and *B. Sanhedrin* 12a).

Know that this ladder corresponds to the mystery of Adam. It encompasses all of the land of Israel. For the shape of the borders of the land of Israel is neither rectangular, nor circular, nor square but rather like a human lying on the ground on his back, with his head to the west and his two arms stretched out—one to the north and one south, and his legs opened—the big toe of one foot pointing to Mount Hor, which is the northwest corner and the big toe of the other foot pointing to the Egyptian river, which is the southwest corner. Between both legs the great sea [i.e., the Mediterranean] is interposed, for it is west of Israel.

Accordingly, you will discover that the land of Israel is divided into large and small strips and the above-mentioned ladder encompasses all of the strips. There are steps on both sides: facing inwards towards Israel and facing outwards, outside of Israel.

Know that anyone who lives outside of Israel is surrounded by 11,000 angels, as is written "One thousand will fall to your left side and 10,000 to your right" (Psalms 91:7). They ascend the steps of the ladder from the outer side, facing outside of Israel. Then they return to their place. As soon as an individual enters the air space of the ladder, immediately 22,000 pure angels descend the inner steps of the ladder. This corresponds to the 22 letters of the Torah [i.e., the Hebrew alphabet]. They accompany him—twenty thousand on one side and two thousand on the other. This is according to the statement "God's chariots are 20,000 and 2,000" Psalms 68:18. Thus, there are 22,000 pure angels, as noted previously.

If one has the misfortune of departing Israel, as he approaches the above-mentioned ladder the 22,000 [angels] leave him and ascend the steps of the ladder and disperse to their places. Thereupon, 11,000 angels descend to accompany him outside of Israel. (*Hesed Le-Avraham*, 19a)

There are also numerous texts from the late eighteenth and early nineteenth century sources that discuss the ladder motif and are worth considering. For example, R. Yaakov Yosef of Polnoyye, the faithful disciple of the Besht, wrote:

The point is that man stands upon the earth and his head reaches Heaven. God's angels ascend and descend within him, for man is referred to as ascending and descending. It is impossible to remain stationary on one level. One must concentrate to unify the Divine attributes, whether he ascends or descends. Everything is connected to the *Shechinah*. Thus it is written, "In all of your paths, know Him" (Proverbs 3:6). Understand this. (*Ben Porat Yosef*, 42a)

Like Azulai, R. Yaakov draws a connection between the human body and Jacob's ladder, though with different results. Herein, the angels of God are connected to Heaven from within the individual.

A hasidic expansion that explicitly refers to the Genesis narrative is the following:

"And he [i.e., Jacob] dreamed" (Genesis 28:12)—the explanation is that in this world a human is like a dreamer, lying in darkness. Indeed no supernal light is revealed to a human in this world. When one awakens by means of serving *HaShem*, namely when one's thoughts come to the supernal realm, then one sees "and behold there is a ladder" (Genesis 28:12) for he himself is the ladder. Even though he is lying on the ground, nevertheless his head reaches heaven. And behold the angels of God [ascend], by means of his study of Torah. (*Or ha-Ganuz*, 22)

This doctrine was also taught by R. Hayyim of Volozhin. R. Hayyim, the pioneer of the Lithuanian *yeshivah* movement, was the leading disciple of the Vilna Gaon and hence the leader of the opponents of Hasidim (i.e., *mitnagdim*). This indicates the universality of this teaching.

Behold, as we have written, man is like a ladder that stands upon the earth and reaches heaven. The angels of God ascend and descend within him. That is to say, they receive ascent or descent from him, as we have written. This is what they said in the *Midrash* [i.e., *Bereshit Rabbah* 68:16]: ladder (*sulam*) corresponds to Sinai.[15] At Sinai the ladder from

15. Sinai and *sulam* (ladder) each have the numerical value of 130. Based on this *midrash*, the *Baal ha-Turim* noted: *sulam* has the numerical value of Sinai, for He showed him (i.e., Jacob) the Sinai event; see *Baal ha-Turim* on Genesis 28:12.

above to below was completed by means of Moses. (*Nefesh ha-Hayyim, Likkutei Maamarim*, 344)

Several other comments of R. Hayyim explore this issue of the celestial roots of the individual and are worth reflecting upon.

Accordingly, the perfect human is like a tree that is planted Above and his shade extends below, which is the body. He is very attached to his root, until he is close to prophecy, for he is very attached to Above and from there to even higher levels extending upwards to the Infinite, Blessed is He. Therefore he is like a pillar that is positioned below, yet he is entirely connected Above, as if by a rope. Thus it is written, "Jacob is a rope that is His allotment" (Deuteronomy 32:9). That is to say, [it is] just like a rope which has one end connected Above and the other below. (*Nefesh ha-Hayyim*, 343)

This image of Jacob as a rope attached to *Ha-Shem* forms the basis for another of R. Hayyim's penetrating discourses:

Each person who believes in the Torah, his soul is attached and grasps the Tree of Eternal Life—grasping onto one of the letters of the Torah that transcends all of the worlds. He is linked, as if by a rope, below to this lowly world. His head, however, is attached above to his root, as it is written "Jacob is a rope that is His allotment" (Deuteronomy 32:9), just like a rope that is connected Above and its end descends below.

If, God forbid, he destroys a spark from his soul, by transgressing a sin that entails cutting off (*karet*), immediately that spark is split from its root—from the rope that it was attached to until now. This is the significance of the following: "And this soul is cut off" (Leviticus 22:3), the explanation is that the small spark that transgressed [is cut off]. The entire soul, however, is not cut off from its root, God forbid. For the part that remains, still rooted and grasping the Holy Torah, redeems him from sin. (*Nefesh ha-Hayyim*, 316)

An extension of this theme is found in the writings of the late nineteenth-century Baghdadi Sage R. Yosef Hayyim. In a discussion of the soul he notes that not everyone can actualize all five levels; nevertheless, there is no need to despair owing to our descent from Adam:

> In any case, every person has a part in primal Adam who comprises all of the created souls. Accordingly, if a person properly participates in Divine service, he will merit connecting the soul to her supernal source. As a result he will be accredited with all [five] levels [of the soul], as previously mentioned.
>
> I shall offer an analogy to this: there is a great rope that hangs in the heart of Heaven. It is many thousand metres wide. A person has a slender string. If he can attach his string to the end of the [celestial] rope that extends to the earth, behold it is considered as if he is holding on to the great rope, "whose head reaches the Heavens" (Genesis 28:12). (*Ben Ish Hai, Va-Yeshev*, 45)

These early modern discussions that employ the image of Jacob's ladder or rope are clearly interconnected. They were likely influenced by two related texts found in zoharic writings: "All knock on the *Shechinah*, which is a ladder with six rungs, and this is the heart. On it the angels of God ascend and descend" (*Tikkunei Zohar*, no. 25:70b).

Here is a more elaborate discussion from the *Raaya Mehemna*:

> The windpipe has six rings, about which it is written "Ascribe to *Ha-Shem*, O Divine beings . . ." (Psalms 29:1). Upon it the voice ascends, dividing into the six voices of the *Shechinah*. The seventh ascends to the mouth, which is the throne. The six rings of the windpipe are like six stairs to the royal throne and the windpipe is a ladder, upon which the angels of God ascend and descend. These are the breaths that arise from the heart and descend to the heart. (*Zohar* 3:235a)

These early texts explicitly refer to the *Shechinah* as a conduit for prayers that are transformed into angels; nevertheless, the anthropomorphic imagery of the Kabbalah makes it easy to transfer this motif to humans.

PROSTRATION

A final posture that is incorporated into the Jewish liturgy is prostration. It is referred to in Hebrew as *nefillat appayim*, lit. falling on one's face. It is practiced daily in a modified form and dramatically enacted on Yom Kippur, during the narrative of the High Priest's activities in the Temple—when the High Priest would utter the *shem ha-meforash* (Ineffable Name), the people would prostrate themselves in awe.

The following biblical text is both a source for the practice, as well as the core of the daily prostration prayer, *tachanun* (petition), or *nefillat appayim*. Having displeased God by undertaking a census, David addressed Gad, the court prophet. "And David said to Gad, I am greatly troubled. Let us fall into the hand of *Ha-Shem* for His mercies are manifold, but into the hand of man let me not fall" (2 Samuel 24:14).

Prostration is performed in the daily morning service after the *Amidah* prayer. Maimonides describes the procedure as follows: "How is the prostration [performed]? . . . He should sit on the ground and fall on his face and utter any petitions that he wishes" (*M.T., Hilchot Tefillah* 5:13).

An even earlier source is found in the *Talmud*: "Prostration [involves] spreading one's hands and feet, as is stated, 'Shall I and your mother and brothers come and bow to you upon the ground?' (Genesis 37:10)" (*B. Megillah* 22b).

Yitzchak Buxbaum has assembled an interesting collection of prayer practices of hasidic masters. Therein we read that certain Rebbes were accustomed to prostrating themselves at various parts of the service. An example is the following description of R. Moshe Teitelbaum. "When he recited the *Shema*, he prostrated himself fully on the ground, with outstretched arms and legs for several hours, and he uttered groans, and all his limbs shook so that his *tallit* would slide off him—though he wasn't aware of that at all" (*Jewish Spiritual Practices*, 170).

In the next chapter, we shall revisit this passage and place it in the context of prayer and martyrdom; for now, it is sufficient to note that prostration was not confined to the *nefillat appayim* prayer, when it was mandatory. Spontaneity and personal intensity are also involved.

The mystical significance of *nefillat appayim* is discussed with much technical detail by R. Hayyim Vital. One aspect of his exposition is the relationship between the *Amidah* and *nefillat appayim*. The former he relates to *olam ha-atzilut*, the World of Emanation namely, the highest of the Four Worlds. Vital then associates *nefillat appayim* with *olam ha-assiyah*, the World of Action, namely, the lowest of the Four Worlds.

> This is what it is necessary to contemplate, while reciting the *nefillat appayim*. Behold, now, when we are reciting the Eighteen Blessings, we are standing in the World of Emanation. . . . Then we cause ourselves to fall from high above in the World of Emanation, where we are currently, and descend below to the depths of the World of Action. This is just like someone who jumps off of a roof to the ground below. This is the secret meaning of *nefillat appayim*. (*Shaar ha-Kavanot, Inyan Nefillat Appayim* 2:303f)

R. Hayyim Vital continues by indicating that once a person has descended to the lowest depths of the World of Action, he is in position to gather the fallen sparks of light that have become trapped in this realm. After they have been gathered, it is possible to elevate them through the Worlds and restore them to their celestial origins. This can only be accomplished if a person dedicates *all* of his spiritual capacities to this task, even to the point of death.

The association of *nefillat appayim* with death was already mentioned in the *Zohar*.

> Come and see. Moses and Aaron handed themselves over
> to death. Why? As is written, "And they fell on their face and
> said, 'God, God of the *ruch[o]t* winds/spirits [of all living
> things]'" (Numbers 16:22). *Ruch[o]t* is written without a *vav*.
> Accordingly, it refers to the Tree of Death. Whenever *nefillat
> appayim* is performed, it is located there. (*Zohar* 3:176b; see
> also 3:121a)

A final exposition on the mystical significance of
nefillat appayim that we shall consider is found in R.
Avraham Azulai's *Hesed le-Avraham*. It is both intricate
and informative, as it connects the calendar with the
celestial realm.

> Know that the number of days of the year that are days of
> sadness (namely when *nefillat appayim* is recited) are days
> served by the intermediate chariot (*merkavah*), which is
> Metatron's chariot, comprising 222 days [equalling *rechev*].
> For Metatron is a *rechev* (carriage) and chariot to the
> *Shechinah*, in the World of Formation. This is the secret of
> "on the Chebar river" (Ezekiel 1:1).[16] On these 222 (*rechev*)
> days Metatron serves with the Holy Creatures and the Four
> Camps [of the *Shechinah*] and the nine celestial spheres. This
> leaves 132 days [of the lunar year] in which *nefillat appayim*
> is prohibited. On these days the throne of Creation serves.
> The letters *k, l,* and *b* [i.e., 132] also spell *kabbel* [i.e., he re-
> ceived]. These are the letters of Kabbalah, for one does not
> transmit the secrets of the *merkavah*, except to the masters
> of the Kabbalah. (*Hesed le-Avraham*, 14a)

The material in this chapter confirms that there has
been intense interest in the role of the body in Jewish
spirituality. Different postures—sitting, standing and
prostration—have been incorporated into the daily liturgy, reflecting the mood of the accompanying prayers.
Our task is to integrate this awareness of the body and
its varying postures into our meditative practice.

---

16. See Chapter 1 for a discussion of this verse. Also, the Hebrew letters of the river Chebar are the same as the word *rechev*,
though in a different order.

5

NOCTURNAL SPIRITUALITY
AND *KIDDUSH HA-SHEM*

Nighttime beckons the seeker. Recall the advice given by R. Yehudah al-Botini (cited in Chapter 2), "It is better, however, if a person meditates at night and he should have many candles burning in the house."[1] In this section, we shall consider various discussions of nocturnal spirituality and conclude with a meditative technique developed by Rebbe Elimelech of Lizhensk. This meditation connects the two themes of nighttime practices and *Kiddush Ha-Shem* (Sanctification of God through self-sacrifice).

In rabbinic and medieval literature, the paradigm for nocturnal spirituality is King David. David's statement, "At midnight I will arise to give thanks to You" (Psalms 119:62), engendered much discussion in the *Talmud*. One of the loveliest commentaries was the following:

---

1. An interesting account of the application of Abulafian techniques and the nocturnal visions that resulted has been preserved by a disciple of Abulafia; see L. Jacobs, *Jewish Mystical Testimonies* (New York, 1977), 67.

"Rabbi Shimon the pious said, 'A lyre was suspended over David's bed. When midnight arrived the north wind came and blew on the harp, which started to play by itself. Immediately David arose and became occupied in Torah, until dawn'" (*B. Berachot* 3b).

The *Zohar* depicts the process of arising at midnight as a cosmic battle between the forces of good and evil.

> Come and see: At the hour when night comes, the celestial doors are closed and the dogs and donkeys roam the world. Permission is given to the evil spirits to be destructive. Everyone is asleep in bed and the souls of the righteous ascend and enjoy being Above. When the north wind is aroused and divides the night, a holy arousal is released in the world, as has been mentioned on a number of occasions. Happy is he who arises at that time and is occupied in Torah study. When he opens up the Torah, he delivers the evil spirits into the holes of the great deep. (*Zohar* 1:242b)

R. Nachman of Bratzlav offered his own perspective on David's practices.

> [R. Nachman] said that King David, of blessed memory, composed the Book of Psalms based on this [i.e., *hitbodedut*/ meditation]. He said that the principal time that King David meditated was lying down in bed. He would cover himself with a blanket and pour out his heart before *Ha-Shem*, may He be blessed. Thus it is written, "Every night I meditated in tears upon my bed" (Psalms 6:7). Happy is the individual who accustoms himself to follow this practice. This the highest [pursuit] of all. (*Sihot ha-Ran*, no. 68:46)

As we have seen, the Psalms have always been a beacon for spiritual guidance. They are also replete with references to noctural spiritual questing.

> Now bless *Ha-Shem*, all servants of *Ha-Shem*,
>   who stand in *Ha-Shem's* house at night.
>   Psalms 134:1
>
> My soul thirsts for God, the living God;
>   When will I come and appear before God? . . .

> By day *Ha-Shem* directs His mercy to me
>   and at night I sing to Him—
>   a prayer to the God of my life.
>   (Psalms 42:3, 9)

God, You are my God; I search for You, my soul thirsts for
You, my body yearns for You, as a parched and thirsty land
that has no water. I shall behold you in the sanctuary, and
see Your might and glory.... I am sated as with a rich feast,
I sing praises with joyful lips when I call You to mind upon
my bed, when I think of You in the watches of the night.
(Psalms 63:2, 6–7, Jewish Publication Society translation)

Nighttime and visions of visiting the Temple, both
earthly and celestial, permeate these verses. The power
of this imagery influenced not only Jews but all who
have been exposed to this material. One need only
mention in passing Mohammed, the founder of Islam.
He had a vision of embarking on a nocturnal journey
to Jerusalem on his legendary steed, Barak. Upon ar-
riving at the Temple Mount, he stood upon the Rock
and ascended to heaven.

It is not surprising that this material likewise had a
profound impact upon R. Yehudah Halevi, the medieval poet laureate of the Jewish people. Halevi's poetry
is replete with nocturnal mystical questing. Here are
a few selections:

Would that I could see Him in my dreams!
I would gladly sleep eternally and never awaken.
If only I could see His face in the interior of my heart,
I would not require my eyes to look outward.
(H. Schirmann, *Ha-Shirah ha-Ivrit be-Sefarad uv-Perovans*, 1:2, 516)

My God, Your dwelling places are lovely
    And Your nearness is in a vision, without riddles.
My dream has brought me to the holy places of God
    And I gazed upon His beautiful liturgies....
I awoke and I was still with You, God,
    And I gave thanks—to You it is so becoming to thank.
(H. Schirmann, *Ha-Shirah*, 517)

My musings on Your Name awakened me,
As I set Your mercies before Me.
They caused me to understand that
    You formed the soul entity,
Which is bound to me—
    She is marvellous in my eyes!
And my heart saw You and believed in You,
As if standing at Sinai.
I sought You in my dream visions;
Your Glory passed by me and descended
    into the clouds.

My thoughts aroused me from my bed,
To bless the Name of Your Glory, *Adonay.*
(*Shirim Nivcharim,* 1)

In one of Halevi's poems, it is clear that his nocturnal questing was part of a larger spiritual movement.

Go outside at midnight
    in the footsteps of the men of renown,
Upon their lips are praises;
    they embody neither guile nor extortion.
Their nights are devoted to prayers;
    Their days to fasts.
Their hearts are pathways to God.
    There are places for them in His throne.
Their way—a ladder upon which to ascend
    To *Ha-Shem,* our God.
(H. Schirmann, *Ha-Shirah,* 518)

Maimonides likewise extolled the virtues of nighttime. He recommended:

When, however, you are alone with yourself and no one else is there and while you lie awake upon your bed, you should take great care during these precious times not to set your thought to work on anything other than that intellectual worship consisting in nearness to God and being in His presence in that true reality that I have made known to you.
(*The Guide of the Perplexed,* S. Pines, trans., 3:51, 623)

Additionally, in his code Maimonides offers both a scriptural and midrashic basis for the superiority of nighttime.

> Even though it is commanded to study during the day and night—one acquires most of his wisdom at night . . . The sages have said, "The song of Torah is only at night" (see *Exodus Rabbah* 47), as is stated, "Arise and sing out at night [at the start of the watches, pour out your heart like water before the presence of *Ha-Shem*]" (Lamentations 2:19). (*M.T., Hilchot Talmud Torah* 3:13)

Undoubtedly, one of the most intriguing developments in medieval Jewish spirituality was the practice of the *sheelat halom*, dream inquiry. The classic example of this is R. Yaakov of Marvege's *Responsa from Heaven*. Prior to going to bed, this rabbinic authority would formulate a halachic question. While asleep he would receive a celestial reply, which he then recorded upon awakening.[2]

An interesting adaption of this practice is found in the diary of R. Hillel Zeitlin (1871–1942), the leading interpreter of Jewish mysticism and Hasidism for early twentieth-century Eastern European Jews. In an entry recorded during World War I, he writes about a series of peculiar dreams he experienced. From the conclusion of this account we see that prior to falling asleep he would meditate upon a particular biblical verse or passage from the *Siddur*.

> I slept enmeshed in great spiritual pain and intense longing for the One who transcends this earth.
> Then the abovementioned dream recurred, but entailing much greater flight. There was no house, no ceiling, nor any

---

2. See M. Verman, *The Books of Contemplation: Medieval Jewish Mystical Sources* (Albany, 1992), 19 n. 46, for bibliographical references on this subject.

obstacle or barrier: no restraint or hindrance. I flew and flew, floating and floating, ascending ever higher, until I hovered above the supernal garden. I saw the garden from a distance, approached it and "peered through the lattice" [Song of Songs 2:9]. I wanted to enter, but the garden was completely closed.

I ascended even higher by means of the biblical verse that I was reciting: "In the thirtieth year, on the fifth day of the fourth month, when I was in the community of exiles by the Chebar Canal, the heavens opened and I saw visions of God" [Ezekiel 1:1].

I ascended higher and higher by means of this recitation, but "visions of God" I did not see. I circled about *Pardes*, but I could not enter *Pardes*.[3]

Usually, I perceive myself ascending by means of a biblical verse or mystical doctrine. Today, this morning, I was able to ascend by means of the prayer: "Please, by the strength of Your right hand's greatness."[4] (*Al Gevul Shnei Olamot*, 176)

One of the benefits of nighttime in promoting spiritual awareness is the relative lessening of activity and the diminution of distractions. A way to artificially create this environment is simply to close your eyes. Moshe Idel has collected a number of sources on this practice. The following comments by an anonymous kabbalist is representative: "And what is the essence of *hitbodedut*? By closing the eyes for a long time, and in accordance with the length of time, so shall be the greatness of the apprehension. Therefore, let his eyes always be shut until he attains apprehension of the Divine, and together with shutting his eyes negate every thought and every sound that he hears" (M. Idel, *Studies in Ecstatic Kabbalah*, 134).

---

3. *Pardes* is a cognate of Paradise and constitutes the locus of rabbinic theosophy; see *B. Hagigah* 14b.

4. The start of a prayer attributed to R. Nehuniah b. Ha-Kanah, which has been incorporated into the morning service and consists of an acrostic for the Forty-two-Letter Name.

Until this point we have been focusing on the relationship between nighttime and private spiritual development. Mention should also be made of the practice by the pious to arise at midnight and mourn for the destruction of the Temple. It is told about R. Avraham Halevi Beruchim: "Always at the midnight hour he ran through the streets of Tzefat, weeping and crying out: Arise in *Ha-Shem*'s name, for the *Shechinah* is in exile, the house of our sanctuary is burned, and Israel is in great distress. He wailed outside the windows of the learned and did not desist until he saw that they had arisen from their sleep" (G. Scholem, *On the Kabbalah*, 149).

R. Avraham lived in sixteenth-century Tzefat, and it was then and there that a formal midnight prayer service was developed. It is known as *Tikkun Hatzot*.[5] After arising an individual would take some ash and place it upon his forehead on the spot where the *tefillah shel rosh* is affixed. He would then remove his shoes, wash his hands, sit on the floor near the doorpost and recite the basic confession. Afterwards psalms and hymns are chanted, beginning with Psalm 137, "By the rivers of Babylon, there we sat and wept when we remembered Zion."

An important source for this ritual is a statement in the *Zohar*: "These are the mourners of Zion. They weep over the destruction of the Temple. At the start of the middle four hours of the night they begin and recite, 'By the rivers of Babylon, there we sat and wept [etc.]' (Psalms 137)" (*Zohar* 1:295b).

We have just seen the connection between nocturnal spiritual practices and the commemoration of the tragedies of our national history. Pursuing this topic

5. On the evolution of this practice, see G. Scholem, *On the Kabbalah and Its Symbolism* (New York, 1969), 146–150.

further will act as a bridge to the culmination of this chapter, namely, Rebbe Elimelech's nighttime meditation.

Martyrdom for the sake of honoring *Ha-Shem* is an integral part of Judaism. It has been our unfortunate lot that thoughout the ages millions of Jews have been compelled to make the supreme sacrifice. The *Shoah* is the most recent and horrific example of this tragic process.

Martyrdom was characterized by the Rabbis as *Kiddush Ha-Shem* (sanctification of the Name). This principle is based on the following biblical passage: "You shall protect and fulfil my commandments: I am *Ha-Shem*. You shall not profane My holy Name, so that I may be sanctified in the midst of the Israelites: I am *Ha-Shem* who sanctifies you—who brought you out of the land of Egypt to be your God: I am *Ha-Shem*" (Leviticus 22:31–33).

Maimonides enumerated the obligations incumbent upon all to uphold this biblical commandment. In part, he wrote,

> All Jews are commanded to sanctify His great Name, as it is stated, "And I shall be sanctified in the midst of the Israelites" (Lev. 22:32). . . . If it is a time of national persecution—such as during the reign of King Nebuchadnezzar, the wicked, and his cohorts—if a decree is issued to nullify our religion or any of the commandments, one should submit to death rather than violate any of the commandments. (*M.T., Yesodei ha-Torah*, 5:1, 3)

While Jewish history is replete with acts of martyrdom, one of the exemplary cases is that of the great sage R. Akiva. The story of his heroic death has been recorded in the *Talmud* and is also retold on *Yom Kippur*. In the *Talmud* it is part of a discussion concerning the significance of the second verse of the *Shema*, "You shall love *Ha-Shem*, your God, with all of your heart and with all of your soul and with all of your might" (Deuteronomy 6:5).

Since it is stated "with all of your soul," why was it also necessary to state "with all of your might"? . . . Rabbi Akiva said "with all of your soul"; this signifies even if he removes your soul [i.e., he kills you].

Our Rabbis taught: Once the wicked [Roman] empire decreed that Jews must not study Torah. Pappus b. Yehudah came upon Rabbi Akiva teaching public classes in Torah. He asked him, "Akiva, aren't you afraid of the empire?" He replied, "I'll formulate a parable for you to explain what this is like—to a fox that was walking along a riverbank. He saw many fish huddled together in various places. He said to them, What are you fleeing from? They said to him, From the nets that humans use against us. He said to them, Why don't you come up onto the dry land and we will dwell together as our ancestors used to? They said to him, Are you really the one who is called the wisest of animals? You aren't smart, but stupid. If we are in our natural environment and we are nevertheless afraid, how much more so if we would be in a deadly environment! So too with us. Now we are sitting and studying Torah, in which it is written, 'for it is your life and a lengthening of your days' (Deuteronomy 30:20) and we are in this predicament; how much more so, if we would go off and abolish it!"

The Rabbis said: It was only a few days later that R. Akiva was captured and imprisoned. They captured Pappus b. Yehudah and imprisoned him as well. R. Akiva said to him, "Pappus, what brought you here?" He replied, "Happy are you, Rabbi Akiva, who was caught while teaching Torah. Woe to Pappus, who was caught while involved in worthless activities."

They took R. Akiva out to execute him at the time of the recitation of the *Shema*. They combed his flesh with iron combs, as he accepted upon himself the yoke of the kingdom of Heaven [i.e., he recited the *Shema*]. His students asked him, "Our Rabbi, even now [you are able to pray]?" He said to them, "All of my life I have been troubled by the expression 'with all of your soul' (Deuteronomy 6:5), signifying even if they take your soul. I said [to myself], When will I be able to fulfill this? Now that the opportunity is at hand, shall I not fulfill it?" He lengthened the word *echad* (one) so that he died while reciting the word *echad*. A heavenly echo called out, "Happy are you, Rabbi Akiva, whose soul departed with the word *echad* . . . Happy are you, Rabbi Akiva, for you have been granted eternal life." (*B. Berachot* 61b)

For almost two millenia R. Akiva's heroism and devotion to *Ha-Shem* have acted as a spiritual paradigm. During the Crusade massacres, thousands of Jews died while reciting the *Shema*.[6] According to the *Zohar*, this act of R. Akiva's should even be emulated during daily prayers: "Next [the one praying] should place himself amongst those who have submitted themselves to the sanctification of *Ha-Shem*. This occurs during the unification of the *Shema*. Anyone who has this intention while reciting this verse is considered to have undergone the sanctification of *Ha-Shem*" (*Zohar* 3:195b).

With this background, we can better understand the actions of R. Moshe Teitelbaum that we quoted previously. "When he recited the *Shema*, he prostrated himself fully on the ground, with outstretched arms and legs for several hours, and he uttered groans, and all his limbs shook so that his *tallit* would slide off him—though he wasn't aware of that at all" (Buxbaum, *Jewish Spiritual Practices*, 170). Thus, R. Moshe had clearly internalized the classical statements on martyrdom and the recitation of the *Shema*. His surrendering to the experience manifested itself in physical prostration.

In order to understand the intensity of this hasidic master, let us consider several general statements on prayer from the Besht, the founder of Hasidism, and his brother-in-law, R. Gershon Kutover. Each underscores the absolute devotion that should be cultivated, in order for an individual to address the Master of the Universe.

---

6. See S. Spiegel's poignant study, *The Last Trial* (New York, 1969), esp. p. 18.

Know that each word [of prayer] is a complete organism (*komah shelemah*). It is necessary for one to devote all of his energy to it, for if not then the word will become deficient, as if it were missing a limb. (*Tzevvaat ha-Rivash*, 6)

I heard them say that the holy Rabbi, our teacher, Gershon, once told our teacher, Rivash [i.e., Rabbi Israel Baal Shem], these words, "Whenever you are still able to recite the prayer 'Blessed are You . . .' out of your own volition, know that you have not yet achieved proper concentration. An individual should achieve such a state of ego dissolution (*hitpashtut*) that he no longer possesses any strength or intellectual energy for the particulars of the prayer."

[R. Yisrael of Koznitz, who transmitted this teaching, added the following comments, thereby underscoring that proper ecstacy does not have antinomian consequences. "It is true that an individual can be so removed from all physicality and desire, being connected only to his Creator, that he is not even aware of reciting his prayers, owing to the extent of his awe and *devekut*. He nevertheless recites all the prayers in their prescribed order—for Heaven is merciful to him and bestows upon him speech and the power to pray, as is written, 'My God, open my lips . . .' (Psalms 51:17)."] (*Avodat Yisrael, Metzora*, cited by M. Hallamish, "*Al ha-Shetikah ba-Kabbalah uv-Hasidut*," in *Dat ve-Safah*, M. Hallamish, ed., 81)

The last source in this series of hasidic texts is likewise from the Besht.

You should think prior to praying that you are prepared to die during that prayer owing to the intensity of the concentration. There are those who pray with such intensity that sometimes it would be natural for them to die after uttering two or three words to Him, may He be blessed. . . . Truly it is a great mercy that *Ha-Shem*, may He be blessed, gives them the strength to complete their prayer and continue living. . . .

Behold, I wish to humble myself in order that I might serve *Ha-Shem*, may He be blessed, in truth and with a complete heart in love and fear, in order that I will bring about His unification; therefore, I desire to humble myself to such an extent that I will offer myself as a sacrifice to Him. (*Tzevvaat ha-Rivash*, 7)

Other horrific events in our history have also acted as a catalyst for spirituality. R. Avraham b. Eliezer Halevi, who settled in Jerusalem following the expulsion from Spain, described in vivid detail a meditation that was developed to escape the pain of inquisitional torture.

> This is a tradition of our Sages. One who resolves to hand himself over for the honor of *Ha-Shem*, no matter what happens to him, this person will not feel the pain of the blows that would be painful to other people, who did not make this resolution. . . . [When he is being tortured], he should meditate on the honorable and awesome Name affixed between his eyes. . . . And the holy Name is a burning fire and its letters spark throughout the expanse of the universe. He can enlarge them according to the power [of his concentration]. Then he can be assured that he will overcome this tribulation . . . nor will he feel the pain of the blows and tortures. (*Megillat Amrafel*, 153)

During the mid-seventeenth century, Eastern European Jewry was ravaged by the Chmielnicki massacres, in which an estimated 100,000 Jews were killed and 300 communities were destroyed. In the ensuing decades, a number of spiritual manuals were composed in which visualizations on martyrdom play an important role, such as R. Alexander Siskind's *Yesod Ve-Shoresh ha-Avodah* and R. Tzevi Hirsh Kaidanover's *Kav ha-Yashar*.[7] The latter text offers an especially graphic visualization.

> When one arrives at a place [during the prayer service] when it is appropriate to sacrifice himself for the sanctification of *Ha-Shem*, he should raise his arms and hands, as if he is submitting to the sanctification of *Ha-Shem*. Thus he should consider himself to be a burnt-offering (*olah*).[8]

---

7. See Y. Buxbaum, *Jewish Spiritual Practices*, (Northvale, 1990), 425, for a discussion of these sources.

8. This notion is in keeping with the verse: "a contrite spirit constitutes sacrifices to God" (Psalms 51:19). On the topic of raising one's hands during prayer see above, Chapter 4.

Sacrificing oneself for the sanctification of *Ha-Shem* is [appropriate] during the recitation of the *Shema* when he says "And you should love *Ha-Shem* with all of your heart and all of your soul" (Deuteronomy 6:5). . . . He should think to himself that it is his lot to reside among idolators. The world is dark around him. He can never repay the goodness that the Holy One, blessed be He, bestowed upon him by not making him an idolator. Certainly, when he realizes this his heart will flame with great happiness. From this happiness and burning love, he should imagine that there is a fire in front of him and they want to force him to convert, God forbid. Then he should jump into the bonfire out of love and affection for the unification of the Holy One, blessed be He and His *Shechinah*. (*Kav ha-Yashar*, ch. 63)

This visualization of jumping into a fire to sanctify *Ha-Shem* constitutes the basis of a spiritual directive formulated by Rebbe Elimelech of Lizhensk, one of the pivotal theoreticians of Hasidism.[9] In *Noam Elimelech*, his oft-printed collection of sermons on the weekly Torah section, he developed the theory of the role of the *tzaddik*, the righteous leader of the hasidic community. The *tzaddik* is a spiritual bridge, spanning the chasm between humans and God. Most editions of *Noam Elimelech* are prefaced by a "short list" of contemplative practices, based on a manuscript from Rebbe Elimelech. The first paragraph of this text offers the following directive:

Each moment when one is unoccupied with Torah study, and especially when sitting idly alone in a room, or lying

---

9. An even earlier text and possible source of influence is the following passage from Bahya's *Hovot ha-Levavot*: "A pious man who used to get up at night and say, 'My God, You have made me hungry and naked, and You have put me in the darkness of night. But I swear by Your power and greatness, that were You to burn me with fire, it would only add to my love for You and my attachment to You.'" Bahya ibn Pakuda, *The Book of Direction to the Duties of the Heart*, M. Mansoor, trans. (London, 1973), 428.

in bed and unable to sleep, one should contemplate this positive commandment, "And I shall be sanctified in the midst of the Israelites" (Leviticus 22:32). He should think and imagine in his mind that a great and awesome fire is burning before him, ascending to the midst of heaven. In order to santify *Ha-Shem*, he should act against his nature and throw himself into this fire, for the sanctification of *Ha-Shem*. "And the Holy One, blessed be He, joins a good thought to a deed" (see *T. Peah* 1:4). He will discover that he is no longer sitting or lying idly, but rather is fulfilling a positive biblical commandment. (*Noam Elimelech*, Introduction)

At first Rebbe Elimelech's suggestion may seem rather extreme and even off-putting. Please do not dismiss it out of hand. In the same way that it is the nature of fire to ascend upwards, so too is it the goal of spirituality to ascend to *Ha-Shem*. It can be noted that the standard, biblical word for sacrifice is *korban*, based on the root signifying "drawing near." This is indicative of all sacrifice, enabling the individual to come close to *Ha-Shem*. Furthermore, the principal biblical sacrifice is referred to as an *olah*, a burnt-offering that is totally consumed by fire; (see Leviticus 1:3). The word *olah* means "that which ascends" and is emblematic of the elevation of the soul.

As an extended footnote to this discussion on *Kiddush Ha-Shem*, let us consider several classical sources on this theme. The biblical paradigm for self-sacrifice associated with fire is the account found in *Daniel*, ch. 3, related to the three communal leaders: Hananyah, Mishael and Azaryah (Shadrach, Meshach, and Aved-Nego), who refused to worship idols and were punished by being thrown into a fiery furnace, where they were miraculously saved. This motif was subsequently incorporated into the *Midrash* and applied to Abraham.[10]

---

10. See *Bereshit Rabbah* 38:19, wherein Abraham, in his youth, was thrown into a fiery furnace by Nimrod.

Interestingly, according to the talmudic Sages the precedent for submitting to martyrdom in fire were the frogs of the second plague in Egypt.

> Todos the Roman expounded: How did Hananyah, Mishael and Azaryah know that they should throw themselves into a burning furnace in order to sanctify *Ha-Shem*? They derived it by extrapolating from the account of the frogs.[11] Frogs are not obliged to fulfill *Kiddush Ha-Shem*; nevertheless, it is written about them, "[The Nile will swarm with frogs, and they will come up and enter] your palace . . . and your ovens and kneading bowls" (Exodus 7:28). . . . [If frogs were willing to do this], since we are commanded to fulfil *Kiddush Ha-Shem*, how much more so [must we]! (*B. Pesahim* 53b)

Incidentally, R. Akiva was intrigued by a linguistic peculiarity in the biblical account of the frogs in Egypt. He concluded that the text described a frog of mythical proportions. Exodus 8:2 literally states: "Aaron stretched his hand on the waters of Egypt, and the frog arose and covered the land of Egypt." Owing to the reference to frog in singular, R. Akiva asserted, "There was one frog that encompassed all of Egypt" (*B. Sanhedrin* 67b).

To conclude, the ultimate self-sacrifice of *Kiddush Ha-Shem* should be viewed as an act of spiritualization, the transference of life from the material to the Eternal. The sustaining power of *Ha-Shem* is neverending. This was exemplified by Moses' initial encounter with *Ha-Shem*, wherein he was confronted by a bush that burned with fire but was not consumed (Exodus 3:2). If you choose to work with Rebbe Elimelech's visualization, always be mindful of *Ha-Shem*'s providential sustenance—"And you who connect with *Ha-Shem*, your God, all of you are alive this day" (Deuteronomy 4:4).

---

11. The devotion of the frog is also echoed in the anecdote recounted in Chapter 3 involving King David.

6

BREATHING

The movement is natural and gentle: air, omnipresent and impalpable, is quietly inhaled. What was outside enters within, filling expansively. The external is transformed into inner vitality and sustenance—then it is expelled. So, too, we shall proceed in this survey of Jewish musings on the significance of breath by considering concepts that are external and then become internalized.

Within Jewish spiritual literature there is much discussion concerning the significance of breath. What follows is an exploration of some of this material. After examining the fundamental concept that all life is dependent upon the breath of God, we shall consider the biblical connection between breath and the soul. This will be followed by an examination of kabbalistic and hasidic texts, culminating with R. Nachman of Bratzlav's teachings on the mystical significance of breath. The thrust of much of this material is theoretical, though one could easily develop specific techniques based upon these sources.

Divine breath animates. *Ha-Shem* blew the "breath of life" into the nostrils of the primordial human, as is written: "*Ha-Shem*, God, formed the earthling (*ha-adam*) from the dust of the earth. He exhaled the breath of life into his nostrils, and the earthling became a living being" (Genesis 2:7). Similarly, in Deuteronomy 8:3 we read that we are not sustained "by bread alone, but each individual shall live on that which comes from God's mouth." Thus Job affirmed, "The spirit (*ruach*) of God has made me; and the breath (*nishmat*) of the Almighty has given me life" (Job 33:4). This was then extended to all of creation: "By the word of *Ha-Shem* the heavens were made, and all the hosts by the breath of His mouth" (Psalms 33:6). At the end of days, it will be the Divine breath that effectuates national resurrection: "You will know that I am *Ha-Shem*, when I open your graves and raise you, My nation, up from them. I will place My spirit in you and you will be revived, and I will settle you in your land" (Ezekiel 37:13–14).

Within *halachah*, the principal criterion for assessing whether an individual is still alive is by checking to see if he or she is breathing. Rashi noted: "[they check] his nose—if there is no life force in his nose, in that he is no longer breathing, assuredly he has died" (*B. Yoma* 85a).

From the Divine perspective our lives are exceedingly short. According to King David, the life span of a human being is but one breath of *Ha-Shem*. "You have designated my days and life span a few handbreadths long; it is nothing to You—the entire existence of a human is merely a breath. Selah!" (Psalms 39:6).

Genesis 2:7, cited above, resonated with many Jewish thinkers. Ramban asserted that the human soul stems "from God's soul (*me-nishmat eloah*)" (*Kitvei Ramban*, 2:285). *Sefer ha-Yashar*—which has been attributed to a number of different authors and was presumably composed in the early thirteenth century—noted that in Genesis 2:7 the human body is formed and created, whereas the soul is unique in her origin. "We can discern from the expression "He exhaled" that He took her [i.e., the soul] and did not create her, rather He emanated one of the facets of His Glory and gave it to Adam" (*Sefer ha-Yashar*, 58).

Reflecting on this issue, a number of medieval and early modern thinkers repeat the statement "one who exhales, exhales from inside of himself," namely, what is essential.[1] A trenchant formulation of this principle is by R. Shneur Zalman of Liadi, the founder of Lubavitch Hasidism.

> The second soul of a Jew is truly a part of God from Above, as it is written, "And He breathed into his nostrils the breath of life" (Genesis 2:7) and "You breathed it [the soul] into me" [*B. Berachot* 60b and morning prayer]. It is written in the *Zohar*, "one who exhales, exhales from inside of himself," namely from his interior and innermost being— for the interior and innermost life-force of man is emitted by exhaling forcefully. (R. Shneur Zalman of Liadi, *Likkutei Amarim*, ch. 2, 6a)

In Chapter 4, we had occasion to discuss at some length the story of Jacob's vision of the heavenly ladder and its association with the spine. In the *Zohar* we find another interpretation. Therein a connection is made between the nose, the life-soul, Jacob's ladder and the Divine throne. Within this framework, the angels that ascend and descend the ladder are interpreted as breath.

---

1. This notion is found in R. Moshe Alshech, *Torat Moshe* (Israel, 1970), 7b, who was paraphrasing Ramban's Torah commentary; see also *Sefer ha-Besht* 1, no. 91, and R. Dov Baer of Mezeritch, *Maggid Devarav le-Yaakov*, ed. R. Shatz (Jerusalem, 1970), 251, where this statement appears in Hebrew. In even later sources, such as the *Tanya/Likkutei Amarim*, ch. 2, f. 6a, it is cited in Aramaic and attributed to an unknown passage from the *Zohar*.

What is the significance of the nose? "He breathed into his nostrils the life-soul" (Genesis 2:7). This [i.e., the life-soul] is the image that is on a human, about which it is written, 'And he dreamed and behold there was a ladder' (Genesis 28:12). The ladder is the life-soul, the throne for the Name, *Ha-Shem*, which comprises fear and love, Torah and commandments. [The Name] resides on her. From this throne are hewn all of the Jewish souls; it is the image on the human head.

"Behold the angels of God are ascending and descend upon it" (Genesis 28:12). These are the breaths that ascend and exit the body, by means of this ladder. (*Zohar* 3:123b)

Philo, the pioneer of Jewish philosophy, offered an additional insight on Genesis 2:7. He asserted that had it not been for this act of Divine infusion, humans would not have the capacity to contemplate God.

"Breathed into" (Genesis 2:7) is equivalent to 'inspired' or 'be-souled' the soulless. . . . [T]hat which inbreathes is God, that which receives is the mind, that which is inbreathed is the [Divine] breath. What, then, do we infer from these elements? A union of all three is produced, as God extends his power through the mediant breath to the subject. And to what purpose, save that we may obtain a conception of Him? For how could the soul have conceived of God had He not infused it and taken hold of it as far as was possible? For the human mind would never have made bold to soar so high as to apprehend the nature of God had not God Himself drawn it up to Himself, so far as it was possible for the human mind to be drawn up, and imprinted it in accordance with the (divine) powers accessible to its reasoning. (*Philo of Alexandria*, D. Winston, trans., 127)

Let us look a little more carefully, at this key verse from Genesis. "*Ha-Shem*, God, formed the earthling from the dust of the earth. He blew into his nostrils the breath of life, and the earthling became a living being" (Genesis 2:7). Thus, we see that the Deity who animated the original human is characterized by two pivotal names: *Ha-Shem* and God [i.e., *Elohim*]. According to the talmudic Sage R. Shmuel b. Nachman, *Ha-Shem* refers to the attribute of Divine mercy—as in *"Ha-Shem, Ha-Shem,* God of mercy . . ."* (Exodus 34:6)—whereas God refers Divine judgment, as in, "the case of both parties shall come before God" (Exodus 22:8) (see *Bereshit Rabbah* 73:2). This pattern is evident in various biblical accounts. For example, Ramban, in his commentary on Genesis 22:12, perceptively noted that in the *akedah* story of the binding of Isaac, it was God who tested Abraham by commanding him to sacrifice his son, whereas it was the angel of *Ha-Shem* who stopped him.

These two Divine Names were incorporated into an interesting breathing technique, developed by an anonymous hasidic master. It is mentioned in the Torah commentary of R. Hirsh of Zydaczow, who heard about it from his brother. "For even one twentieth of a twenty-four hour period he [i.e., the unnamed *tzaddik*] did not cease to adhere to the Creator. . . . With each and every breath, when he inhaled he focused on the Name, *Elohim,* and when he exhaled he focused on the Name, *Ha-Shem,* blessed is He and blessed is His Name" (*Tefillah le-Moshe,* 10b).[2]

R. Eliahu de Vidas offers a theoretical discussion on the relationship between breathing and the Four-Letter Name:

> There are 1,080 parts to an hour, corresponding to the Four-Letter Name, which has 1,080 different letter-vowel permutations. These 1,080 parts of the hour correspond to 1,080 breaths that a person breathes [each hour]. Each breath corresponds to one of the letter-[permutations] of the Four-Letter Name, giving life to each breath. Thus, "[not by bread alone,] but each individual shall live on that which comes from God's mouth" (Deuteronomy 8:3). (*Reshit Hochmah ha-Shalem, Shaar ha-Yirah* 1:10:26, 184; cf. R. Isaiah Horowitz, *Shnei Luhot ha-Brit Shaar ha-Otiyyot,* 2:47a)

---

2. Thanks to Dr. Zeev Gries for providing me a copy of this text; see also Y. Buxbaum, *Jewish Spiritual Practices* (Northvale, NJ, 1990), 109.

This verse from Deuteronomy also serves as a spring-board for an important reflection. Since we are animated by the Divine spirit, why do we need to sustain ourselves physically? R. Hayyim of Volozhin summarized the answer given by R. Hayyim Vital as follows:

> This is the real issue. Certainly the soul (*neshamah*) is not nourished by physical bread. At the moment that the Holy One, blessed be He, said, "let the earth sprout vegetation" (Genesis 1:11) and all such statements, from the air of His mouth, may His Name be blessed, the potential was created for this entity and its ability to exist. The absence of Divine Providence would negate the physical existence of this entity. The power that sustains it is spiritual. Accordingly, each food substance is comprised of two elements: one physical and the other spiritual. (*Nefesh Ha-Hayyim*, 383)

R. Hayyim's contention is that our bodies are nourished by the food that we eat and simultaneously our souls are nourished by the spiritual force that has brought this food into existence.

Before leaving this particular issue on the relationship between the body and soul it is worth considering a doctrine formulated by Maimonides. He contends that each person possesses two essentially different souls, which he designates *neshamah* and *nefesh*. An individual's life force (*neshamah*) needs a body to support it. At death the *neshamah* perishes; whereas the Divine soul (*nefesh*), which comprises pure consciousness (*daat*), returns to *Ha-Shem*, its source (see *M.T., Yesodei ha-Torah*, 4:8, 9).

The Divine spirit-breath was viewed as the first cosmic principle (*Sefirah*) in the classic cosmological work, *Sefer Yetzirah*: "There are 10 non-corporeal *Sefirot*. The first is the Spirit of the living God, who is blessed, and blessed is the Name of the eternal living. Voice and breath and speech, this is the Holy Spirit" (*Sefer Yetzirah* 1:9).

The thirteenth-century mystical theologian, Rabbi

Elhanan ben Yakar, in one of his commentaries on *Sefer Yetzirah*, wrote about the Divine Spirit as follows: "*Ruach*, this is the Primal Ether which was the exhalation that issued forth, resulting from the formulation of the *alef*" (*Tekstim be-Torat ha-Elohut*, 54). The universe was fashioned through the permutation of the letters of the primordial alphabet, the Divine *ruach* being a product of the silent vocalization of the first letter.

The external, which is Divine in origin, is paralleled by an inner dimension, the God-image in which Adam was created. All biblical words that express the concept of the soul are related to the Divine breath: *ruach*, the spirit; *neshamah*, the soul/breath of life; and *nefesh*, a tranquil sigh, as evidenced in Exodus 31:17, "and on the seventh day He ceased and rested (*va-yinafash*); (see also Exodus 23:12). Commenting on this verse, Rashi explains that the root word "*nofesh*" indicates a restoration of one's soul and calm breathing.

The linguistic link between *neshamah*, soul, and *neshimah*, breath, is noted in midrashic literature. "Rabbi Levi taught in the name of Rabbi Hanina, With every breath (*neshimah*) that one breathes, one should praise his Creator. What is the scriptural basis for this? "Every living soul (*neshamah*) shall praise God (Psalms 150:6). [Read instead] each breath shall praise God" (*Bereshit Rabbah* 4:11).

An anonymous hasidic writer used this *Midrash* as a basis for viewing prayer as a cosmic cycling of breath from the human individual to God and back again: "For breath goes out from him, from below to Above, and returns to him from Above to below. Certainly with ease one can join the Divine part within man to its root" (*Likkutey Yekarim*, 12a).

This brief statement can most assuredly be used as the basis for a powerful meditative technique—focused, God-centered breathing. With each inhalation be mindful of the breath as a gift from *Ha-Shem*. As you exhale, realize that you are returning the breath to its source.

Note that there is a twofold significance to the term *ruach*, depending on whether it is Divine or human breath. This is discussed in the quasi-philosophical treatise, entitled "A Chapter on Happiness" and ascribed to Maimonides. Therein, the process of Divine revelation, empowered with resurrecting the souls of the dead, is compared to breathing. "For it is just like breathing that gives life to the heart and is the source of its health, curing it from any sickness which afflicts it. Additionally, *ruach* has two meanings: sometimes referring to the breathing process and sometimes referring to prophecy" (*Perakim be-Hatzlachah*, 1–2).

Herein we see the association of *ruach*, the mundane breath, and *Ruach ha-Kodesh*, the sacred breath of prophecy. This conceptual relationship is evident even in English, Divine inspiration being derived from *spirare*, which is Latin for "breathing." Likewise animation is derived from the Latin *anima*, signifying breath and soul.

All three soul concepts are brought together in the analogy of the glass-blower. This metaphor is mentioned in passing in the *Talmud* (*B. Sanhedrin* 91a) and was subsequently elaborated upon by numerous kabbalistic writers, including the mid-thirteenth-century text, *Perush Shem ben Arba Otiyyot*, R. Moshe Alshech and Rabbi Hayyim Vital.[3]

Let us consider Alshech's discussion, as it is the most extensive.

> With this, we can understand the description of the exhalation that was mentioned in connection with God's giving a soul to Adam. It is like one who exhales into a glass vessel.

---

3. For the latter source, see A. Kaplan, *Meditation and the Bible* (York Beach, 1978), 18; see also, R. Hayyim of Volozhin, *Nefesh Ha-Hayyim* 1:15, 50.

The air that is in his mouth adheres to that which is in the vessel. So it was when God gave Adam a soul. The part [of the soul] that was inside of Adam was attached to that which was inside of God. There is however a difference between a human blowing into a glass vessel and God blowing into Adam. In terms of the human exhalation, when the vessel is finished the connection is severed between what is inside of the vessel and the human's breath, because it is a physical object. The exhalation of God is not like this, the breath of His exhalation remains eternally bonded. (*Torat Moshe, Bereshit*, 8a)

As noted above in Chapter 4, R. Eleazar b. Judah asserted that the two nostrils, divided by the septum, form an inverted *shin*. R. Eleazar prefaced this by noting that *shin* represents cosmic fire. This can be deduced from the fact that the Hebrew for fire is *esh*, a short word in which the letter *shin* dominates. R. Eleazar continues: "It seems that an inverted *shin* is on the nose. From there the *neshamah* (soul) breathes and the *ruach* (spirit) exits from there constantly" (*Hochmat ha-Nefesh*, 145).

A related example of the symbolism of the inverted *shin* is found in several passages from the *Bahir*, in which the letter *shin* is described as forming the roots of the cosmic Tree of Life (see A. Kaplan, *The Bahir*, 30, 45). In this instance as well, the inverted *shin* plays a life-giving role.

An interesting relationship between one's nose and soul is delineated in the *Zohar*. Before quoting this source, some introductory remarks are necessary. According to the Rabbis, when one sleeps, one's soul temporarily departs the body; hence, sleep is viewed as mini-death.[4] Upon awakening in the morning, it is customary to thank *Ha-Shem* for compassion in being

---

4. In *B. Berachot* 57b sleep is characterized as one-sixtieth of death.

revived, by reciting the *modeh* prayer. Next, the following blessing is recited. (Note that *soul* is a feminine noun in Hebrew and is translated accordingly.) "My God, the soul that You have given me is pure. You have created her; You have formed her; You have breathed her into me. . . . Blessed are You, *Ha-Shem*, who restores souls to the corpses of the dead" (*Siddur Rinnat Yisrael*, 15).

The *Zohar* expands upon this notion, concluding with a practical application of this theory.

> The human soul in this world departs from the individual every night. In the morning she is returned to him. She resides on the person's nose and does not enter or resettle in his innards until he blesses the Holy One, blessed be He, and he prays for his life. Only then does she resettle in her place. . . . If not, [i.e. if he does not recite the appropriate blessing], then she flies away and departs and the individual will lack the sanctity of the soul. Since he lacks his soul, "what is his value?" (Isaiah 2:22). Absolutely nothing. It is as if he does not exist. Accordingly, it is prohibited for someone to bless his friend, before he blesses his Master at the start of the prayer service. (*Zohar Hadash* 90d)[5]

Immeasurable is the power of God-centered breathing. R. Pinchas of Koretz, an early hasidic leader, discussed the function of breath and its celestial impact as it clears the Divine Mind. In so doing he focused on the metaphor of clouds as spiritual obstacles. This image is based on Lamentations 3:44. "You have covered Yourself with a cloud, so that no prayer may pass through." R. Pinchas's comments on achieving clarity through focused breathing are applicable to us, as well.

> The reason that the Heavens sometimes cloud over without reason is because there are clouds that cover the Mind, as is

---

5. See *B. Berachot* 14a; cf. L. Englander and H. Basser, *The Mystical Study of Ruth* (Atlanta, 1993), 160, for the full text.

mentioned in the *Tikkunim*.[6] The proof is found in the *Talmud* (B. *Berachot* 32b) for Rava did not declare a fast on a cloudy day, as it is written, "You have covered yourself with a cloud" (Lamentations 3:44).

The dispersion of the clouds is by the breath, namely the movements—the way one moves during prayer. For the movements come from the lung which corresponds to breath, as is mentioned several times in the *Zohar* and the *Tikkunim*. Understand this.

Afterwards [Rabbi Pinchas] added, "If I had said this several years ago, everyone would have served *Ha-Shem*, may He be blessed, in this manner for a time and dispersed the clouds, but now no one pays any attention." (*Midrash Pinhas*, no. 29:10a)

An earlier discussion of the clouds as a negative symbol that may have influenced R. Pinhas is from the early eighteenth-century savant, R. Moshe Hayyim Luzzatto: "When the clouds converge, permission is given to the evil spirits (*sheidim*) to roam the world. That is why clouds are referred to as *seirim* (goats/rain showers)—during their designated time, bands of evil spirits battle each other, shooting arrows at each other, and humans need protection" (R. Moshe Luzzatto, *Daat Hochmah*, 35b).

R. Pinchas discussed the topic of dispersing the clouds in another context, as well.

I heard in his name [i.e., in the name of R. Pinchas], when an individual is totally nullified in his own eyes, then the

6. The zoharic sources of R. Pinchas and the ensuing statement by R. Moshe Hayyim Luzzatto include: *Tikkunei Zohar* 21: 50b, wherein Lamentations 3:44 is related to "Greater Rome and Lesser Rome, covering over the prayers"; *Zohar Hadash, Tikkunim* 97a, wherein Lamentations 3:44 is used as an example of when the *Shechinah* has been separated from the upper *Sefirot*, and *Zohar Hadash, Midrash ha-Neelam, Shir Ha-Shirim*, 61b, wherein clouds are associated with the pernicious arch-angels of the nations of the world.

clouds and rain are dispersed. One who has achieved self-abnegation has no need for clouds and rain or anything else. Therefore, in the time of Rabbi [Yehudah, the Prince]—who was extremely humble, as it says in the *Gemara,* "with the death of Rabbi, humility [and the fear of sin] disappeared" (*M. Sotah* 9:15)—there was never any rain and nevertheless "he plucked radishes from the ground [etc.]" (*B. Avodah Zarah* 10a). Similarly, Moses, our Rabbi, who was the most modest human ever, during his lifetime there was no need for anything, as manna descended from Heaven. Reflect well [on this issue.] (*Midrash Pinchas* #36, 6a)

From this second source we see that the removal of the obstacles is dependent upon achieving the state of *ayin,* or self-abnegation.

The Maggid of Mezeritch, a contemporary of R. Pinchas, also refers to the "clouds." Commenting on "*solu* (extol/clear) a path for Him who rides the clouds; YH is His Name" (Psalms 68:5), the Maggid contended that if one prays fervently "the Holy One, blessed be He, would rest upon him, then the Spirit [i.e., *Tiferet*] would disperse the clouds" (*Maggid Devarav le-Yaakov,* R. Shatz, ed., 73).

Let us turn now to mystical significance of the nostrils. Beginning in the thirteenth century, there are numerous references to anthropomorphic imagery of the Divine Being, in which nostrils play a role. In an early commentary on the *Sefirot,* the two highest levels are referred to as Primal Intellect and Fixed Intellect—corresponding to *Keter* and *Hochmah,* in the more conventional kabbalistic terminology.

How is it? The first *Sefirah,* which is the Primal Intellect, is in the head at the place where the *tefillin* are worn. This place has two windows, namely the Primal Intellect and the Fixed Intellect, having their counterpart in the two nostrils of the nose. Behold, these two aspects are situated in one place and they comprise the Balanced Unity. (*Perush le-Eser Sefirot, Kitvei Yad,* Scholem ed., 204–205)

Thus, the nostrils are situated so as to correspond to the two windows of the Intellect, located in the forehead, where the *tefillah shel rosh* is affixed.

In the *Zohar*, there are highly technical discussions of the Divine Anthropos, namely, God imaged humanly. Therein the left nostril is associated with *Gevurah*, Divine Power and Judgment, whereas the right nostril is related to *Hesed*, Divine Grace.

> Rather in the house there are two windows: concerning the left [nostril], it is written, "and smoke arose in His nose" (Psalms 18:9). What is the significance of "arose"? Rather, it ascended from the heart which is the left, corresponding to *Gevurah*. From the right, from the side of *Hesed*, descended the breath to cool it and quiet His anger—for the brain is there, which is *Hochmah*, located on the right. Thus, one who wants to become wise should turn to the south.[7] *Binah* is in the heart, corresponding to the left. One who wants to become rich should turn to the north. (*Zohar* 3:224a)

Accordingly, the nostrils have distinct functions: the right nostril draws the cool, compassionate air down from the brain, and the left uplifts the hot air from the heart.[8] Although no specific technique is advocated; nevertheless, this theory could certainly be applied.

In another section of the *Zohar*, this topic is elaborated upon, based implicitly on the verse, "The breath of our nostrils, God's Messiah" (Lamentations 4:20):

> Come and see what is the difference between the *Atika* [the Ancient One, i.e., the highest of the *Sefirot*] and the *Zeir Anpin* [Impatient One, i.e., the lower levels of the *Sefirot*]. This one is Master of the Nose—from one nostril comes life and from the other nostril comes the life of life. This nose is a receptacle from which the breath of life is drawn to the *Zeir Anpin*. And we call it forgiveness, and it is equanimity, the perfuming of the breath.

---

7. Namely, to the right if facing east; see *B. Baba Batra* 25b.

8. A parallel discussion is found in *Zohar* 3:235a.

> For the breath issues from these nostrils, one breath goes out to the *Zeir Anpin* to awaken it in the Garden of Eden. The other is the breath of life which is reserved in the future for the son of David, in order to know wisdom. From this nostril the breath is awakened and issues forth from the hidden brain. It is reserved to dwell upon the King Messiah, as it is written, "And the breath of God shall rest upon him, the breath of *Hochmah* and *Binah*, the breath of counsel and *Gevurah*, the breath of knowledge and the fear of God'" (Isaiah 11:2). (*Zohar* 3:10b)

Here, too, the nostrils play discrete roles. The left sustains the lower Divine realms and their functions in the present world, while the right channels the breath of life into the future, messianic world.

A further discussion of the role of nostrils, with practical implications, is found in the unpublished treatise on alchemy, written by R. Hayyim Vital. Therein, R. Hayyim offers an explanation for an important phenomenon in human respiration—we breath primarily with only one nostril and at different times of the day the dominant nostril changes.

> Know that the nostrils of a person are connected to the regulated hours of the day in this fashion. From the beginning of the first hour of the morning—according to the equality principle, wherein each day is divided into 12 daytime hours and 12 nighttime hours—the strength of the breath of the nostrils increases with the right nostril and there is a diminution of the left nostril, until the end of the first hour. During the second hour, most of the strength of the breath comes from the left nostril . . . Accordingly, during the first regulated hour of the day or night, most of the breath will exit the right nostril. (*Alchemical Text*, Mousayeff manuscript)

In breathing, as in this essay, there is a continuous movement from external to internal, and then back out again. Yet there is a moment, like that of the pendulum at the nadir of its arch, when movement stops. It is a time of preparatory inactivity, which can be transformed into a medium for dynamic spirituality. An anonymous thirteenth-century mystic described this moment as the basis for creation itself. This passage is one of the sources of the seminal kabbalistic theory of *tzimtzum*, the act of Divine self-contraction—a prerequisite for creation: "And how did He produce and create His universe? It is like a man who holds his breath; for by contracting His Unity, the universe remained in darkness and from this darkness He cut the forms and hewed the rocks" (Florence 2:18, 101a).

The Maggid of Mezeritch takes a different perspective on the intake of air in preparation for exhaling. As is typical of many of the hasidic teachings that we have seen, the boundaries between the Divine and the human domains are blurred.

> "Make *Ha-Shem* great with me, [let us exalt His Name together]" (Psalms 34:4). The mystical allusion is that the *Sefirah* of *Malchut* is associated with the Realm of Speech [i.e., the lowest level]. The Maggid, of eternally blessed memory, said that all the time a person is preoccupied with trying to speak, his mind is not open to thinking as previously—'as long as it is exuding, it is not absorbing'.[9]
>
> This is what King David was teaching Nathan in the midst of the holy nation of Israel, "Make *Ha-Shem* great," namely the Realm of Thought [i.e., the upper *Sefirot*]. You shall become great and expansive. How shall the Realm of Thought become great?—"with me," for I am the Realm of Speech. When breath is inhaled in preparation for speaking, then the Realm of Thought becomes great and expansive. (*Torat Ha-Maggid*, 2:51, in the name of *Or ha-Meir*, *Ruth*)

Until this point, we have viewed breathing as a consciously controlled undertaking that can have a spiritual component to it. One can go beyond this framework of self-generated limitation. A key facet of the hasidic theory of *devekut*, attachment to God, is that

---

9. This expression is actually a halachic principle associated with draining meat of its blood.

through the negation of the ego, one can actualize the Divine spark within. Rabbi Shneur Zalman of Liadi applied this theory of self-negation to breathing. In so doing he evoked the notion of acosmism[10] (namely, that *Ha-Shem* is the only reality), as a necessary corollary of Divine unity.

> One who contemplates this matter will thoroughly understand how all that has been created and exists, is in reality to be considered as nought and veritable nothingness in relation to the power of the Actualizer and the breath of His mouth, which is within the actualized and which animates him. . . . For it is the breath of His mouth which alone, continually transforms him from nothingness and nought into that which exists, for it animates him. Accordingly, "There is nothing outside of Him" (cf. Isaiah 45:6), in truth. (*Shaar ha-Yichud ve-ha-Emunah*, ch. 3)

The nostrils are the medium for the transmission of the Divine breath. They form a bridge between the mundane and the spiritual. If ego-negation is attempted through conscious, oppositional thought, the resulting inner turmoil will only nourish the ego-system. Instead, let the ego walk out over the nostril bridge. Passively watch the ebb and flow of Divine breath. In this state of relaxed God-centered awareness, the boundaries marking internal and external, so delineated by the mind, will gradually dissolve.

Among the hasidic masters who emphasized the significance of breathing, R. Nachman of Bratzlav, the great-grandson of the Baal Shem Tov, stands out. He was especially attuned to this issue owing to his persistent breathing problems. Ultimately, he perished from tuberculosis.

---

10. For a more extended discussion of this important concept, see the end of Chapter 8.

In a straightforward discussion, preserved in one of
R. Nachman's own manuscripts, we read about the role
of sighing in the process of repentance.

> One who truly wants to return to *Ha-Shem*, may He be
> blessed, must transform himself into a new creature. Know
> that in a sigh one can transform oneself into a new creature.
>
> A human cannot cease to breathe. For at each moment
> that he breaths, he exhales and inhales air. This is the es-
> sence of his being. This air is rooted Above.
>
> There is the good air of the righteous and the bad air of
> the wicked. The righteous continually draws air from the
> realm of holiness and the wicked draws air from the realm
> of impurity. Therefore when one wants to undertake *tesh-
> uvah*, [returning to *Ha-Shem*], he must ensure that he pre-
> vents the bad air from entering. Accordingly, he should sigh.
> This sigh lengthens the inhaling and the exhaling, and ex-
> tends the air by increasing it. This increase is referred to as
> "they increase their breath and perish" (Psalms 104:29), that
> is death. Before death, air fills the individual and at death
> the air departs.
>
> When one sighs the air increases and then it is cut off.
> Thus, he releases himself from the channel of impure air
> and connects himself to the channel of pure air. He then
> receives this air and is sustained by the pure air. By means
> of a sigh for one's transgressions, an individual can release
> himself from the root of impurity and connect himself to
> the root of holiness. (*Hayyei Moharan*, no. 27:28)

A more complex discussion is found in three of
R. Nachman's discourses, each formulated somewhat
differently. We shall cite one of these. In the following,
multileveled exposition, R. Nachman explicitly connects breathing with the purifying of intellect and compares this process to a candle burning. Implicit are
basic kabbalistic associations, which he explains in
statements scattered throughout his homilies. He identifies oil/wax/fat as *Malchut*, the lowest of the *Sefirot*;
(see also *Likkutei Moharan* 1, 49:7). Lungs are associated
with *Tiferet*, the nucleus of the *Sefirot* (cf. 1, 92) and intellect is connected with *Hochmah* (1, 8:7).

This is the meaning of, "an understanding individual is a cold wind" (Proverbs 17:27). By means of a cold wind—that is, the cold wind of the breath—by these means they merit the understanding that comes from wealth (as mentioned previously).

This is the meaning of, "And the breath of the Almighty causes them to understand" (Job 32:8)—for the basis of understanding is by means of the breath, which is associated with the cold wind, as discussed above. The basis of the restoration (*tikkun*) of the intellect is by means of the breath. The essence of the intellect functioning properly so that it can contemplate is by means of the oils/fats in the body. For the intellect is like a burning candle and it burns by means of the oils that are drawn to it and they are like the oil that is drawn to the burning wick. When there are no oils in the body, the intellect cannot burn in contemplation. This results in insane people when the moisture in the body dehydrates. The brain becomes defective when there are no oils to burn.

All the moisture and oils in the body are a result of the breath. "If it were not for the wings of the lung that blow on the heart, the heart would set the whole body on fire" (*Tikkunei Zohar*, no. 13, f. 28a; no. 21, f. 49a; no. 25, f. 70a). Accordingly, the basis of the existence of oil and moisture in the body is due to the breath. The lungs receive the cold wind from outside, in order to cool the heart, and this also enables the intellect to burn in contemplation, as discussed above. This is the significance of "the candle/lamp of *Ha-Shem* is the soul/breath of man" (Proverbs 20:27). The existence and restoration of the candle of *Ha-Shem*, namely the intellect, is dependent upon the breath. (*Likkutei Moharan* 1, 60:3; cf. 225; 2, 8:12)

Herein R. Nachman makes the following argument: in the same way that flames are sustained by oil, we are nourished by our physicality and the Divine realm is supported by human activity. The ultimate goal is to elevate and transform matter on every level, into pure light (i.e., intellect). This is accomplished through the medium of breathing.

Breath requires a twofold movement, in and out. Thus, too, is the pendular bond between humans and

God. The primal Divine act is exhalation, blowing
the life-force into Adam's nostrils. This parallels the
flow of the *shefa*, Divine energy, channeled downward
through the *Sefirot*. We inhale this energy and then
exhale, redirecting it back upward through our spiritually oriented activity. By connecting kabbalistic
symbolism with the image of the burning candle, R.
Nachman offers a powerful tool for appreciating the
mystical significance of breathing. The flame is within,
glowing with each breath that is devoted to Divine
awareness.

7

MUSIC AND CHANTING

Music can be magical and transforming, if you but listen. R. Moshe Hayyim Ephraim of Sudylkow, commenting on the sounds accompanying the revelation at Mount Sinai, transmitted a parable in the name of his grandfather, the Baal Shem Tov:

> Once someone was playing very beautifully on an instrument, with great sweetness and melody. All who heard could not restrain themselves, owing to the sweetness and pleasure, such that they danced with boundless enthusiasm, almost to the ceiling. The closer one got to the music, the more pleasurable it sounded and the more energetic the dancing.
>
> In the midst of this celebration a deaf person arrived. He could not hear the music at all. He only saw people dancing fervently and thought they must be crazy. . . . Had he been wise, he would have understood that the celebration was caused by the sweet and pleasurable music. Then he too would have danced there.
>
> The meaning of this analogy is transparent. (*Degel Machaneh Ephraim, Yitro*, 35a)

In the previous chapter, we traced the role of breath in meditation. One of the techniques that is dependent upon breath regulation entails chanting. In the latter part of this chapter, we shall investigate this issue. By way of background, we shall first explore the connection between music and meditation.

There is general agreement that spiritual elevation through meditation requires extensive preparation and a proper mindset. Joy and equanimity are two prerequisites. In order to promote this attitude, music is frequently recommended. R. Yehudah Al-Botini, quoted in Chapter 2, noted that a key element in preparing to meditate was making music. He suggested the following: "Moreover, he should try to play on all types of musical instruments, if he has them and knows how to play them. If not, he should sing verses from Psalms and the Pentateuch, in order to please the animal soul, which is a partner with the rational soul and intelligence" (*Sulam*, ch. 10).

R. Eleazar Azikri takes this notion even further by asserting that singing to *Ha-Shem* is the fulfillment of a biblical commandment. Codifiers of biblical prescriptions list the obligation to love *Ha-Shem* as one of the fundamental obligations—based on Deuteronomy 6:5 "You shall love *Ha-Shem*, your God, with all of your heart." Azikri discussed the implementation of this commandment as follows: "It is the way of a lover to sing, since the love of our Creator is more marvellous than human affection, a person who loves Him full heartedly will sing for the Blessed One, just like Moses, the Israelites, Miriam, Deborah, Joshua, the descendents of Korah, David and Solomon, sang by means of the Holy Spirit" (*Sefer Haredim*, ch. 9, 56).

Azikri belonged to a group of like-minded contemplatives, whom he referred to as "the association of hearkening friends." (This expression is based upon Song of Songs 8:13.) They would gather and chant

Divine love songs. One of Azikri's compositions that the group sang was the classic poem, *Yedid Nefesh*, which eventually became incorporated into the *Siddur* and is traditionally sung in the synagogue on *Shabbat* evening, as well as during the third meal on *Shabbat* afternoon (see Chapter 9).

Azikri prefaced this song: "As we have previously written, one of the principal branches of the ecstacy of Divine desire is that the lover will sing a love song to Him. Accordingly, I shall set down before you a few love songs which we sang joyously in the 'association of hearkening friends.'" (*Sefer Haredim* 161).

As Azikri noted above, numerous biblical figures composed songs to *Ha-Shem*. In fact, one of the weekly Sabbaths is named *Shabbos Shirah*, the Sabbath of Song, since the Torah portion for that week includes the "Song of the Sea" (Exodus 15:1–19) and the *Haftorah* that is chanted is Deborah's song (Judges 5:2–31).

It is also customary to feed birds on *Shabbos Shirah*. The traditional reason involves a story about how birds preserved Moses' integrity, in connection with the descent of the manna, which is also part of this biblical narrative. R. Pinchas of Koretz offered a different rationale: "Why is it customary to throw kashi to birds on *Shabbos Shirah*? They are referred to as masters of song, for there is nothing that can sing like a bird among all of the creatures, with the exception of humans, because the birds rule the air and songs come from the air. Similarly musical instruments require air" (*Midrash Pinchas* 16b, no. 39).

R. Pinchas then connected music's dependency upon air to the scribal custom of writing the "Song of the Sea" in a peculiar manner in Torah scrolls, such that there are gaps (of air) in each line.

Owing to the importance of song in Jewish spirituality, it is, therefore, not surprising that music played a significant role in promoting prophesy, as attested in several biblical narratives. For example, the great prophet Samuel encouraged the newly crowned King Saul to join "a band of prophets coming down from the shrine, preceded by lyres, drums, flutes, and harps, and they will be prophesying" (1 Samuel 10:5). Similarly, the prophet Elisha summoned a musician. "While the musician played, the hand of *Ha-Shem* came upon him" (2 Kings 3:15). On the basis of this incident, the Rabbis concluded that happiness was a prerequisite for receiving "the holy spirit," namely, prophecy (see *B. Shabbat*, f. 30b). By extension, joyousness is also congruent with successful meditation.

The Psalms are replete with musical invocations:

> Sing out, righteous people to *Ha-Shem*. . . .
> Praise *Ha-Shem* with a harp,
>   With a ten-stringed lyre sing to Him.
> Sing a new song for Him.
> (Psalms 33:1-3)

> My heart is resolute, God;
>   I will whole-heartedly sing and play.
> Awake, harp and lyre!
>   I shall wake the dawn.
> (Psalms 108:2-3)

These passages gave rise to the Rabbinic legend (cited previously in Chapter 5) concerning a special harp that would awaken King David each night at midnight. "Rabbi Shimon, the pious, said, 'A harp was suspended over David's bed. When midnight arrived the north wind came and blew on the harp, which started to play by itself. Immediately David arose and became occupied in Torah, until dawn.'" (*B. Berachot* 3b).

This image of the primal harp was evoked in a poem by R. Avraham Yitzhak Kook.

> The First One drew me with His rope
> To the Holy of Holies of His dwelling-place.

> From the strings of his lyre
> My soul listens to His song.
> (Habermann, "*Shirat ha-Rav*," 17)

Music also played a significant role in R. Abraham Abulafia's theory of meditation and the attainment of prophecy. This theme has been systematically studied by Moshe Idel in his *The Mystical Experience* (53–71). An especially interesting presentation is Abulafia's assertion that music directly effects the body, as well as the spirit. In the following selection, he compares the human body to a garden and then to King David's *kinnor* (lyre).

> Just as the owner of a garden has the power to water the garden at will by means of rivers, so does the one making music with the Name have the power to water at will his limbs by means of his soul, through the Almighty, Blessed Name; and this is [the meaning of] "and it came to pass, when the minstrel played, that the hand of the Lord came upon him" (2 Kings 3:15)—this is the *kinnor* that hung above David's bed, which used to play of itself and praise Him with the *nevel* and *kinnor*. But this would only be after receiving the divine effluence, which is called the seventy-two letter name, together with the understanding of its paths. (M. Idel, *Mystical Experience*, 56)

Abulafia also refers to the analogy of music when he describes his meditative technique of *tseruf*, combining letters.

> Know that the method of *tseruf* can be compared to music; for the ear hears sounds from various combinations, in accordance with the character of the melody and the instrument. Also, two different instruments can form a combination, and if the sounds combine, the listener's ear registers a pleasant sensation in acknowledging their difference. The strings touched by the right or left hand move [i.e., vibrate], and the sound is sweet to the ear. And from the ear the sensation travels to the heart, and from the heart to the spleen [the centre of emotion], and enjoyment of the different

melodies produces ever-new delight. It is impossible to produce it except through the combination of sounds, and the
same is true of the combination of letters. It touches the first
string, which is comparable to the first letter, and proceeds
to the second, third, fourth and fifth, and the various sounds
combine. And the secrets, which express themselves in these
combinations, delight the heart which acknowledges its God
and is filled with ever fresh joy. (G. Scholem, *Major Trends
in Jewish Mysticism*, 134. This passage was also translated in
M. Idel, *Mystical Experience*, 53)

As noted above in Chapter 3, an early Jewish source
on music is Philo of Alexandria. Some 2,000 years ago,
he wrote that "heaven is ever making music, producing in accordance with its celestial motions the perfect
harmony" (Winston, *Philo of Alexandria*, 115). According to Philo, it was this music that Moses listened to
for the forty days and nights that he was atop Mount
Sinai, receiving the Torah.

In his commentary on the Ten Commandments,
Philo contended that the reason that God revealed the
Ten Commandments at Sinai was that ten is the perfect number. He then related this to geometrical and
musical patterns.

Here our admiration is at once aroused by their number,
which is neither more nor less than is the supremely perfect. Ten. . . . Ten also contains the properties observed in
triangles, quadrilaterals and other polygons, and also those
of the concords, the fourth, fifth, octave and double octave
intervals, where the ratios are respectively 4:3, 3:2, 2:1 and
8:2. (*Philo*, F. H. Colson, trans., 7:15–17)

Philo's ideas were embellished by the great sixteenth-century Italian homilist, R. Judah Moscato, who
associated musical patterns with the four letters of the
Tetragrammaton:

Concerning the most sublime of inner matters, we should
believe that the creation of the melodies of music is blessed

with complete unity, wherein all the forms are united. It is the natural order for all that exists—whether Above or below. Let Him come, come and relate the correctness of His essential and unique Name, whose letters allude to all the intervals of music. The *yod* is indicative of the eighth, which is called octave. For this is just like the number ten, which includes all the numbers. This is what the sage, Rabbi Yedidya [i.e., Philo], wrote in his book entitled *The Decalogue*, explaining the Ten Commandments—how this number includes all the interval patterns. . . . And included in the *yod* is the interval called the third, which is the root of the tenth. The *hay* is indicative of the interval called the fifth and the *vav*, the sixth. And the *hay* is doubled to complete the sum of the four letters, to correspond to the interval called the fourth, and also to teach about the mixture of the intervals: one with the other. For *vav* and *hay* correspond numerically to eleven—the essence of which is the fourth. Similarly, the initial *yod* is joined with its neighboring *hay*, corresponding numerically to 15, which is the *quintodecima* [i.e., 15th], namely the double octave. (R. Judah Moscato, *Nefutzot Yehudah, Derashah* #1)

In the early eighteenth century, a special institute was established in Jerusalem named Beit El. Its purpose was to train kabbalists in the recondite meditative techniques for praying developed by R. Yitzhak Luria and R. Hayyim Vital, as codified by the Yeminite luminary, R. Shalom Sharabi—who headed the academy in the mid-eighteenth century. This school still exists. A fascinating account of the spiritual activities of the Beit El mystics is found in Ariel Bension's monograph, *The Zohar in Moslem and Christian Spain*. Bension's father was an active member of this group. What follows are several selections from Bension's account, especially as it pertains to the theme of meditation and music.

The members of the mystical group in Beth-El [Beit-El] were known under the name *Mechavenim*, i.e., those who make prayers with meditation. The harmony that ruled Beth-El followed the *Mechavenim* into their public as well as their private lives. At home and abroad, Beth-El was at peace. (244)

In Beth-El, joy was attained by no artificial means, but by silent meditation, by introspection in an atmosphere in which music, blending with men's thoughts, induced a forgetfulness of externals. Each man's eyes were turned inwards. Seeking to mine the wealth of his own soul, he found there the soul of the universe. Amazed at his own discovery of this hidden treasure the mystic pursues his course upwards until he attains the ecstasy that brings him to the mystery of creation, where sits Joy enthroned. In a silence in which alone the soul may meet its God, destroyed worlds are reconstructed and restored to their pristine perfection. And this is the aim of the *Kavanoth*—the meditation on the mystic meaning of certain prayers with intention to bring restoration.

In a song which follows the meaning-full word, continuing and deepening its meaning—even as a pause in the rendition of a symphony is but the continuation of the music—, this wordless song attains that which cannot be reached through the medium of words. And the word of prayer, arising at a given moment from the throats of all Israel, attains its highest form in the silence of Beth-El, imaged in song by the Master seated on his divan and surrounded by silent, thought-inspired mystics. (243-244)

Beth-El also introduced something new to Jewish liturgy: melodies to mark the period of meditation. The meditation is sung aloud by the *Rav HaChassid* to stimulate and inspire the silent meditation of the *Mechavenim*. At first, it had been the custom to carry on the meditation in a deep silence—the meditation on a single word, sometimes lasting for fifteen minutes. But with the introduction of the musical interludes the *Kavanoth* began to be performed during the intoning of a melody that was at the same time suggestive of the form which the meditation was to take. So true are these tunes, in searching out and expressing the emotions of souls dwelling on the mystic meaning of the prayer, that even the listener, uninitiated though he may be, feels himself transported into the realms of thought, where dwell those who commune with the Infinite. Under the magic of these tunes *Mechavenim* and listeners, animate and inanimate objects, become one in true pantheistic sense.

Thus, on hearing the Master sing the *Umevi Go'el* ("and He will bring a Redeemer unto their children's children for His Name's sake in love")—hearing his voice rise in triumphant rapture to the words—"In Love"—when the *Mechaven* must be prepared to die for the sanctity of the Ineffable Name "In Love"—the listener feels himself a heroic spirit ready to do battle for pure love. And he is able to understand the ecstasy of saints and martyrs as they joyfully gave themselves to the flames of the stake "In Love."

And hearing the Master sing the *Shmah* ("Hear, O Israel, the Lord our God, the Lord is ONE!"), it is as if a great music had come into the soul washing away all its imperfections, bringing man nearer to his fellow-men: his hates transformed, his world unified and ennobled. Thus it came about that the *Kavana*—sent forth in the hope of bringing together the conflicting fragments of the shattered *Sephiroth* and of re-creating them into the perfect UNITY—first pours its healing balm into men's souls, bringing them into unity with things eternal.

The life of the Sephardi Chassidim of Beth-El was a life of beauty, of sanctity, of melody, of silence. And it was in this fashion that Beth-El in Jerusalem kept alight the flame of Sephardi mysticism down to the present day. (245–246)

Even if you do not have access to an environment like Beit-El, you can still become attuned to spiritually elevating music. There is a prevalent theory that for each individual there is a special song that flows from the source of one's soul. This notion is alluded to in the first text that we shall cite and is made explicit in the next:

It will happen sometimes that as you sing, without intending it, you will spontaneously begin to speak words of prayer to God. If at first these words may be associated with the life and desires of the body, the more you become spiritually aroused, and your soul comes out of its sheath to fly upwards, the more will you leave this world and its concerns and from the depths of your heart you will cry out in pure prayer to God. And lest you think that such prayers are somehow less important than those written down in the Siddur, you should know that prayers such as these come from the very same quarry from which the soul itself is hewn. (R. Kalonymous Kalman of Peasetzna, *Hachsharat ha-Avrechim*, translated by Y. Buxbaum, *Jewish Spiritual Practices*, 485)

Consider the following remarks by R. Dov Baer of Lubavitch, the second Lubavitcher Rebbe in his *Tract of Ecstasy*:

> What is the nature of melody? There is a well-known saying that the Faithful Shepherd [i.e., Moses] used to sing every kind of melody in his prayers. For he included the six hundred thousand souls of Israel and each soul can only ascend to the root of the Source whence she was hewn by means of song. This is the category of essential ecstasy, mentioned above, with "love of delights," according to the manner in which the soul is rooted on high in the supernal delight. He who included them all was the Faithful Shepherd who, therefore, used to sing with every kind of melody. (*On Ecstasy*, L. Jacobs, trans., 76f)

Not always are these melodies readily evident. In the same way that Jewish life is played out in a state of exile, awaiting redemption, so too many holy songs have been dispersed among the nations and await recovery. A well-known example of the restoration of lost melodies is that of the Hungarian master, R. Yitzhak Eizik of Kalov. As a young boy he heard shepherds singing lovesongs. Slightly altering the words he would sing: "*Shechinah, Shechinah,* how far away you are! Exile (*galus*), exile, how enormous you are! If the exile would be removed, we could be together again." When asked by Rebbe Leib Sarah's what the shepherds actually sang, Eizak replied: "They sing about a beloved instead of the *Shechinah* and about a forest instead of *galus*— but who is the beloved if not the *Shechinah* and what is the forest that separates us, if not *galus*?" (M. Buber, *Or ha-Ganuz*, 308).

By discussing a series of biblical verses, R. Nachman of Bratzlav formulated an intriguing theory of shepherd's songs. In so doing he refers to *Perek Shirah* (Chapter of Song), which we discussed in Chapter 3. (This ancient text delineated the songs sung by the various creatures of the world.)

Know that when Jacob sent the ten brothers to Joseph [in Egypt], he also sent a melody from the land of Israel with them. This is the secret meaning of "take some *zemrat* (choice produce/song) from the land with your belongings" (Genesis 43:11). . . . Know that every shepherd has a special melody according to the grasses and place, wherein he is pasturing [his flock]—for each animal requires a special kind of grass to eat. Furthermore, he doesn't always pasture in the same place and according to the grasses and place there is a particular melody, since every grass has its own song that it recites. This is the message of *Perek Shirah*. . . .

Therefore King David, who knew how to play music, was a shepherd—likewise all the Patriarchs raised animals. This is the meaning of the verse: "from the corner of the land we heard songs" (Isaiah 24:16). Thus songs and melodies emanated from the corners of the land: melodies are formed by the grasses that grow on the land. Since the shepherd knows the melody, he invigorates the grasses thereby providing sustenance for the animals to eat.

This is the meaning of "the blossoms appeared in the land; the time of *zamir* (pruning/singing) has arrived" (Song of Songs 2:12). Thus, the blossoms flourish in the land owing to the songs and melodies that pertain to them. . . .

Melodies are also beneficial to shepherds. Since the shepherd is continuously among animals, it is possible that they might draw him down from the spiritual level of a human to that of an animal . . . by means of the melody he is saved from this, for melodies promote the purification of souls . . . for the essential quality of melodies is to gather and purify good souls. (*Likkutei Moharan* 2:63, 68f)

Like the shepherds, *hasidim* tended to prefer *niggunim*, wordless melodies that are rhythmically hummed, rather than songs with lyrics. Especially significant are the *tish* (table) *niggunim*, that were chanted when the *hasidim* had gathered around their master's table—usually for the last *Shabbat* meal, Saturday afternoon. It was then that the Rebbe would give his weekly discourse. To put all assembled into the proper mood, reflective *niggunim* would be sung.

Niggunim can be even more effective than erudite discourses. The Lubavitcher Hasidim tell the following story about their founder, R. Shneur Zalman of Liadi.

> It is well known that a *niggun* is a high level of the World of Emanation. . . . Once, when the Rebbe [R. Shneur Zalman of Liadi] had publicly delivered a hasidic discourse concerning a profound topic, he noticed that opposite him at the *tish* (table) sat an elderly Jew. Although it was obvious that this person was deeply attached to the Rebbe and enjoyed seeing his face, the holy words that the *tzaddik* had uttered didn't make any impression upon him.
>
> Realizing that the lesson was lost on this simple disciple, the Rebbe spoke with him privately and learned about the hardships of his life. Moved by the plight and sincerity of this elderly follower, the Rebbe told him: "*Nu*, listen to me— I will explain my lesson to you with a *niggun*. And so he began to sing."
>
> Now, according to the *hasidim*, wordless melodies are filled with meaning:
>
> Each *niggun* is permeated with a sea of Torah, a sea of faith, a sea of longing for *Ha-Shem* with attachment to the Infinite, a sea of contemplation, filled with love for the Creator of the universe. . . . [I]n sum, the *niggun* comprises all of Hasidic doctrine, the entire teaching of the Baal Shem Tov, may his merit protect us.
>
> The more the Rebbe sang, the more the aged *hasid* absorbed the sound and with it he began to understand the profundity of the world. He eventually comprehended the grandeur of the holy Torah and finally cried out with all of his strength:
>
> "Rebbe, now I can unite with *Ha-Shem*! Your *niggun* has given me the proper *devekut* to the Master of the Universe."
>
> From this time on after each of his lessons, the Rebbe would chant this particular melody, which became known as "The Rebbe's *Devekut*." (M. Indritz, *In Di Gezelten fun Habad*, 47–49)

R. Shlomoh Zalman of Kopust (1830–1900), a great grandson of R. Shneur Zalman of Liadi, while discussing the sound of the *shofar*, provides an interesting theoretical discussion on the nature of melody and its similarity to color theory:

The explanation of this issue pertaining to the sound of the *shofar* is that its sound is simple, without embellishment; therefore, it does not produce pleasure like other music. Just the same way that loveliness and beauty in colors comes from the blending of several colors together, as opposed to a solitary color, which is not so beautiful—so it is exactly with melody. Essential pleasure comes from the blending of opposing notes and sounds that are mixed together: namely those notes that gladden the heart and notes that produce sadness and neutral ones, as well. This will result in joy and sweetness for the listener's soul. (*Magen Avot*, 2:35a)

We have already noted that Rav Nachman of Bratzlav frequently discussed the role of *niggunim* in Jewish spirituality. We shall conclude this section with a partial translation of his discourse on the impact of music in overturning Divine judgment. R. Nachman connects music to prayer and the *keshet* (bow/rainbow), all of which are the domain of the *Shechinah*. In the kabbalistic framework of the *Sefirot, Shechinah/Malchut* receives Divine energy from the upper *Sefirot*. Herein, Rav Nachman focuses on the central *Sefirot: Hesed* (Grace), *Gevurah* (Valor), and *Tiferet* (Beauty), which likewise correspond to the three Patriarchs: Abraham, Isaac, and Jacob. He also associates these attributes with the colors of the rainbow and the primal elements: water, fire, and air. All of these various symbols are understood as being aspects of music/prayer.

"He [i.e., *Ha-Shem*] took note of their distress, when He heard their song" (Psalms 106:44). Behold, music can sweeten harsh judgments. Thus, it is written in the holy *Zohar* (*Pinchas* 3:215), the rainbow represents the *Shechinah*. The three colors of the rainbow correspond to the Patriarchs and they are the garments of the *Shechinah*. Whenever She is clothed in radiant garments "when I [i.e., God] see it, I will remember the eternal covenant" (Genesis 9:16); furthermore, "then the wrath of the king subsided" (Esther 7:10).

This is analogous to a king who was angry with his son. When the king saw the queen wearing her radiant garments then he had compassion for his son.

The letters of prayer are the *Shechinah*, as is written "Lord, (*Adonay*) open my lips" (Psalms 51:17). Speech corresponds to the Name *Adonay*. It is also referred to as rainbow, as Rashi explained "with my [i.e., Jacob's] sword and bow" (Genesis 48:22) connotes prayer. The sound of music is comprised of the three colors of the rainbow, for sound comprises fire, water and air, which correspond to the Patriarchs. . . . Accordingly, when one chants the letters of prayer and the sound of the music is positive and shines brightly, then the *Shechinah*—namely the letters [of prayer]—is clothed in radiant garments. When the Holy One, blessed be He, sees Her, then "the wrath of the king subsides.". . .

This explains the significance of "And *Shaddai* attends your suffering" (Job 22:25)—for the name *Shaddai* comprises the Patriarchs (*Zohar* 3:231). Accordingly, the *shin* possesses three branches of the Tree, which are the Patriarchs. They are the three Names in the unification: ". . . *Ha-Shem*, our God, *Ha-Shem*" (Deuteronomy 6:4). These Names have 14 (*yod dalet*) letters, which correspond to the *yod dalet* of *Shaddai*. The initial [Hebrew] letters of Abraham, Isaac and Jacob, correspond to the initial (Hebrew) letters of "*Ha-Shem*, our God, *Ha-Shem*." (*Likkutei Moharan* 1:42, 124f)

Chanting is a form of musical breathing. All discussions of chanting within the Jewish tradition revolve around the thirteenth-century savant, R. Abraham Abulafia, the master of prophetic *Kabbalah*. He developed a special technique that he taught to his disciples, which was revived in the sixteenth century, when his voluminous writings enjoyed a renaissance.

First, let us consider a passage from Abulafia, which illustrates his special approach to breathing. Herein, the nostrils are described as *Aravot*, Heavenly Plains, and correspond to the two cherubs atop the sacred Ark. Much of this treatise was written in a peculiar fashion such that the *gematria* (numerical value) of the important words and expressions is equivalent. In the case of the following passage, all the key terms add up to 678. These equivalences have been italicized: "Behold, you possess *two nostrils* whose name is *Aravot*. Understand that they are *nostrils of the soul*. And *they secretly correspond* to the *two cherubs*, and they are *two composite beings, which force the Divine Presence* to dwell on earth and to speak with man from on top of the curtain between the *two cherubs*" (*Hayyei Olam ha-Ba*, 770).

Representative of Abulafia's special technique for chanting are the following directives concerning the proper vocalization of the Divine Name:

> One should take each letter [of the Ineffable Name] and nod according to the duration of the breath, such that one would breathe only once between each pair of letters—a breath as long as possible and afterwards resting the length of one breath. In this manner he should proceed with each letter, such that there would be two breaths for each letter: one [breath] to allow for exhalation at the time of expressing the vowel of the letter and a second [breath] for resting between each letter.
>
> It is known to everyone that each breath [cycle] is composed of taking air in from outside, that is from *bar* (outside) to *gav* (inside). The secret of this points to the truth of the attribute of *Gevurah* (Valor) and its nature—for with it an individual will be called *gebor* (hero), that is to say *gav bar*, according to his ability to conquer his passions [cf. *M. Avot* 4:1]. (*Mafteach ha-Shemot*, cited by Idel, *Rav Avraham Abulafia*, 257; cf. Idel, *Mystical Experience*, 24)

We see that Abulafia's technique entails regulated breathing, vocalizing each syllable independently, and accompanying this chanting with certain head movements. Abulafia describes in detail his technique in *Or ha-Sechel* (Light of the Intellect). Several centuries later, this same process was explained by R. Yehudah al-Botini (and somewhat later by R. Moshe Cordovero, in *Pardes Rimmonim* 21:1). Although the technique described in each of these sources is the same, the instructions and preparatory comments complement each other. Accordingly, we shall first offer an abridged translation of Abulafia's instructions and then al-Botini's more expansive and edifying directives.

It is necessary to keep in mind that Hebrew letters are essentially consonants. The different vowels are not independent letters, but simply dots or lines that are associated with the consonants. Abulafian chanting combines the pronunciation of each consonant with a motioning of one's head according to the shape of the accompanying vowel. For example, the *holam* is an "oh" vowel that consists of single dot placed above any consonant. When chanting a consonant that is vocalized with a *holam*, Abulafia recommended that you raise your head upwards, thereby evoking the dot above the letter.

Abulafia's depiction of his chanting method begins:

> When you desire to vocalize this Glorious Name . . . prepare yourself and isolate yourself in a place where your voice will not be heard. Purify your heart and soul from thoughts of this world. Contemplate that at this moment your soul will depart from your body and you will die from this world and be revived in the World To Come, which is the source of all life. . . .
>
> When you begin to pronounce the letter *alef* with any of the vowels—since the *alef* refers to the secret of unity—only prolong its pronunciation for the length of one breath, nor should you interrupt this breath for any reason. You should prolong this breath for as long as you can. Similarly, each letter should be pronouned with awe, fear and dread, combined with the spiritual joy of providence, which is its compensation.
>
> The form of the chanting of each letter should resemble its vowel. Thus, a *holam* should ascend. When you begin to pronounce it, you should face eastward, neither down nor up. Sit cloaked in clean white garments, over your clothes, or wrapped in a *tallit* over your head that is crowned in *tefillin*, facing eastward—for that is the direction where light comes into the world. (Abulafia, *Or ha-Sechel*, Florence ms. 44:16, f. 97b–98a)

Al-Botini presents this same method more elaborately:

The ninth chapter deals with vowels and how they are visualized in the inner heart and the manner of [expressing]
them through nodding of the head and other external limbs.
From this you will know the marvelous way of reciting the
Holy Names, such as the High Priest would utter when the
Temple stood and also other righteous and pious persons
who conjured the Holy Names. [This chapter will explain]
how they would recite them with their appropriate vocalization and vowels. But before this explanation it is necessary to know that the vocalization of a letter is, as it were,
its soul and its moving force. If you tried to pronounce any
letter without its vocalization, it would be impossible, according to the nature of speech—"For voice, air and speech:
this is the Holy Spirit" (*Sefer Yetzirah* 1:9). "Voice" is divided
into five vowels, which utilize the "air." Thus, "speech" is
composed of both of them. . . .

Know that the nodding of each letter is according to its
vocalization with the inner heart and external limbs in this
manner. Behold, when the High Priest, prophet or any righteous person would conjure the Holy Names, or when you
will pronounce any letter that is vocalized with a *holam* [i.e.,
"oh" vowel], you should direct your heart and mind and nod
according to the form of this vowel, as follows. Do not turn
your head either to the right or left at all, nor down or up,
rather straighten your head, as if it hung in a balance, as if
you were talking face to face with someone who was as tall
as you. As you begin to pronounce the vocalized letter move
your head upwards, towards heaven. Close your eyes and
open your mouth. Speak clearly and clear your throat of any
phlegm, so that it will not interfere with the pronunciation
of the letter. The upward movement of your head should
correspond to the duration of your breath, such that your
breath and head movement will stop simultaneously. The
vocalization of the *holam* entails moving your head upwards,
as if you were acknowledging the sovereignty of your Creator—ever higher above all the celestial beings.

The *kamatz* ["ah" vowel] is like a straight line drawn by a
scribe, from left to right and below the line there is a dot.
When you pronounce it with any letter, first turn your head
to your left shoulder and pronounce the letter with a pleasant, clear voice and move your head from left to right, re-
sembling the straight line drawn by someone vocalizing a
text. Afterwards return your head facing east, which should

be straight ahead, for this is the direction that one faces when uttering the Name, as well as the direction of the Temple that one faces while praying to *Ha-Shem*, may He be blessed. Next bow your head slightly for this nodding corresponds to the dot that is under the straight line of the *kamatz*. The entire movement should be completed with one breath, as indicated above. Thus the movement of the *kamatz* is from left to right and then facing ahead and bowing, as if you were acknowledging the sovereignty of your Owner to the north, south and lower regions.

The *tzayray* ["ay" vowel] is composed of two dots: one to the right and one to the left. When you vocalize any letter with it, begin by nodding your head to the right and then left. This is the opposite of the straight line of the *kamatz*, for the *kamatz* is considered to be the Great *Kamatz*, whereas *tzayray* is the Little *Kamatz*. It is as if you were acknowledging *Ha-Shem*'s sovereignty from south to north.

The *heereek* ["ee" vowel] is a single dot under the letter. When you vocalize any letter with it, nod your head downwards in the form of a bow before *Ha-Shem*, may He be blessed, as if you were speaking with Him and He were standing before you. This is the opposite of the *holam*, for you are hereby acknowledging His sovereignty in the lower regions.

The *shoorook* ["oo" vowel] is a single dot in the middle of the letter, called full mouth. When you pronounce it with any letter straighten yourself and start to draw your head from in front of you, until the end of the extension of your neck behind you, as straight as you can. Don't raise or lower your head or turn it to the left or right, but a straight line forwards and backwards, as if you were acknowledging *Ha-Shem*'s sovereignty from the east to the west. Consequently, by the movement of these five vowels you will have affirmed your Owner's dominion over the six directions. . . .

The *patach's* [another "ah" vowel] movement is like the straight line of the *kamatz*, from left to right. And the *sheva*, which is two dots, one on top of the other, has two movements: the upper dot is like the *holam* and the lower is like the *heereek*. The two dots of the *segol* that are to the right and left of each other are like the *tzayray*. And the third dot which is below them is like a *heereek*. The *shoorook*, which is three dots, diagonally arranged—the highest dot is like a *holam*, the middle like a *shoorook* and the lowest like a *heereek*. (*Sulam ha-Aliyah*, ch. 9, G. Scholem, ed., 166–167)

Although it will take some practice to master the head movements, insofar as they follow the shape of the vowels, they are relatively straightforward.

The Abulafian chanting method can be applied to the pronunciation of any Hebrew word. A good choice is *shalom* (peace), for according to the Sages, it is also an epithet for God (see *B. Shabbat* 10b). This word has two syllables. The first is "sha," which is vocalized with a *kamatz*, while the second syllable, "lom," is vocalized with a *holam*.

To apply Abulafia's technique to the chanting of *shalom*, start by sitting, facing eastward and looking straight ahead. Close your eyes and inhale. Turn your head to your left shoulder and begin to intone the first syllable, "sha." As you chant "sha," you should move your head from your left shoulder to your right shoulder. Then bring your head back to the center and bow it downwards. With these movements you have acknowledged *Ha-Shem*'s dominion over the north, south, and lower realms.

This entire process should last the duration of one exhalation, such that you are chanting "sha" the entire time that you are moving your head. This syllable is completed with your head bowed. Inhale and return your head to the center in preparation for the next syllable. As you exhale and begin to chant "lom," very slowly move your head upwards to Heaven, thereby acknowledging *Ha-Shem*'s sovereignty above all celestial beings. You should try to synchronize the end of your head movement upwards with the conclusion of your exhalation.

After you become proficient at combining the head movements and chanting, you might decide to work with the complex vocalizations of the vowel permutations of the Four-Letter Name that Abulafia himself advocated. A chart of this intricate procedure is found in Aryeh Kaplan's *Meditation and Kabbalah* (90).

8

AN ANCIENT MEDITATION

Let us now focus on a meditation that was first described in the *Talmud* more than 1,500 years ago. This concise meditation was subsequently incorporated into numerous medieval Jewish religious law codes. Owing to its "canonization" in normative *halachah*, it has been continuously practiced for almost two millenia. Even today, countless Jews use this technique twice daily. Accordingly, it is one of the most significant forms of meditation developed within any religious tradition.

This ancient practice instructs an individual how best to recite the *Shema*, a biblical prayer that is at the heart of the Jewish liturgy. It begins, "Hear (*Shema*) Israel, *Ha-Shem* is our God, *Ha-Shem* is oneness (*echad*)" (Deuteronomy 6:4). According to the rabbinic Sages, this biblical passage and its successive verses are to be recited morning and night, in fulfillment of a biblical commandment, (as reflected in Deuteronomy 6:7). The initial verse—with its compelling affirmation of faith—

requires special attentiveness. This is inherent in the word *Shema* (hear/listen) itself.

In order to create a proper mind-set for this critical recitation, let us consider Maimonides's counsel: "The first thing that you should cause your soul to hold fast onto is that, while reciting the *Shema* prayer, you should empty your mind of everything and pray thus" (*The Guide of the Perplexed*, 2, 3:51, 622).

Once you have removed extraneous thoughts from your mind, you will be able to engage in the meditation. It focuses on the concentration that an individual should have while reciting the word *echad* (one). The Rabbis attached particular importance to the last letter of the word *echad*—the *dalet*—which is written overly large in all Torah scrolls. Since the letter *dalet* corresponds to the number 4, it was interpreted as alluding to the four compass points. The pivotal discussion of this issue in the Talmud is the following:

> And it was taught: Symmachos said: Anyone who prolongs the pronunciation of *echad* (one), his days and years will likewise be prolonged. R. Aha b. Jacob said: This refers to the letter *dalet*. R. Ashi said: Moreover, one should not shorten the letter *chet*. R. Jeremiah was seated before his teacher, R. Hiyya b. Abba. The latter saw that he was greatly prolonging [the recitation] and said to him: Once you have acknowledged His sovereignty above and below, and in the four directions [literally, winds], more than that is not required of you. (*B. Berachot* 13b)

The text continues by noting that the leading rabbinic authority, Rabbi Judah the Prince, would cover his eyes with his hand while reciting the *Shema*. This, too, has been incorporated into the normative practice. An interesting discussion of this technique is found in the prayer book commentary of the *Hasidei Ashkenaz*. It connects the talmudic requirement to acknowledge *Ha-Shem's* sovereignty in six dimensions (i.e., above, below, and the four directions) with the special characteristics of the angels.

> And I, Asher b. R. Yaakov ha-Levi, heard directly from R. Eleazar ha-Darshan, of blessed memory, they prolong the *dalet* of *echad* in order to acknowledge His sovereignty in Heaven and on earth and in the four directions. These are the six aspects as is written, "Each [of the *seraphim*, i.e., fiery angels] possessed six wings: with two he would cover his face, with two he would cover his legs and with two he would fly" (Isaiah 6:2). (*Siddur of Rabbenu Shelomoh b. R. Shimshon of Worms*, 93)

This passage concludes by noting that the flight of the angels constitutes songs of praise to God.

A much expanded discussion of the *Shema* meditation is found in the seminal twelfth-century legal code, *Sefer Ha-Eshkol*, which was compiled by Rabbi Abraham b. Isaac of Narbonne. According to the testimony of Rabbi Abraham, it was the custom of the eleventh-century Babylonian Sage, Rabbi Hai Gaon, to nod his head in the six directions: that is—up, down, east, west, south, and north, while reciting the word *echad*. This particular order was derived from a key passage in the classic mystical work, *Sefer Yetzirah* (The Book of Creation), in which God is described as sealing the six planes of our three-dimensional universe with permutations of the Ineffable Name.

After referring to the above-quoted passage from the *Talmud*, R. Abraham comments:

> We have learned that one does well to shorten the *alef*, and it is commanded to do so. We can deduce this from R. Ashi's stipulation that specifically the *chet* should not be shortened. The fact that he did not mention the *alef* implies that one does well to shorten it. It has been stated that one should lengthen the *chet* to a count of three and the *dalet* to twice three. First, one should acknowledge sovereignty below and above while reciting the *chet*, and then do the four directions during the *dalet*.

When contemplating the four directions, one should nod
one's head first east, then west, then south, then north. We
learn this practice from the *Hilchot Yetzirah* (The Laws of
Creation), as is taught there (Chapter 1:13). . . .

"At the fifth [stage], He chose three simple letters: *yod, hey,
vav*, and fixed them for His great Name. He sealed the six
directions with them. He sealed the heights and turned
upward and sealed it with *yod, hey, vav*. The sixth [stage] He
sealed below and turned downward and sealed it with *yod,
vav, hey*. The seventh [stage] He sealed the east and turned
before Himself and sealed it with *hey, yod, vav*. The eighth
[stage] He sealed the west and turned backwards and sealed
it with *hey, vav, yod*. The ninth [stage] He sealed the south
and turned to His right and sealed it with *vav, yod, hey*. The
tenth [stage] He sealed the north and turned to His left and
sealed it with *vav, hey, yod*."

Since we are taught this, it is proper that we acknowledge
the sovereignty of the Creator of the universe, during our
recitation of the *Shema*, following the same pattern with
which the Creator created and sealed the universe. And our
teacher, Hai, of blessed memory explained [that one should
prolong the recitation of *echad*] long enough to motion with
one's head in the six directions and thereby accept the dominion of Heaven. And Rabbi [Judah the Prince] would
cover his eyes with his hands, [when facing his students
during the recitation]. Our sages explain that he was protecting himself from having his students see his eyes when
he was rotating them in the various directions. [This text was
translated from the printed edition of *Sefer ha-Eshkol* and
corrected by referring to Paris ms. H-91-A, 3b]

It should be noted in passing that an interesting
parallel to the pattern of this nodding is the ritualized
shaking of the *lulav* (palm frond) on Sukkot, which
follows a similar circuit. The only difference is that the
four directions precede the up and down movement.
Presumably, this change is indicative of the importance of the four winds in bringing life-sustaining rain,
which is of primary concern during Sukkot. The pertinent talmudic text begins: "R. Yohanan said, 'Extend
and then draw in [the *lulav*] for He who possesses the

four winds; next elevate then lower [the *lulav*] for He who possesses Heaven and earth" (*B. Sukkot* 37b).

Although there have been numerous rabbinic discussions of the *Shema* meditation, one of the most significant is found in R. Isaac of Corbeil's thirteenth-century presentation of the 613 biblical commandments, *Sefer Mitzvot Katan (SeMaK)*. R. Isaac focused on the key word *echad* (one), which concludes the opening line of the *Shema*. In order to appreciate his reasoning, it is necessary to be aware of the numerical significance of the three letters that constitute the word *echad: alef* (=1), *chet* (=8), and *dalet* (=4). R. Isaac expounded upon the second biblical commandment as follows:

> {We are commanded] to unify the name of the Holy One, blessed be He, as it is written, "Hear, Israel, *Ha-Shem* our God, *Ha-Shem* is one" (Deuteronomy 6:4). This represents accepting the yoke of the sovereignty of heaven. Concerning unification, R. Saadia Gaon explained that accompanying our belief that our God is the universal ruler, we must also believe that there is no other ruler. . . . [F]rom this it is derived that He is unique on earth and in the seven Heavens. This is alluded to in the *alef* and *chet* of *echad* and the *dalet* refers to the four directions. In the future everyone will believe this, as is written, "On that day the Lord will be one and His name one" (Zechariah 14:9). The explanation of this is that the entire world will believe that He is one. (*Sefer ha-Semak me-Zurich*, R. Isaac Rozenberg, ed., 1:50)

A brief discussion and elucidation of this exposition is by Rabbi Joshua Falk, in his sixteenth-century commentary on the *Tur* code (*Prishah, Orah Hayyim* 61:9). He quotes the *Semak* and in so doing slightly modifies the key phrasing to make it clearer. "This is what it says in the *Sefer Mitzvot Katan:* When reciting the *alef*, one should consider that He is One; at the *chet*, that He is united in the seven heavens and on earth, which makes eight; and the *dalet* alludes to the four directions. In the future, all will declare that He is One."

To summarize, *echad* has three distinct and interrelated components. While reciting the initial syllable *eh* for one beat, focus your consciousness on the oneness of the Holy One. Next, pronounce *cha* to a count of three and raise your head up and then down, indicative of God's dominion above and below. Finally, vocalize the "d" of *dalet* to six beats, and nod your head first east, then west, then south, then north. Additionally, based on the prophecy of Zechariah, both Rabbis Isaac of Corbeil and Joshua Falk asserted that during the Messianic era everyone—Jew and Gentile alike—will participate together in this act of unification.

A related, though somewhat different presentation is found in the writings of R. Ezra of Gerona. R. Ezra, who was a leading religious figure in early thirteenth-century Spain, was an older contemporary of Ramban (Nachmanides). R. Ezra was a kabbalist and one of the earliest, possibly the first, to write full-fledged treatises using the kabbalistic terminology of the *Sefirot*. Included among his writings are a commentary on the *Aggadot* of the Talmud and a commentary on the Song of Songs, which was eventually attributed to Ramban. The following is his discussion of the recitation of the *Shema*.

> You should know about Divine unification that when one mentions various Names and matters, he should be careful to unify everything to the Infinite (*Ayn Sof*), thereby acknowledging that He is the cause of everything and everything is from Him. He should not be afraid of any separation or cutting off in the universe, as a result of mentioning the Names. In the same way that the branches of a tree are numerous and all protrude from the trunk in the middle, when you reflect upon each in turn, so too with the issue of Divine unification.
>
> The essence of reciting the *Shema* is to unify everything. Each word possesses a special significance; therefore, one must concentrate upon each word according to its significance and unify everything at the word "one" (*echad*). The *alef* of the word hints at what one's thought cannot

abstract.[1] The *chet* hints at the eight *Sefirot*. And the *dalet* is large, hinting at the tenth *Sefirah* [i.e., *Malchut* = Sovereignty], in order to designate Him as king over the four directions, which correspond to the four Camps [of the *Shechinah*].

It is necessary to be precise when pronouncing every letter, neither adding nor subtracting anything. The significance of the recitation of *Shema* is like the seal of a king, which he has sent to his subjects. They recognize the image of his seal and stand erect and shout ecstatically and call out to him in awe, trembling and fearfully. The Holy One, blessed be He, however, did not trouble Israel to recite the *Shema* standing erect and shouting ecstatically, rather they recite it normally, by precisely pronouncing the letters and neither adding nor subtracting what has been written down. (G. Scholem, pub., "*Seridim Hadashim* . . . ," in *Sefer Zikaron Le-Asher Gulak*, 222)

Other kabbalistic suggestions for the proper recitation of the *Shema* are recorded by R. Yosef Hayyim of Baghdad. Initially, he cites a visualization found in a manuscript entitled *Keter Malchut*: "One who recites [the *Shema*] should visualize with his mind's eye all of the letters of the verse" (*Ben Ish Hai* 81).

R. Yosef also recommends that while reciting the word *echad*, one should concentrate on the collation of the two Divine Names: *YHVH* and *ADoNaY*, thereby yielding the unified Name: *YAHDVNHY*. (This practice is known as *yichudim*, meaning unifications, and is the subject of Chapter 11). Finally, he suggests that when one recites the word *malchuto* (His kingdom) from the passage that immediately follows the first verse of the *Shema*, he should lower his head. R. Yosef explains the reason: "There is in this matter the mystery of bringing down the Divine illumination to the *Shechinah*, [namely] *Malchut*, who is the Mistress of the House" (*Ben Ish Hai* 82).

---

1. This corresponds to the highest *Sefirah, Keter*; cf. R. Yitzhak of Acco, *Meirat Aynayim*, "*Va-ethanan*" (Jerusalem, 1975), 274.

Among the many reflections on the significance of the *Shema* meditation are the following comments by the Maggid of Mezeritch, who attributed the supernatural powers of the hasidic masters to its proper recitation.

> I heard from the Maggid, of eternally blessed memory, concerning the explanation of their statements about reaching the word *echad* and nodding one's head in the six directions. One wonders what is gained by this [procedure]? If one were to nod to all of the corners of the universe and his heart is unaware what his head is doing?
>
> He explained that when one unites himself in union with *Ha-Shem*, may He be blessed, then there is a complete union with the Holy One, blessed be He. Thereupon, he would have the potential to invalidate His [harsh] decrees and also to decree and have [his desires] fulfilled, as was stated [by the sages] of blessed memory, "The Holy One blessed be He issues decrees and the *tzaddik* (righteous) invalidates [them]" (see *B. Moed Katan* 16b).
>
> This is the proper intention [that one should have] upon reciting the word *echad* and uniting oneself with the Creator of the universe in a complete union. Its benefits are great. When one has the power to nod in the six directions, which were the six planes upon which the universe was built, he can shake and direct them according to his will and desire. He can change the times and transform the seasons (cf. Daniel 2:21) since he has achieved complete union with the Supernal Unity, which transcends time. (*Torat ha-Maggid* 2:48.)

Another profound extension of this meditation is evident in several comments by R. Hayyim of Volozhin, the early nineteenth-century pioneer of the *yeshivah* (Rabbinical Seminary) movement.

R. Hayyim asserted:

> Accordingly, when engaged in the unification of the first verse of the recitation of the *Shema*, at the word "one" it is appropriate for a true servant to contemplate in the holiness of his thoughts that He, may His Name be blessed, from the

Divine perspective is actually one, even in respect to all of the created beings. He exists alone in pristine oneness, as was the case prior to the creation of the universe. (*Nefesh ha-Hayyim*, 166.)

He also wrote,

Concerning the unification process associated with the first verse [of the recitation of the *Shema*], in conjunction with the word "one," the individual should contemplate that *Ha-Shem*, may He be blessed, is unique. He is one in respect to all of the worlds and all of the created beings. He exhibits a pristine oneness and everything else is considered to be none existent—for there is nothing else other than Him, at all (cf. Deuteronomy 4:39). (*Nefesh ha-Hayyim*, 162)

A final comment that he makes on this theme is that in the *Shema* God is referred to as both *Eloheinu* and *Ha-Shem*. The reason that this passage refers to *Eloheinu* (i.e., our God) is:

One should contemplate that He, may He be blessed is *Eloheinu* (our God), the Master of Divine powers and the source of our souls and our life forces, and of all created beings and worlds. Even though He created and brought into existence the powers and worlds and creatures; nevertheless, from His own perspective He is in a state of pure being and absolute oneness, such that no creature can intrude, forfend, in any way upon His pristine oneness, may He be blessed, which infuses everything. Thus, even now [i.e., after the creation of the universe] He is absolute existence and oneness. (R. Hayyim, *Nefesh ha-Hayyim*, 178)

In these statements, R. Hayyim is expressing a doctrine that is known as acosmism, literally a negation of the cosmos.[2] It is the teaching that God is the only essential reality and that everything else is ephemeral

---

2. For an expanded discussion of this concept, see M. Verman, "Panentheism and Acosmism in the Kabbalah," *Studia Mystica* 10:2 (1987).

and without true being. Although this doctrine was not particularly evident in Jewish circles until the late eighteenth century, R. Hayyim and certain hasidic masters (especially R. Shneur Zalman of Liadi and his disciple, R. Aaron), based themselves upon a literal interpretation of Deuteronomy 4:39, "And you shall know today and place it upon your heart that *Ha-Shem* is God in Heaven above and on the earth below; there is no other."

Thus, we see that each letter of *echad* has a special significance that is expressed meditatively in our daily affirmation of Divine unity. By casting your awareness in all directions, you can traverse the universe in one word. Through concentrating on "one," you can perceive the vastness of the cosmic kingdom that our Creator has formed and in which we have been placed.

9

PERCEIVING THE LIGHT

Light is primal. Light is the beginning. The first act of God in the creation of the universe was fashioning light; hence the initial utterance of Divine speech was "Let there be light" (Genesis 1:3). It is not surprising that the most common metaphor in Jewish mystical writings that connotes Divine manifestation is spiritual light. This is readily evident in the titles of the classic books of Jewish mysticism: *Sefer ha-Bahir* (The Book of Brilliant Light); *Sefer ha-Zohar* (The Book of Radiance); *Shaarei Orah* (The Gates of Light). In discussing this topic, we shall offer a brief selection of classical texts and then focus on the writings of the renaissance mystic, R. Eleazar Azikri, who expounded extensively upon contemplation of Divine light. This sustained discussion will be followed by subsequent elaborations on this theme. We shall conclude with several concise techniques involving eye movements, and finally the *Zohar's* candle-gazing meditation.

Ha-Shem is identified at the start of the first blessing that precedes the morning *Shema* recital as the "Creator of Light. . . . The One who illumines the earth and [all] those that dwell upon it with compassion." This blessing concludes, "May You shine a new light on Zion and may we all speedily merit its light. Blessed are You, *Ha-Shem*, Creator of the lights." Similarly, the last blessing of the morning *Amidah* invokes Divine light: "Bless us, our Father, all of us together in the light of Your Presence, for in the light of Your Presence You have given us, *Ha-Shem* our God, the Torah of life."

Not only is *Ha-Shem* the source of light, but light imagery serves as an epithet or signifier for *Ha-Shem*. For example, the prophet Isaiah proclaimed, "The Light of Israel will be fire and [Israel's] Holy One a flame" (Isaiah 10:17). The ancient text *Sefer Ha-Razim* (The Book of Mysteries) is part of the *Hechalot* corpus and describes the seven Heavens. Its account of the seventh and highest stratum begins:

> The seventh firmament, all of it is sevenfold light, and from its light all the heavens shine. . . . There is no calculation or limit to the great light within it, and the fullness of the light illumines all the earth. The angels are fixed in pillars of light, and their light is as the light of the brilliant star [i.e., Venus] and cannot be extinguished, for their eyes are like flashes of lightning, and they stand upon the margins of [the Divine light], and glorify in fear the One who sits upon the throne of glory. (*Sepher Ha-Razim*, M. Morgan, trans., 81)

Turning now to R. Elezar Azikri, who lived in Tzefat —a lovely town in the hill country, near the Sea of Galilee. Now famous as an artist colony, it was once the home of spiritual artisans, the medieval kabbalists of Israel. Many of these pillars of the Jewish mystical tradition are well-known figures: R. Moshe Cordovero, R. Yitzhak Luria, and their student and literary virtuoso, R. Hayyim Vital. We have already encountered each of them many times throughout this book.

R. Eleazar devoted his life to an intense spiritual practice. This focus was a straightforward, yet powerful meditative technique, based on biblical directives. It is rooted in the injunction to continuously attach oneself to God: "I have set *Ha-Shem* before me always" (Psalms 16:8). This verse convinced Azikri that meditation should not be confined to a specific time or setting, but rather it must be an ongoing activity, undertaken throughout the day.

Instead of contemplating the more transcendent aspects of the Divine Being, Azikri concentrated on the *Shechinah*, the Divine In-Dwelling, God's immanent presence in the world. According to classic thirteenth-century kabbalists, like R. Yosef Gikatilla in the opening chapter of his *Shaarei Orah*, whoever desires to contemplate the *Sefirot* must start with the lowest level, *Malchut*. This corresponds to the standard rabbinic term, *Shechinah*, and is seen as a gate through which all cosmic energy flows, from Above to below and below to Above.

R. Eleazar contended that the Divine Presence is manifest as spiritual light, and accordingly one must be ever mindful of being enveloped by the Divine effulgence. This is clearly reflected in Azikri's well-known song, *Yedid Nefesh* (Lover of the Soul), which is traditionally sung as a prelude to the *Shabbat* evening service. He introduced this lovely hymn by noting that its theme is Divine unity and love, and that it is based on an acrostic; each stanza corresponding to one of the letters of the Four-Letter Name.

The second stanza begins:

> Splendorously beautiful, light of the universe,
> My soul is lovesick for You.
> Please, God, please cure her,
> By revealing to her the delightfulness of Your light.
> (*Sefer Haredim*, 163)

In this century, Azikri's famous poem was echoed by Rav Kook:

> My soul longs
> For the supernal light
> For infinite light
> For the light of the God of truth. . . .
> Please satisfy my desire;
> Satiate me with the light of Your revelation.
> Fulfill my thirst for Your light,
> Let Your Countenance shine that I might be saved.
> (A. Habermann, "Shirat Ha-Rav," 18)

Both Azikri and Rav Kook are rooted in the Jewish mystical tradition, which viewed light as the principal image of the Divine realm. They were also influenced by Maimonides' statement, "Just as we apprehend Him by means of that light which He caused to overflow toward us[,] . . . we are always before Him, may He be exalted, and walk about to and fro while his *Shechinah* is with us (*Guide of the Perplexed*, 3:52, S. Pines, trans., 629).

In his extremely popular handbook, *Sefer Haredim* (The Book of the God-Fearers), Azikri wrote:

> In several treatises it is recorded that the Jewish pietists used to engage in *hitbodedut* (seclusion), withdrawal and *devekut*, attachment; that is to say when they were alone they would remove all worldly concerns from their thought and connect their thoughts to the all embracing Lord. Similarly our teacher and rabbi, Rabbi Y. [Yitzhak Luria], the aforementioned kabbalist, taught that it is sevenfold more beneficial for the soul than study.[1] According to the perseverance and capacity of the individual, one should withdraw and go into seclusion one day a week, or once a fortnight, or at least once a month. Ramban, of blessed memory, commented on the

---

1. Azikri relied on a manuscript text from R. Yitzhak Luria entitled *Beit Middot*; see R. Eleazer Azikri, *Sefer Haredim* (Jerusalem, 1984), 253, 309.

verse referring to the patriarch Jacob, "Get up and go to Beit El and dwell there" (Genesis 35:1), what does the phrase "and dwell (ve-shev) there" mean? It is the same as "in sitting still (be-shuvah) and rest you shall be saved" (Isaiah 30:15). That is to say, one should direct one's thought by securing one's mind with Him, may He be blessed.

It is taught that the ancient pietists would wait for an hour and then pray, in order to direct their hearts to the Place [i.e., Ha-Shem]; (see M. Berachot 5:1). The commentators explained that this indicates that they would empty their minds of worldly matters and attach their thought to the Lord of all, may He be blessed, with awe and love. Behold, for nine hours [daily] they would desist from their study and be engaged in meditation and attachment. They would imagine the light of the Shechinah upon their heads, as if it had spread out all around them and they were sitting inside the light. So I have found in an ancient pamphlet of the early ascetics. Then they would tremble naturally and rejoice in the trembling, as it says, "Serve Ha-Shem in fear and rejoice in trembling" (Psalms 2:11). (Sefer Haredim 254)

R. Eleazar also kept a diary spanning many years in which he jotted down a series of observations on spirituality. This work has been preserved in a unique manuscript. What follow are two selections from it.

Realize that you are standing before your Creator. When you are studying the Torah, you are gazing on the light of His garment. And when you are walking in the market-place or sitting anywhere, you are encountering the light of the Shechinah. For "His glory fills the whole world" (Isaiah 6:3); face to face you shall meet Him. When you speak with someone it is as if He is speaking, for from His power everyone speaks. (J. T. S. ms., Adler 74, f. 205a)

Let the light always shine on your face. Speaking with Him, and walking with Him, and being silent with Him, and asleep with Him, and awakening with Him, and sitting with Him, and standing with Him, and lying down with Him; all my movements are for Him. The King rests on His throne and the servant runs to Him and serves Him personally, not through an agent. I fulfill the conditions of a servant and am not at all stubborn. I unify His Names, may He be blessed, at every moment, in joy and trembling, and flee from social contact, as much as possible. Complete silence in the fiery light; alone, fearful and crawling. Make the light which is always upon your head a teacher, and acquire it for yourself as a friend. (f. 202a)[2]

Azikri's intoxication with love for God, echoes the following comments by Maimonides. It should be noted that "love of *Ha-Shem*" constitutes one of the foundational commandments as formulated by Maimonides in *M.T., Yesodei ha-Torah*, 2:2. He subsequently expanded upon this:

What is the love that is appropriate for a person to love *Ha-Shem*? It should be a love that is surpassingly great, exceedingly strong such that one's very soul is bound up with the love of *Ha-Shem*. It happens when one is completely infatuated with someone, as if they are love-sick and their mind is never free from thinking about that person. They are constantly infatuated, whether sitting or standing, even when they are eating and drinking. Even more than this should the love of *Ha-Shem* be in the hearts of His lovers. They are infatuated with her [i.e., love of *Ha-Shem*] always, as we are commanded "with all your heart and all your soul" (Deuteronomy 6:5). This is what Solomon said by way of analogy, "for I am love-sick" (Song of Songs 2:5), for all of Song of Songs is an analogy for this topic. (*M.T., Teshuvah* 10:3)

One can find many echoes of Azikri's light-centered spirituality. R. Moshe Hayyim Luzzatto, in the introduction to his famous *138 Doorways to Wisdom*, offers a beautiful exposition on the nature of the study of *Torah* and the supreme value of every single letter of the text. This recalls our earlier discussion, in Chapter 2, on this theme.

---

2. Note that the last sentence is an interesting reworking of *M. Avot* 1:6.

Consider a coal that is not burning and the flame is hidden and closed inside. When someone blows upon it, then it spreads and flares and it continues to expand. Within this flame there are many different colors, which were not apparent initially; nevertheless, everything is coming from the coal.

So too with this Torah that is before us. Every one of her words and letters are like a coal. When one sets them out as they are, they appear like coals, somewhat dim. If an individual endeavors to study her, then from each letter a great flame bursts forth, filled with many colors. These are the data that are hidden in each letter. This was already explained in the *Zohar* concerning the *alef beit*. This is not an analogy, but literally something that is indeed essential, for all of the letters that we see in the Torah correspond to the twenty-two lights that exist Above. These supernal lights shine on the letters. From here is derived the holiness of the Torah, the Torah scrolls, the *tefillin*, *mezuzot* and all sacred writings. According to the sanctity with which they were written, so too will grow the Divine inspiration and illumination of these lights on the letters. Therefore a Torah scroll that has only one mistake is totally invalidated, for there is not the appropriate illumination by reading from it, from which will flow sanctity to the nation. (*KL"CH Pitchei Hochmah*, 3)

The following lines from *Keter Shem Tov*, the traditional anthology of the teachings of the Baal Shem Tov, is virtually identical to Azikri: "The soul becomes a throne for the light of the *Shechinah* above the head. And it is as if the light spreads around him and he is within the light, sitting and trembling with joy" (*Keter Shem Tov*, cited in Buxbaum, *Spiritual Practices*, 378).

R. Isaac Safrin (1806–1874) was a fascinating hasidic master. In his secret diary, *Megillat Setarim*, he recorded his earliest vision.

While studying Talmud, in the middle of the day. Suddenly a great light fell on me. The whole house became filled with light, a marvelous light, the *Shechinah* resting there. This was the first time in my life that I had some little taste of His light, may He be blessed.... Afterwards I fell once again for a time

> so I came to realize that I must journey to the saints who would draw down His light, blessed be He, upon me since I already had a refined vessel wherewith to receive the light. (Jacobs, *Jewish Mystical Testimonies*, 240)

R. Aaron Roth, a twentieth-century hasidic master who eventually settled in Jerusalem, also connected the issue of love of God with perception of light.

> I shall explain the matter to you by means of a parable, all having to do with the idea of love. A man is in prison where he has sat so long in darkness that he is unaware that there is any such thing as light. Adjacent to his prison is a room in which there shines a brilliant light. Suddenly a small aperture is opened and he sees the light. . . . Even though the light which comes through this aperture is as nothing compared to the light which shines through the open doors, yet since it shines directly on the recipients a great and holy illumination is theirs. When a man is worthy of seeing this light his soul longs and is set on fire without limit until he feels that he is about to expire [in ecstasy]. In his great longing he risks his life to break open the door of his dungeon and springs energetically to enjoy the light. But as soon as he emerges [from the dungeon] the light is concealed. (Jacobs, *Jewish Mystical Testimonies*, 249–250)

The parable continues and ultimately ends with a lesson on the benefit of attaching oneself to a *tzaddik* and thereupon receiving help.

When Azikri discussed the theory of *hitbodedut*, as cited above, he mentioned that he had found some of his material in "an ancient pamphlet of the early ascetics." It is quite likely that the text he was referring to is the anonymous thirteenth-century treatise, "A Chapter on Concentration [*kavvanah*] by the Early Kabbalists, of Blessed Memory." This important, though enigmatic text advocated the visualization of sitting inside the Divine light. Near its beginning we read, "You should imagine in your mind that you are light and that all of your surroundings, from each corner and side, are comprised of light. In the midst of the light is a throne of light."[3]

Let us also consider two other thirteenth-century texts, in order to have a fuller picture of the mind-set that lay behind the meditative techniques that we will shortly present. *The Fountain of Wisdom* is one of the most complex and challenging writings of this period. It was attributed to Moses, who purportedly received it from a mysterious angel. Therein, one finds a description of the Primal Darkness that preceded creation and from which ten colored lights emanated.

> These ten colors flow from the Darkness. They are the following: light from light, radiance from radiance, lustre from lustre, radiance from light, light from radiance, lustre from light, light from lustre, lustre from radiance, radiance from lustre, and flaming fire from flaming fire. Behold, there are ten. The first is Marvellous Light; this is light from light. The second is Hidden light: this is radiance from radiance. (Verman, *The Books of Contemplation*, 59)

Undoubtedly, this text influenced the "Chapter on Concentration," as did the well-known *Iggeret ha-Kodesh* (Holy Letter), which is traditionally attributed to Ramban.

> Know that [in the case of] a spring of water, since it flows from an elevated place to a lower place, there exists the possibility of raising the water to another elevated place, corresponding to the elevated place from whence it origi-

---

3. Originally published by G. Scholem, *"Der Begriff der Kawwana in der alten Kabbala,"* *MGWJ* (1934): 511. This work has also been translated by Aryeh Kaplan, *Meditation and Kabbalah* (York Beach, 1982), 119–122. The complete Hebrew text, along with R. Hayyim Vital's commentary is found in *Ketavim Hadashim le-Rabbenu Hayyim Vital,* "Shaarei Kedushah," (Jerusalem, 1988), 15–18.

nated. Similarly, it is known to the masters of the *Kabbalah* that the source of human thought is the rational soul, which emanated from the supernal spheres. Thought is capable of expanding, elevating and reaching her place of origin. When she reaches the source, she adheres to the Supernal Light from which she was emanated. Then they will become one entity. When this thought emanates again from Above to below, everything will become like one line and the Supernal Light will be drawn below by the power of the thought to draw it below. Then the *Shechinah* will reside below. As a result of this [process] the Radiant Light will be drawn down and expand within the place where the sage is sitting. Thus, the ancient pietists attached their thoughts to the supernal spheres and drew down the Supernal Light. As a result [their] activities prospered and were blessed by the power of thought.[4]

Note how the author interprets the classic talmudic statement about the meditative practices of the ancient pietists, according to his theory about the celestial origins of thought. The reason that their deeds were blessed was owing to the Supernal Light, which was drawn downwards by their meditation.

Jewish mystics developed specific techniques to promote the contemplation of Divine light. For example, the *Zohar* recommends special eye movements for perceiving the supernal lights. "This is the secret. Close your eye[s] and roll your eyeball[s]. Those colors that are luminous and radiate will be revealed. It is not permitted to see them, except with closed eyes for they are hidden (*Zohar* 2:23b).

One can even find biblical support for this practice of eye-rolling in the following verse: "*Gal* (open/roll) my eyes that I might see the wonders of Your Torah" (Psalms 119:18).

---

4. "Iggeret ha-Kodesh," in R. Moshe b. Nachman *Kitvei Ramban*, (Jerusalem, 1763), 2:333. This text was also published and translated by S. Cohen, *The Holy Letter* (Ktav, 1976).

In an early thirteenth-century text by R. Elhanan b. Yakar, an even more dramatic procedure is mentioned. It is potentially harmful and could cause permanent eye damage. Accordingly, I am definitely *not* suggesting that anyone experiment with it! It is offered simply as an illustration of the scope of medieval Jewish explorations of Divine light.

> The soul is a red light that resides on the brain, between two membranes. It is the size of a hazel-nut. If you shut your eye and place your finger at the tip of your eye adjacent to your nose and massage there with your finger, you will perceive a red, circular light on your eyeball. This is the light of the soul shining on your eye. At the time of death this small light grows and assumes the shape of the individual from whom it emanated. The proof of this is the prophet Samuel.[5]

Another technique that is found in the *Zohar* entails candle gazing. It is rooted in the verse from Proverbs 20:27, "*Ha-Shem*'s candle/lamp is the soul of man, searching all the internal organs (literally, rooms of the belly)." (A similar concept is found in the *Talmud, B. Shabbat* 22b, wherein the light from the *menorah* attests to the *Shechinah* residing in the world.) According to the *Zohar*, not only does the relationship between the flame and the candle exemplify the union of upper and lower, but even within the flame itself there are two dimensions, paralleling the upper and lower realms within the Divine Being. This text is a good example of the interplay between light and colors in Jewish mystical writings.

> Rabbi Shimon began by stating, There are two verses, "For *Ha-Shem*, your God, is a consuming fire" (Deuteronomy 4:24), and it is also written there, "But you that are attached

---

5. *Sod ha-Sodot* in *Tekstim be-Torat ha-Elohut shel Hasidut Ashkenaz*, Y. Dan, ed. (Jerusalem, 1977), 28. The concluding statement is an allusion to 1 Samuel 28.

to *Ha-Shem*, your God, are all alive today" (Deuteronomy 4:4). These are two verses I have explained on several occasions, for my colleagues were stirred up by them.

Come and see: "For *Ha-Shem*, your God, is a consuming fire." This has already been clarified among the group that there is a type of fire which consumes fire. It consumes and destroys it. For there is one type of fire which is more potent than another, as previously explained.

But come and see: One who desires to know the mystery of the Holy Unity should gaze on the flame that rises from the coal or from a lit candle, for a flame cannot ascend except if it is holding on to coarse matter.

Come and see: An ascending flame has two lights, a white luminous light, and another which clings to it and is either black or blue. The white light is higher and ascends in a straight path. Underneath is either a blue or a black light which acts as a chair for the white, and this white light rests on it. Each grasps the other such that everything is one.

For the black or blue light is a Throne of Glory for the white light. This is the secret of the *tachelet* [i.e., the blue thread of the *tallit*]. Moreover, the blue/black throne is attached to something else, which is below it, enabling it to burn, and it [i.e., what is below the blue/black flame] encourages it to grasp onto the white light. Sometimes the blue/black light becomes red; however, the white light which is above it never changes—for white is perpetual but blue changes to these colors: sometimes blue or black and sometimes red. This light is joined on two sides.

It is joined above to the white light and joined below to what is under it, which is transformed because of it, enabling it to shine and grasp onto it. This light constantly consumes and destroys whatever lies beneath it. The blue light destroys and consumes whatever is attached to it from underneath and it rests on, as it is its nature to destroy and consume. The destruction of everything and the death of all is dependent upon it. Accordingly, it consumes everything that is attached to it from below. But the white light, which rests on it, never consumes or destroys, and its light never changes.

And Moses had this in mind when he said, "For *Ha-Shem*, your God, is a consuming fire." [This fire] assuredly consumes; it consumes and destroys whatever resides underneath it. Accordingly, Moses specified "*Ha-Shem*, your God" and not "our God," for Moses was associated with the upper white light, which does not destroy or consume. (*Zohar*, 1:50b–51a)

Consider that there are two basic ways of looking at something, as suggested by Martin Buber in *I and Thou*. Usually, we affirm that there is a gulf separating us from that which is being perceived. The existence of this gap is continually supported by constant monitoring of the Self as it is engaged in the act of perception.

There is another way to perceive and experience the world—by "dis-regarding" the Self, one can identify with what is being perceived.

Darken the room and light a candle. Sit in a comfortable position. Take a few deep breaths. Relax and candle-gaze. Work with the above-quoted statement from the *Zohar*, "One who desires to know the mystery of the Holy Unity should gaze in the flame . . . for a flame cannot ascend except if it is holding on to coarse matter."

Identify with the candle, by closing the perceptual distance that seperates you from the candle. Identification can move in two directions. Either you can bring the candle image in your mind closer, until it is within, or you can allow yourself to be drawn toward and ultimately into the candle. Both approaches can result in a unity of awareness. Merge with the candle. Let its light illuminate you, from within. Remember, this light is your soul—*Ha-Shem*'s lamp.

As a postscript, it is worthwhile to consider the interpretation of this material by R. Eleazar Azikri. Note especially the association of the congregation of Israel with the candle-wick. The various colors of the flame allude to different *Sefirot*, with *Malkut* (Sovereignty = *Shechinah*) being the lowest.

The nine *Sefirot* altogether are called the white light, and *Malchut* is the blue light, being a throne for the white light.

Together they are a throne for the Emanator, may He be blessed, for all ten comprise a single unity, without any division. This is analagous to the light of the candle. Above is the white light and below, the blue light. The blue light is a throne for the white. And He commanded the nation whom He chose to attach their thought to this blue light. They are compared to the wick that is joined to the blue light and on which is the white light—thereby they are joined to both of them.

This is what it says, "But you that are attached to *Ha-Shem*, your God, are all alive today (Deuteronomy 4:4). That is to say that even though you are compared to the wick which is linked to the blue, destructive light as is stated, "For *Ha-Shem*, your God, is a consuming fire" (Deuteronomy 4:24)— and concerning it is written in Chronicles, "When Solomon concluded praying a fire descended from heaven and consumed the *olah* and *zevachim* [i.e., sacrifices]" (2 Chronicles 7:1)—nevertheless, you will not be consumed. On the contrary, owing to your attachment to *Ha-Shem*, you shall continue to live. This is explicit in the section on Genesis in the *Zohar*, f. 51." (*Sefer Haredim*, 34)

We shall end this section on the quest for Divine light with a description of the practices of a small network of Israeli meditators who refer to themselves as the *Hugei Argaman* (Circles of Royal Purple). I encountered them in Jerusalem a dozen years ago. At the time they also had a group in Tel Aviv. Perhaps they are still active.

They based their spiritual practice on the teachings of an itinerant Polish kabbalist named Max Théon (1848–1927). Théon had a disciple, David Themanlys, and it was Themanlys's son, Pascal, who heads the *Hugei Argaman*. Théon published voluminously at the start of the century in an arcane, theosophical journal, *Revue Cosmique*. Under Themanlys's direction, the group culled Théon's writings and compiled an anthology entitled *Shaar le-Sodot ha-Hitbonenut* (Gateway to the Mysteries of Meditation). They sold this slender, yet fascinating, volume in a bookstore devoted to

Kabbalah and Hasidism called "The Hidden Corner" (alas defunct), which was operated by several members of the group.

The *Hugei Argaman* met weekly. The dozen or so members sat in a circle, read and discussed passages from the *Gateway*. Someone then recited a preparatory text that shall be presented shortly. A central component of this text is that the titles of the initial four *parshiyyot* (sections) of the Torah are interpreted as spiritual guideposts. The recitation was followed by half an hour of silent meditation. Afterwards, the individuals shared their experiences. The perception of violet light was especially valued in the group.

Text of the Concentration before Meditation and Serenity

We view this meditation as part of holy service—to help build the bridge between this world and the higher realms.

We must try to open ourselves to receive blessings, lights and powers from Above, to open [our] spiritual senses, according to the tradition of the prophets, kabbalists and hasidic masters.

Especially according to the teaching of the holy ARI [i.e., R. Yitzhak Luria], who brought his disciples to drink the living waters of the well of Miriam, the prophetess.

We hope to dedicate this meditation, to reach inner quiet, introspection, heartfelt prayer and serenity, until [achieving] *devekut* (attachment), as the early pietists did—according to *Berachot* [i.e., M. Berachot, 5:1].

For the covenant of serenity is one aspect of the mysteries of *Shabbat*.

We sit in the violet light of the tabernacle (*sukkah*) of peace.

The order of the *parshiyyot* (sections) of *Genesis* hint at the levels of spiritual ascension:

"In the beginning," "Noah," "Go forth," "And He appeared." "In the beginning"—wisdom, "Noah"—serenity (*menuchah*), "Go forth"—ascension of the soul, "And He appeared"—for *all* the Israelites saw the thunderings [lit. voices] while standing at Mount Sinai (Exodus 20:15).

> May He remember us so that Your *Shechinah*
>   will reside upon us,
> And the spirit of wisdom and understanding
>   will shine upon us,
> And we will fulfill the scriptural verse:
> 'The spirit of *Ha-Shem* shall rest upon him,
> The spirit of wisdom and understanding,
> The spirit of counsel and valor,
> The spirit of the knowledge and fear of
>   *Ha-Shem*' (Isaiah 11:2).

"In the beginning" "Noah"—in the beginning [*la-nuach*] one must rest, as it is written, "you shall be silent" (Exodus 14:14). (*Shaar le-Sodot ha-Hitbonenut*, 83)

10

HEART-CENTERED SPIRITUALITY

> R. Hiyya bar Abba said, "Where do we find that
> the Holy one, blessed be He, is called Israel's
> heart?—from this verse, 'God is the rock of my
> heart and my portion forever'" (Psalms 73:26).
> —*Shir ha-Shirim Rabbah* 5:2

Jewish spiritual literature has always focused on the
heart. From biblical times to present, the heart has
been the fulcrum for Jewish meditation. After explor-
ing some of the jewels from the treasury of sources
on heart spirituality, we shall conclude this chapter
with a powerful, heart-centered meditative technique
formulated by R. Isaac of Acco, an early fourteenth-
century figure.

Heart spirituality permeates the Hebrew Scriptures.
Well known is the passage from the *Shema*, "You shall
love *Ha-Shem* with all your heart and all soul and all of
your strength" (Deuteronomy 6:5). Rededication to *Ha-
Shem* is characterized by receiving a new heart. King

David, after sinning with Bathsheba, petitioned: "Create a pure heart for me, God, and renew a resolute spirit within me" (Psalms 51:12). This theme was developed by Ezekiel, wherein *Ha-Shem* promises the exiled Israelites: "I will give you a new heart and embue you with a new spirit. I will remove the heart of stone from your flesh and give you a heart of flesh. . . . Then you will dwell in the land that I gave to your fathers, and you shall be My nation and I will be your God" (Ezekiel 36:26–28; cf. 11:19, 18:31).

A complementary biblical image for spiritual transformation is that of the circumcision of the heart: "Then *Ha-Shem*, your God, will circumcize your heart and the heart of your seed to love *Ha-Shem*, your God, with all your heart and soul that you may live" (Deuteronomy 30:6; cf. 10:16, Jeremiah 4:4).

For those interested in numerology, the first letter of the Torah is a *bet* = 2 and the last letter is a *lamed* = 30. When combined, these two letters form the word *lev*, which is the Hebrew for heart and yields the numerical value thirty-two. Moreover, *Elohim* (God) appears thirty-two times in Genesis 1. It is presumably for these reasons that the classic text of Jewish theosophy, *Sefer Yetzirah* 1:1 begins: "With thirty-two marvellous paths of wisdom *Ha-Shem* inscribed . . . His Name and created the universe."

The Rabbis endorsed the centrality of the heart. "All the limbs [of the body] depend upon the heart" (*Y. Terumot* 8:4, 47a). "Why was wisdom given to the heart? Because all of the limbs depend upon the heart" (*Yalkut Shimoni, Mishlei*, no. 929).

The heart is also the focus of numerous interesting halachic rulings. For example, the heart is attributed with sight. Based on Ecclesiastes 1:16, "My heart has seen much wisdom," the Rabbis decreed that one's genitals must be covered during prayer, so that the heart will not see them and become distracted (*B. Berachot* 24b). Another regulation pertains to *Shabbat* observance and the restriction on not walking more than approximately half a mile beyond a city's boundaries. The *Mishnah* specifies how one should hold the tape measure for establishing the parameter: "One should not measure except at the level of the heart" (*M. Eruvin* 5:4). Additionally, the verse, "The heart knows a person's bitterness" (Proverbs 14:10) is the scriptural basis for permitting someone to eat on Yom Kippur. The Rabbis ruled that one should even disregard medical advice and listen to the individual (*B. Yoma* 83a).

Referring to another situation, the talmudic commentator Meiri noted: "Even if a person is a transgressor, if someone is present at the moment when his soul departs, [the observer] is obligated to rend [his garment]; just like a burnt Torah, the commandments of the human heart are like letters on a Torah scroll" (*Beit ha-Bechirah Shabbat*, 405).

Two fascinating issues pertaining to the heart are raised in the collection of customs attributed to R. Yitzhak Luria. The first pertains to the practice of beating on one's chest with one's right hand during the Confession (*vidui*), which is recited repeatedly on *Yom Kippur*. In this text there is reference to the standard kabbalistic symbolism, which associates the right side with *Hesed* (Mercy):

> We have previously explained about the secret of the human heart which is located in the chest—that is where the illumination of the Mercies and Harsh Judgments, which issue forth from *Yesod* (Foundation), stop. Accordingly, it is necessary for an individual to strike his heart completely to signify that he is causing the Mercies to ascend from the hidden place. . . . The secret of the right hand is the secret of the Mercies, as is well known, and therefore one beats with one's right hand. (*Shulhan Aruch ha-Ari* 37:32)

The next text is predicated upon the kabbalistic doctrine of *gilgul*, namely, transmigration/reincarnation.[1]

One should refrain from eating meat and drinking wine during the week, in order to avoid sinning even unintentionally. One should be particularly careful to avoid eating the heart of an animal or bird because the animal spirit resides therein. If a person eats it, then the animal spirit will adhere to him and cause stupidity and forgetfulness. Sometimes a soul transmigrates into an animal or bird and adheres to it [i.e., the heart] for the sanctuary of the soul is the heart. (*Shulhan Aruch ha-Ari* 58:9)

As the talmudic sages noted, spiritual passion is highly valued by *Ha-Shem*—"The Holy One, blessed be He, desires the heart" (*B. Sanhedrin* 106b). Maimonides expanded upon this expression: "The Merciful One desires the heart and according to the intention of the heart are all things judged" (*Iggerotav*, 23b). This is wonderfully illustrated by the classic story of the unschooled herdsman who each day would affirm that if *Ha-Shem* had any cattle, he would tend them for free. Once a scholar happened to hear this naive proclamation and decided to teach the herdsman how to pray "properly." After a time, the herdsman forgot the standard prayers, but was reticent to resume his personal affirmation, as it had been disparaged by the scholar. He therefore ceased praying altogether. One night the scholar had a dream in which he was commanded to ensure that the herdsman resume his daily proclamation.

The narrative continues:

Behold, here there is neither Torah [study] nor works [obedience to the Law], but only this, that there was one who had it in his heart to do good, and he was rewarded for it, as if

---

1. An informative discussion of this theory is found in G. Scholem, *On the Mystical Shape of the Godhead* (New York, 1991), 197–250.

this were a great thing. For [tradition teaches that] "the Merciful One desires the heart." Therefore let people think good thoughts, and let these thoughts be turned to the Holy One, blessed be He. (*Sefer Hasidim*, cited in M. Fishbane, *Judaism*, 16)

The scriptural basis for *Ha-Shem's* focus on the heart is found in the story of David's selection to replace Saul as king. Recall that Saul was originally chosen as a stop-gap measure, in response to the clamoring of the masses for a monarch. Saul's principal qualifications were his physical characteristics, "there being none of the Israelites more handsome than he; none of the people reached his shoulder" (1 Samuel 9:2). Owing to his impatience and numerous errors in judgment, Saul was a failure and eventually lost Divine support. When the prophet Samuel was sent by *Ha-Shem* to anoint one of Jesse's sons as Saul's successor, as soon as he was introduced to Eliav, the handsome and statuesque eldest son, Samuel naturally assumed that he was the chosen one.

Ha-Shem said to Samuel, "Do not look upon his appearance, nor his height, for I have rejected him; what matters is not what a man perceives, for man perceives the eyes, whereas *Ha-Shem* perceives the heart" (1 Samuel 16:7). Thus, Samuel was instructed to pass over Jesse's seven adult sons in favor of David, the youngest—a red-faced shepherd.

Not only does *Ha-Shem* focus on the heart, but the heart is portrayed as being the medium for perceiving God. Numerous poems by R. Yehudah Halevi refer to the human heart as the source of visionary experience.

> To behold Him the eye fails,
> But from my flesh He is revealed to my heart.[2]

---

2. This and related passages are cited by Elliot Wolfson, "Merkavah Traditions in Philosophical Garb," *Proceedings of the American Academy for Jewish Research* 57 (1990/1991): 225–231.

Although we assume that the mouth is the organ of speech, sincere speech is rooted in the heart. "My mouth speaks wisdom; the utterance of my heart is insightful" (Psalms 49:3). This honesty is expressed by the popular rabbinic maxim: "what comes from the heart, enters the heart."[3] The Divine response to human commitment is characterized by heartfelt reciprocity. "And they shall be My nation and I will be their God, when they return to Me with all their heart" (Jeremiah 24:7).

"Prayer is dependent upon the heart" (*Sefer Hasidim*, no. 1590). It has long been contended that the heart is the home of prayer. The connection between the heart and prayer is so strong that the talmudic Sages characterized prayer as *avodah she-be-lev* (service of the heart) (see *B. Taanit* 2a). Thus, we find that *the* prayer par excellence, the *Amidah*, is concluded with the following biblical verse: "May the words of my mouth and the meditation of my heart be acceptable to You, *Ha-Shem*, my rock and redeemer" (Psalms 19:15).

The biblical paradigm for sincerity in prayer was Samuel's mother, Hannah: "Now Hannah was speaking to her heart; only her lips moved, but her voice was not heard" (1 Samuel 1:13). R. Hamnuna asserted that this verse contains many basic regulations pertaining to ardent prayer, including the need to direct one's heart to *Ha-Shem* and praying quietly but with precision (see *B. Berachot* 31a).

The *Midrash* offers an interesting insight into the difference between Divine and human nature.

> If a human owns a vessel, as long as it is whole, he is pleased with it. As soon as it breaks, he no longer wants to see it. The

---

3. A. Hyman, *Otzar Divrei Hachamim u-Fitgameihem* (Tel Aviv, 1972), 198, notes that this maxim is not found in the *Talmud* but is nevertheless based upon the statement, "The words of a God-fearing person are accepted" (*B. Berachot* 6b).

Holy One, blessed be He, is different. If a certain object is whole, He does not want to see it. If it is broken, then He desires it. What is this object belonging to the Holy One, blessed be He?—the human heart. If the Holy One, blessed be He, sees that a person is haughty—[literally, high-hearted]—He does not want him, as is written "all the haughty are an abomination to *Ha-Shem*" (Proverbs 16:5). If he is shattered, then He says, "This is Mine"—as is written, "*Ha-Shem* is close to the broken-hearted" (Psalms 34:19). (*Midrash ha-Gadol* on Genesis 38:1)

Esteeming the brokenhearted supplicant is an important motif in Jewish spiritual literature. "Although the ancients were able to concentrate on the proper *kavvanah* (intention) that was appropriate for each context, nowadays we lack *kavvanot*—the only response is a broken heart, which is an opening for everything" (Maggid of Mezeritch, *Or ha-Emet*, 14a).

Connected with this theme is the notion of the heart as a sanctuary/altar:

An altar will I construct from my shattered heart. . . .
[T]he shards of my spirit are Your offerings.
(*Shir ha-Yichud le-Yom Rishon, Machazor Rabba*, 78)

Consider also the following from the philosophical text, "A Chapter on Happiness": "Know that the sanctuary of your heart is the sanctuary of the ark, sequestering the Tablets of the Testimony. Similarly it is sequestered in your heart and inscribed on the tablet of your heart. Thus you will see that they have said: '. . . O people who bear My Torah on their heart' (Isaiah 51:7)" (*Perakim be-Hatzlahah*, 2).

A lovely expansion of this theme constitutes a popular song based on R. Nachman's teachings:

I will build a sanctuary in my heart,
    to adorn His Glory.
In this sanctuary I will place an altar,
    for the rays of His Splendor.

> For the eternal flame,
>   I will take the fire of the Binding [of Isaac].
> For a sacrifice
>   I will offer to Him my sublime soul.

Our final selection on this topic is from R. Hayyim of Volozhin: "Each person individually is a Temple, comprising all of the worlds, but is more sacred than any of them. The heart is even more sacred still and is comparable to the Holy of Holies, as is written '[during prayer] direct your heart to the Holy of Holies' (*B. Berachot* 30a)" (*Nefesh ha-Hayyim* 309).

From the twelfth century and onwards, there was a pronounced influence of Islamic mysticism upon Sephardic Jewish spirituality.[4] This is especially true in matters of the heart, as is evidenced by the pioneering classic of this genre, R. Bahya ibn Paquda's *Duties of the Heart*. Bahya begins by noting: "Religion itself is divided into two parts. One is the knowledge of the external duties of the body and its members; the other is the internal knowledge of the secret duties of the heart" (*The Book of Direction to the Duties of the Heart*, M. Mansoor, trans., 87).

Duties is nothing less than a presentation of the stages of the Sufi *tariqa* (path) to God, using Jewish motifs. Each of its ten chapters describes another level on the spiritual quest, beginning with the unity of God, continuing with such topics as repentance and asceticism and concluding with love of God.

In justifying the study of Sufi practices, R. Avraham, the son of Maimonides, asserted: "And do not regard as unseemly our (comparison) of that to the behavior of the Sufis, because the Sufis imitate the prophets and walk in their footsteps, not the prophets in theirs"

---

4. An excellent overview of the synergy between Judaism and Sufism is Paul Fenton's introduction to his translation of Obadayah Maimonides' *Treatise of the Pool* (London, 1981), 1–71.

(Abraham Maimonides, *The High Ways to Perfection*, 2:321).

Thus, R. Avraham argued that the Sufis had preserved authentic Jewish prophetic practices and that it was worthwhile to study their behavior and thereby recover this aspect of the Jewish heritage. As we noted in Chapter 4, he even advocated specific liturgical innovations, such as kneeling during prayer and frequent bowing and hand-raising. He was nevertheless very distressed at this course of events:

> Observe then these wonderful traditions and sigh with regret over how they have been transferred from us and made their appearance among someone else than our nation and had been hidden from us, about situations like which they have said, blessed be their memory. . . . "My soul shall weep . . . because of the pride of Israel that was taken away from them and given to the nations of the world" (*B. Hagigah* 5b). (*High Ways*, 323)

Owing to this perceived affinity between Judaism and Sufi spirituality, in the early thirteenth century, several Sufi texts were paraphrased and translated from Arabic into Hebrew. One such treatise was a work by al-Ghazali, which was repackaged by R. Avraham bar Hasdai as *Moznei Tzedek* (Scales of Righteousness).

> So the Sage[5] has said, heresy begins like a black dot in the heart. This [heresy] can increase until the heart becomes totally black. Similarly, faith begins like a white dot. As faith increases so does the whiteness. If a person's faith is complete, then his heart becomes totally white. So it is written, "Even though your sins are scarlet, they can become snow-white" (Isaiah 1:18). (*Moznei Tzedek*, 81)

---

5. This was originally attributed to Ali, though in the *Hadith* literature it is attributed to Mohammed; cf. A. Schimmel, *Mystical Dimensions of Islam* (Chapel Hill, 1975), 135.

This process of cleansing the heart was rooted in biblical directives such as, "wash your heart clean of wickedness, Jerusalem, that you may be saved" (Jeremiah 4:14). Another relevant biblical formulation is the verse from *Proverbs* 27:19, "As one face [mirrors] another face in the water, so too does one heart to another heart." Heart-centered spirituality associated with water was developed by Sufism and eventually reintegrated into Jewish thought. It became the central motif of an intriguing mid-thirteenth-century spiritual text, *The Treatise of the Pool*, composed by Obadyah Maimonides, son of R. Avraham Maimonides and grandson of R. Moses Maimonides. The significance of the pool metaphor is described in some detail:

> Imagine a certain person who, possessing a very old pool, desireth to cleanse the latter of dirt and mire and to restore it. Certainly a Divine favour hath been bestowed upon him. He must therefore ensure that the pool cease to be polluted, occupying himself with its gradual cleansing until it is completely purified. Only after having ascertained that there remaineth therein no impurity can the *living waters that go forth from the House of God* flow therein, concerning which it is said, "And a source from the House of God" (Joel 4:18). The foregoing is an allegory alluding to the purification, cleansing and purging of the heart, the correction of its defects and failings and its being emptied of all but the Most High. He who accomplisheth this will comprehend invaluable notions which were hitherto hidden from him, deriving therefrom that which none else can acquire (even) after much time and with plenteous knowledge, as Solomon hath said, "above all that thou guardest keep thy heart; for out of it are the issues of life" (Proverbs 4:23). (Obadyah Maimonides, *The Treatise of the Pool*, 91)

Even in this century, there are Jews who have focused on Sufi heart-spirituality—the best-known being Samuel Lewis, the pioneer of Sufi dancing in this country. Some of his musings on the heart evoke traditional Jewish themes and include the following:

For nothing stands between God
　　and the human heart,
Nothing tarnishes the altar within the heart.
(*In the Garden*, 94)

Whereby with the opening of the heart
The heart can regain heart,
Man comes face to face with his Creator,
The soul finds its eternal resting-place,
And the purpose of existence is revealed. . . .
Within the secret confines of the heart
There lies the sacred door.
(*In the Garden*, 176)

Lewis also formulated a "meditation of the heart":

This meditation is a difficult task:
For it is not of the body, neither is it of the mind . . .
Its very simplicity is its difficulty . . .
Let us turn, in silence let us turn to the heart,
Let us seek the secret asylum of the heart,
For therein lies the city of refuge,
　　great beyond conception,
There is repose, there is salvation. . . .
Feel this love, find this love, follow this love. . . .
This is *tauba* [Ar.], this is *shuvo* [Heb.], this is repentance,
This is the Way toward Love.
(*In the Garden*, 178–179)

Having traced a history of Jewish heart-spirituality, we can now go back to the early fourteenth century and the profound meditation formulated by R. Yitzhak of Acco. His kabbalistic commentary on the Torah is essentially a super-commentary on Ramban's famous Torah commentary. *Deuteronomy* 11:22 ends, "to love *Ha-Shem*, your God, to walk in His ways and to attach yourself to Him." In discussing this verse, Ramban wrote, "You should remember *Ha-Shem* always, and your love should never be removed from your thoughts." These comments served as a catalyst for R. Yitzhak of Acco's meditative technique.

I, Yitzhak the youth, the son of Rabbi Shmuel, may the Compassionate One guard him, from Acco, may it be rebuilt and restored, say both to specially trained individuals and the general public, that one who wants to know the secret of connecting one's soul Above and attaching one's thoughts to the Supreme Master, will acquire the World to Come through this perpetual, uninterrupted thought process. *Ha-Shem* will be with you, now and in the future.

You should place the letters of the Unique Name [i.e., *YHVH*], may He be blessed, against the eyes of your mind and thought, as if they were written before you in square letters in a book. Each letter should appear infinitely large to your eyes; that is to say, when you place the letters of the Unique Name opposite your eyes, your mind's eyes should focus on them and your heart's thought should be concentrated on the *Ayn Sof* (The Infinite). Together, both your visualization and your thought should be as one. This is the true attachment as it is written, "Adhere to Him" (Deuteronomy 30:20), "and in Him you should adhere" (Deuteronomy 10:20), "and you who adhere [etc.]" (Deuteronomy 4:4).

As long as your soul is attached to *Ha-Shem*, may He be blessed, in this manner, no evil will befall you. . . . Owing to the honor of *Ha-Shem*, may He be blessed, be careful not to attach your thought to Him except in a clean place, not in dirty alleyways, nor with unclean hands, nor in a place of idolatry, etc." (*Meirat Aynayim*, 278f)

Rabbi Yitzhak stressed that this meditation is for anyone who sincerely desires to adhere to God. It can be practiced any place that is appropriate to Divine contemplation. There are two distinct, yet simultaneous concentrations. With your mind's eye, visualize the four letters of the Unique Name—*yod/hey/vav/hey/* —as if they are infinitely large. At the same time, open your heart to the *Ayn Sof*, the infinite, undefinable, and hiddenmost aspect of the Divinity.

The Four-Letter Name was viewed by the early kabbalists as the pivotal name. R. Yosef Gikatilla, who composed his classic book, *Shaarei Orah*, a few decades prior to R. Yitzhak, stated that all the other holy Names in the Torah depend on It. He compares this Name to the trunk of a tree, which possesses many branches.[6]

Or consider the early kabbalistic homily:

> After the destruction of the Temple, only the Great Name remained for them. The righteous and pious individuals and the men of good deeds would go into isolation and unify the Great Name, may He be blessed. They would light a fire in the altar place of their hearts—and with pure thought, they would unite all of the *Sefirot*: joining one to the other, progressing to the flame source, whose exaltedness is infinite. (Scholem, *Begriff*, 506)

Detailed directives on the concentration appropriate for each letter of the Ineffable Name are found in the Hasidic anthology, *Or ha-Ganuz la-Tzaddikim*:

> Concerning the topic, "I have continuously placed *Ha-Shem* before me" (Psalms 16:8) one should always visualize the Ever-Existent Name. The proper concentration is that the *yod* of the Name alludes to the attribute [*Sefirah*] of *Wisdom* that is the Source of Life, animating everything; therefore one should concentrate on the attribute of *Wisdom* animating him. This leads to the attribute of Love [corresponding to *heh*]. In the same way that a person loves his being and his life, such is the love of *Ha-Shem*. Moreover, Fear is included in Love. This is the Fear of separating, God forbid, from the source of life, which is *Ha-Shem*. The first *heh* is the attribute that fills all of the worlds encompassing the six directions of the worlds, alluded to by the *vav*. The final *heh* corresponds to *Malchut* (Sovereignty), which brings him into existence from nothingness—like the great light of the sun and the shield of *Ha-Shem* of the Hosts, radiating and bestowing upon him life and existence from the Source of Life. (*Or ha-Ganuz la-Tzaddikim*, 5)

The letters of the Name are like paths leading the mind to the palace of consciousness of the eternal

---

6. An excellent translation of this incomparable book has recently been published: Joseph Gikatilla, *Gates of Light: Shaare Orah*, trans. A. Weinstein (San Francisco, 1994).

Divine Presence. There is, however, another realm that cannot be perceived through the intellect. It is the root and source of the tree, hidden below the surface. The *Ayn Sof* can only be approached via the heart, which expands and contracts, emulating the Divine.

Two different modes: a conceptual exercise designed for the mind, and an encounter with Infinity for the heart—simultaneously, two complementary meditations, like arms reaching out to embrace the Divine that is within.

11

YICHUDIM: UNIFICATIONS

In this penultimate chapter, we shall discuss the technique of *yichudim* (unifications). In many ways, it can be seen as the culmination of the Jewish meditative tradition, owing to its widespread utilization during the Middle Ages. Themes that we have previously considered, such as focusing on Divine Names and the connection between spirituality and sexuality, are brought into sharp relief in this practice.

Many of the meditative techniques that we have discussed up to this point can be characterized as private meditations. We have also seen examples of communal practices, such as the ancient meditation connected with the *Shema*, undertaken twice daily during public prayer services. *Yichudim* (unifications) were also associated with the daily liturgy. Basically, *yichudim* entail the merging of two distinct Divine Names, which correspond to upper and lower intraDivine states, as well as male and female Divine attributes. This technique originated in the thirteenth century and was comprehensively developed in the sixteenth century. Although vestiges of it remain, it is not currently widely practiced.

The major proponent of *yichudim* was the sixteenth-century luminary R. Yitzhak Luria. In fact, much has been published on the role of *yichudim* in his mysticism.[1] Lurianic techniques are highly complex and rather convoluted. They were never intended for the general public, but solely for circles of adepts. Rather than reprising this material, we shall instead focus on the medieval kabbalists, who first formulated the technique of *yichudim*. While still challenging, this material is more accessible, yet little known. In addition to providing substantial information about the *yichudim*, the selections that we shall consider offer significant insight into the mechanics of the early *Kabbalah*.

Although various combinations of Divine Names have been used in *yichudim*, the most important is the merging of *YHVH* with *ADoNaY*, thereby yielding *YAHDVNHY*. As we mentioned in Chapter 1, the Four-Letter Name, *YHVH,* which is indicative of eternal existence, is the most sacred; therefore, it is not vocalized. Instead, it is traditional to substitute *ADoNaY* (My Master/Lord), when pronouncing the Four-Letter Name. These two Names have therefore been interconnected for millenia and the technique of *yichudim* is simply a contemplative focusing on this relationship.

Insofar as these two Names are standardly associated in the *Kabbalah* with the *Sefirot, Tiferet* (Beauty), and *Malchut* (Sovereignty), it is quite understandable that the compilation *YAHDVNHY* would be used to repre-

---

1. See the material presented by Aryeh Kaplan, *Meditation and Kabbalah* (York Beach, 1982), esp. 218–260; as well as Lawrence Fine's essay, "The Contemplative Practice of Yihudim in Lurianic Kabbalah," in *Jewish Spirituality 2*, A. Green, ed. (New York, 1987), 64–98, and the panoramic overview by R. Patai, *The Hebrew Goddess*, (Detroit, 1990), 161–201.

sent the unification of these *Sefirot*. Thus, *yichudim* are indicative of harmony in the intraDivine realm.[2]

An apt conceptualization of this process of unification is from the Baghdadi Sage R. Yosef Hayyim: "It is known that from the letters of the Name, *YHVH*, the vitality and existence of Heaven are derived, and from the letters of the name, *ADoNaY*, the vitality and existence of the earth are derived. Thus he said, "Our help is through the Name of *Ha-Shem*, who makes Heaven and earth" (Psalms 124:8)" (*Ben Ish Hai, Va-Yeira*, 19).

In another discourse, R. Yosef Hayyim explains the significance of the fact that the collated Name, *YAHDVNHY*, begins and ends with the letter *yod*. He asserts that the initial *yod* corresponds to the first letter of *Yisrael*, the exalted name that was bestowed upon the Patriarch Jacob when he wrestled with an angel (see Genesis 32:29). The final *yod*, however, corresponds to the first letter of Jacob's original name, *Yaakov*, which is derived from the Hebrew *akev* (heel), alluding to Jacob's birth, whereupon he held onto the heel of his brother Esau (see Genesis 25:26). R. Yosef Hayyim adroitly relates these two *yodim* to the ten (i.e., *yod*) *Sefirot*: "This is the aspect of *Malchut* that is the *akev* (heel) of the *Sefirot*, and is alluded to the name *Yaakov*, which has the letters *Y[od] akev*, that is to say the *yod* that stands at the heel. This is the opposite of the name *Yisrael*, which alludes to *Y[od] le-rosh* (at the beginning)" (*Ben Ish Hai*, 263f).

Although the technique of *yichudim* achieved prominence in the sixteenth century, it was first developed in the corpus of texts commonly referred to as the writings of the "Circle of Contemplation." This term was coined by Gershom Scholem, owing to the

---

2. On the liturgical use of the unification of the *Sefirot*, see L. Jacobs, *Hasidic Prayer* (New York, 1973), 140–153.

centrality of a short theosophical work, *The Book of Contemplation.*[3] It is attributed to an individual known only as R. Hammai (i.e., Seer/Contemplator). Although Scholem contended that this text originated in Provence in the twelfth century, my research into its various recensions has lead to the conclusion that it was a product of mid-thirteenth century Castile (i.e., western Spain).[4]

One of the more important treatises of the "Circle" and one which contains significant material related to *yichudim* is the *Commentary on the Four-Letter Name* (hereafter *Commentary*).[5] Towards the end of the *Commentary*, there is a discussion of four pivotal Divine Names: *YHVH, ADoNaY, YYAY* and *EHYeH*. The author asserts that by combining their letters in a specific manner their *hotamot* (seals) will be formed. These seals are said to "guide and sustain" previously formulated letter permutations derived from the opening verse of Genesis. Hence, they have a cosmological significance in that they are associated with the creation of the universe. "Now you shall mix their letters and discover their seals. How? *Y* from the Four-Letter Name which is *YHVH, A* from the name *ADoNaY, Y* from *YYAY, A* from *EHYeH*. You shall place this by itself and it will yield for you the name, *YAYA*" (Florence ms. 2:41, 200b).

In all, four new Names—*YAYA, HDYH, VNAY,* and *HYYH*—were formed by combining successive letters from each of the Divine Names. Owing to the elaborate detail of these instructions one can presume that this procedure for generating new Names was not

---

3. See G. Scholem's *Origins of the Kabbalah* (Princeton, 1987), 309–364.

4. See M. Verman, *The Books of Contemplation: Medieval Jewish Mystical Sources* (Albany, 1992).

5. This text was partially translated in J. Dan's *The Early Kabbalah* (New York, 1986), 54–56.

widely known and may have even been pioneered by this anonymous author.

It is significant that these seals, along with the permutations from Genesis are asserted to have a liturgical role. For example, *YAYA* is to be used, "when you direct your heart in prayer" (200b). A more specific liturgical usage, connected with the recitation of the *Shema*, is the following directive:

> Afterwards you should return and join and collate the four seals one against the other. They are: *YAHA, HDYH, VNAY*, and *HYYH* and your concentration should focus on this seal: "*Ha-Shem*, our God, *Ha-Shem* is one" (Deuteronomy 6:4). Guard this unity of seventeen, corresponding to good, in order that you shall know from this that everything comes from One and exists in One and returns to One. . . . Happy is he who concentrates on the perfect One who is Master of all the unities, blessed is His Name for ever. (201a)

The "unity of seventeen" presumably refers to the seventeen Hebrew letters that constitute the expression "*Ha-Shem*, our God, *Ha-Shem* is one." Additionally, this represents the *gematria*, i.e. numerical value, of *tov* (good). It is interesting that although the first of the seals, *YAHA* was derived from the initial letters of four Divine Names, it also happens to correspond exactly to the initial letters of the four words from the verse under discussion.

A further liturgical association entails the recitation of the *Amidah*, the standing prayer. "When you stand to pray and are completing each of the eighteen blessings, upon reciting each Divine Name of the blessings, concentrate your mind and remember one of these four aforementioned seals that are seals of truth. You will be answered from Heaven and your prayers will not return empty" (201a–b).

From the previous passages we see clearly that the primary function of *yichudim* in the *Commentary* is to promote contemplation during prayer.

At one point the author asserts that these four seals constitute a sixteen-letter entity, "one Name from end to beginning" (201a). Although this composite Name is not presented in the *Commentary*, it forms the crux of another work from the "Circle," entitled *This Is the Knowledge of the Blessed Creator* (hereafter, *Knowledge*). It is a brief piece which has been preserved in only two manuscripts.

Knowledge commences with a Neoplatonic discussion of the Four-Letter Name. It asserts that the four letters correspond to four *panim* (aspects), of which two are masculine and two are feminine. Together they constitute "the essence of the *shekel*, (i.e., a biblical weight), which was weighed by the Prime Mover" (Florence ms. 2:53, 23b). This peculiar use of the term "*shekel*" calls to mind both the Hebrew writings of R. Moshe de Leon and the *Zohar* itself.[6]

The text continues by depicting the primordial state as one in which the forces coexisted in "crystalline, balanced unity." Thereupon, "the masculine embraced the feminine, as it were, and the separate powers emanated from them and were formed like an embryo in an expansive womb. From them were generated the thirty-two marvellous paths of wisdom. These are *YOD HA HA*" (23b).[7]

After a brief discussion of the concept of "balanced unity," the focus shifts to the composite name *YAAYHHDYVYNAHHYY*, which is said to represent its *yichud*. This seems to be the first instance of the compilation of Divine Names referred to by the technical term, *yichud*. Eventually this becomes standard usage. Like the Four-Letter Name Itself, *YAAYHHDYVYNAHHYY* also consists of two male and two female components.

---

6. See, for example, R. Moshe de Leon's *Shekel ha-Kodesh*.

7. It should be noted that the numerical value of *YOD HA HA* is thirty-two.

The text offers a scriptural allusion to substantiate this characteristic—"a woman shall encircle a man" (Jeremiah 31:22).

It is noteworthy that in *Knowledge,* no guidance is offered as to how this name was generated. Perhaps, familiarity with the instructions in the *Commentary,* was assumed by this author. Finally, in *Knowledge,* as in the *Commentary,* the *yichud* is depicted as having a liturgical function. "You shall imagine this form during the hour of prayer. When there is no prayer do not imagine it" (Florence ms. 2:53, 23b).

As we have just seen, a fundamental element of the principle of unification in these texts is the intimate connection between spirituality and sexuality, a theme that we originally discussed in Chapter 4. The sources of this notion are surely ancient. For example, mention can be made of R. Akiva's championing of King Solomon's sensual love poems that constitute the Song of Songs, as the "Holy of Holies." "R. Akiva declared . . . "For the entire world is not as worthy as the day on which the Song of Songs was given to Israel, for all the Writings are holy, but the Song of Songs is the Holy of Holies" (*M. Yadayim* 3:5).

Even more ancient is the statuary of the Cherubs atop the ark, initially in the Mosaic Tabernacle and eventually in the First Temple. These angelic figures, representing the Divine Presence, were positioned facing each other. According to the Rabbis, they were embracing "like a man with his consort" (*B. Yoma* 54a–b, based on 1 Kings 7:36).

In an enigmatic text, *The Kabbalah of R. Meshullam the Zadokite,* which is possibly the earliest of the writings of the "Circle of Contemplation," there is an interesting discussion concerning the sexuality of the Cherubs. "*Hashmal* is the great Cherub: sometimes it is transformed into a male and sometimes into a female" (Verman, *Books of Contemplation,* 208). In a related text from the "Circle" we read: "'[Cherub, lions and palms] according to the spacing of each, and wreaths [encircling]' (1 Kings 7:36). There is in this the secret of the Cherubs: an allusion for one who understands what is written in Scripture—'male and female He created them . . . and He called their name Adam' (Genesis 5:2)" (M. Verman, *Books of Contemplation* 201).

Returning to the evolution of *yichudim*, another text from the "Circle" that is pertinent is a commentary on the *Sefirot* published by Gershom Scholem.[8] The anonymous author discusses the *Sefirot* in three distinct ways. Initially, he divides them into two groups of five each. The first group bears names indicative of intellectual capacity, such as *sechel kadmon* (Primal Intellect), whereas the second group is associated with light: for example, *or ha-bahir* (Shining Light). These terms also appear in other writings from the "Circle."

The upper *Sefirot* are then discussed in terms of kabbalistic doctrines. Finally, in the third phase the initial five *Sefirot* are associated with *shemot*, Divine Names. These involve permutations of the combination of *YHVH* and *ADoNaY: YAHDVNHY, YHNDVNHY, YNHDVNHY, HYNDVNHY* and *HHNDVNHY*. The first of these is the basic *yichud*. The next three are interrelated. *YHNDVNHY* was presumably formed by taking the final three letters of the initial combination (i.e., *NHY*) and transposing them, thereby producing the mirror image, *YHNDVNHY*. This is followed by two standard permutations of these three letters. First *YHN* is transformed into *YNHDVNHY* and then *HYNDVNHY*. If the pattern would have continued, the fifth should have read *HNYDVNHY*. It is unclear why it commences instead *HHNDVNHY*.

Although one cannot date the writings of the "Circle" with any precision—owing in part to the fact that all

---

8. G. Scholem, *Kitvei Yad ba-Kabbalah*, 204–206.

of these texts are either anonymous or pseudony-
mous—there is another, early occurrence of a *yichud*
that may be easier to pinpoint. It is found in a prayer
attributed to R. Yaakov ha-Cohen and published by
Gershom Scholem.[9] For various reasons Scholem was
somewhat hesitant to accept its authenticity; nevertheless, it is preserved in a manuscript dated 1298 and is
accordingly relevant to our discussion, whoever the
author may have been.

The *Prayer* consists of numerous acrostics. One of its
stanzas focuses on the theme of Divine unicity. It concludes with a proclamation concerning God's salvific
power that yields the *yichud, YAAHHDVYNHHY*. This
represents a combination of the three Names: *YHVH,
EHYeH* and *ADoNaY*; (Scholem, "*Kabbalot*," 60).

Another datable attestation is found in *Sefer ha-Ot*,
one of R. Abraham Abulafia's later works, written in
1288. Owing to Abulafia's great interest in letter permutations of Divine Names, it is somewhat surprising
that one does not find more such instances. At the end
of the second section of this prophetic work Abulafia
writes, "We want Your salvation *YAHDVNHY.*"[10] A more
interesting usage is found near the conclusion of the
book. "And happiness, joy, levity and gaiety are joined
in the heart of all that seek *Ha-Shem*, through the name
YHAVHDYHNVHYYHVH."[11] This consists of the first two
letters of the Four-Letter Name, followed by the first
letter of *ADoNaY*, then the concluding pair of Four-
Letter Name letters, followed by the second letter of

9. G. Scholem, "Kabbalot R. Yaakov ve-R. Yitzhak," *Maddaei ha-Yahadut* 2 (1927): 58–64.

10. A. Abulafia, *Sefer ha-Ot*, ed. A. Jellinek, in *Jubelschrift des H. Graetz* (Breslau, 1887), 69; cf. Vatican ms. 245, f. 20a.

11. Jellinek's edition, 75, is problematic for it divides the name thusly, *YHAVHDYHNYH YYDVD*. We have followed the reading in Vatican ms. 245, f. 56b.

ADoNaY, and then the pattern repeats. It is concluded with a third reference to the Four-Letter Name.

Other pertinent material is evident in the writings of R. Yosef Gikatilla, an important late thirteenth-century figure. In his *Ginnat Egoz*, there is a sustained discussion of the esoteric implications of the *Shema* based on *gematriot*. Gikatilla writes,

> And in truth in this palace (*hechal* = 65) called *ADoNaY* (=65) the Unique Name is hidden. . . . You should know that this *hechal* contains the secret of the *yichud*. . . . Therefore you shall discover that *hechal* (=65) includes the secret of the Name, which is *YHVH* (=26), plus the secret of its explanation, which is "*YHVH echad*" [i.e., *Ha-Shem* is one = 39).[12]

This theme is repeated in Gikatilla's *Shaarei Orah*, without the numerical underpinnings stated explicitly. Gikatilla begins with the assertion that "*ADoNaY* is a *hechal* for the Name, *YHVH*." He concludes: "Accordingly there is no way to enter into the knowledge of the name, *YHVH*, except by means of *ADoNaY* . . . and this shall be a sign for you, '*YHVH* is one and His Name is one' (Zecheriah 14:9). That is to say that *YHVH* is *ADoNaY* through the reading of 'one' (*ba-keriat echad*)."[13]

The concluding statement is admittedly ambiguous; however, it is understandable in light of the *gematriot* cited above that R. Yosef Gikatilla had worked out in *Ginnat Egoz*. Thus *YHVH* can be transformed into *ADoNaY* by means of *echad* as follows: *YHVH* (26), plus *echad* (13), plus *YHVH* (26), equals *ADoNaY* (65).[14]

---

12. J. Gikatilla, *Ginnat Egoz*, "Shaar ha-Hechal" (reprint, n.d.) 14b; cf. the discussion by E. Gottlieb, *Ha-Kabbalah be-Kitvei Rabbenu Bahya ben Asher* (Jerusalem, 1970), 152f.

13. Y. Gikatilla, *Shaarei Orah*. 1, ed. Y. Ben-Shlomoh, (Jerusalem, 1981), 87.

14. Yosef Ben-Shlomoh, ibid., n. 107, offers a different explanation by interpreting the phrase *ba-keriat echad* as a simultaneous reading. "*YHVH* and *ADoNaY* are joined simultaneously

R. Moshe de Leon was a colleague of R. Yosef Gikatilla, as well as being the disseminator of the *Zohar*. In his Hebrew writings, there is evidence of *yichudim*. For example, in *Mishkan ha-Edut* there is an interesting assertion that links the unification of the Divine Names to the angelic beings that Ezekiel saw. "The mystery of the Living Creatures (*hayyot*), which are called *Hashmal*, when they are united is the mystery of *YAHDVNHY* that is known in the depths of wisdom. It is the mystery of the supernal creatures, when they are joined in one Name" (Cambridge ms., Dd. 4.2. f. 53a [29a]).

There is also a general statement on the process of unification that is found in one of the earliest strata of the *Zohar* itself. The topic is the respective roles of the priests, levites and Israelites in bringing sacrifices during the Temple period. "The essential element of the sacrificial offering is the priest's. He must concentrate on the holy Name and arrange the exalted levels and unify everything in a complete union, thereby bringing joy to the upper and lower realms, by means of his will and intention" (*Zohar Hadash, Midrash Ruth,* 82a).

To be sure, there are a number of other references to *yichudim* in the writings of R. Yosef Gikatilla, R. Moshe de Leon, and the *Zohar* proper.[15] They are, on the whole, brief and relatively sparse. The situation is very different when one considers the latest strands of the zoharic corpus: *Tikkunei Zohar* and *Raaya Mehemna.* These two substantial works were presumably composed by the same anonymous author, which would account for their interdependence. This individual

---

when the Ineffable Name is referred to by its epithet, *ADoNaY.*" Not only is this rendering grammatically problematic, but the material from *Ginnat Egoz* appears to be more to the point.

15. For additional references, see M. Verman, "The Development of Yihudim in Spanish Kabbalah," *Jerusalem Studies in Jewish Thought* 8 (1989): 32–33.

may have been a student of R. Yosef Gikatilla. Although *Tikkunei Zohar* is published as an independent work, *Raaya Mehemna* has been incorporated into the standard editions of the *Zohar*.

An examination of *Tikkunei Zohar* and *Raaya Mehemna* reveals more than a dozen discussions of *yichudim*. As *Tikkunei Zohar* (hereafter *T.Z.*) offers a richer presentation of this material, we shall use it as the basis for our analysis. The primary focus of *T.Z.'s* lengthy introduction are the interrelated themes of exile and reunification. Exile is characterized by the biblical injunction concerning trapping birds, "send the mother bird and take the chicks (*banim*)" (Deuteronomy 22:7). This is interpreted according to kabbalistic symbolism. "Mother" is associated with "Supernal *Shechinah*" (i.e., *Binah*). Furthermore, Deuteronomy 22:6 states, "don't take the mother and her *banim*." According to *T.Z.*, "*banim* are the masters of the *Kabbalah*" (1b). Among those listed as *banim* are seers and prophets. Later on, we are told that seers and prophets derive specifically from the *Sefirot*, *Netzach* and *Hod*, "for in them are included the two names that are *YAHDVNHY*, which contains eight letters corresponding to the eight prophetic books, and 'prophets' are two, yielding ten, corresponding to the ten *Sefirot*" (*T.Z.* 2a). Thus, initially the *yichud* is considered in terms of the merging of the right side of the Sefirotic superstructure, represented by *Netzah*, with the left side, *Hod*. The point of contact of these *Sefirot* is *Yesod* and, as we shall see, most discussions of *YAHDVNHY* in *T.Z.* are connected with either *Yesod* or, occasionally, *Tiferet*, its more elevated counterpart.

The discourse continues with various interpretations of the two *yodim* of the *yichud*. The first *yod* is associated with the sign of *brit milah* (covenantal circumcision, an allusion to *Yesod*), and the latter, with the sign of *Shabbat* (*T.Z.* 2a). A similar analysis connects the initial *yod* from *YHVH* with the sign of circumcision, naturally considered to be masculine, whereas the concluding *yod* from *ADoNaY* is considered to be feminine and to represent the sign of the *tefillin*.[16] An interesting complement to this is found in a subsequent discourse on the significance of the two *yodim,* based on the exegesis of Psalms 145:16 "Open your hand." "Don't read your hand (*yadecha*) but *yodecha* [i.e., your *yodim*]. This corresponds to *YY* from *YAHDVNHY*" (*T.Z.* 7b).

Another discussion of the two *yodim* focuses on the bowing that is part of the recitation of the *Amidah.* This process entails two acts: bowing and straightening up. Each of these actions engender the unification of the ten *Sefirot.* The act of bowing causes the Divine energy to flow from the upper *Sefirot* to the lower *Sefirot,* and straightening up reverses this process from below to Above. In this connection, bowing is associated with the final *yod* from *ADoNaY* and straightening up is associated with the initial *yod* of *YHVH;* (see *Tikkunim, Zohar Hadash* 115a).

Most of the expositions in *T.Z.* concerning *YAHDVNHY* are predicated on its numerical value corresponding to 91. For example, in our discussion on the role of the spine in Chapter 4, we already cited at length a passage from *T.Z.* no. 18, in which *YAHDVNHY* is associated with *AMeN* (= 91).[17] The first discourse in *T.Z.* that develops this theme focuses on the *sukkah* (festive booth/tabernacle), which likewise equals 91. Initially "Mother" (i.e., *Binah*) is compared to a *sukkah,* insofar as both shield and protect. The association of the other ritual objects

---

16. *T.Z.* 2b. Soon after, in f. 3a, the two *yodim* of *YAHDVNHY* are said to correspond to knots of the *tefillin* of the head and arm. Moreover, *YHVH* is related to the four biblical sections which constitute the *tefillin* and *ADoNaY* corresponds to their four compartments; see also f. 34b.

17. There is a source that predates *T.Z.,* which offers the basic association *amen* = 91 = *YHVH* plus *kinnuav* (Its epithets), see the *Responsum of R. Yekutiel,* cited in R. Shem Tov ibn Gaon, *Baddei Aron,* 229.

of *Sukkot* (The Feast of Booths) with the *Sefirot* continues. The three myrtle branches are said to correspond to the "Patriarchs," (i.e., *Hesed, Gevurah,* and *Tiferet*); the two willow branches represent the aforementioned "prophets," *Netzach* and *Hod*; the palm frond is connected with the "righteous one" (i.e., *Yesod*), and finally, the citron is associated with the *Shechinah*, namely *Malchut*. This totals eight, which corresponds to the eight letters of *YAHDVNHY*.[18]

This theme is further developed in the sixth homily, with a discussion of the phrase *sukkat shalom* (tabernacle of peace), which is designated by *YAHDVNHY* (*T.Z.* 22b). Here, too, *sukkah* is associated with *Binah*, and "peace" is said to correspond to *Tiferet*. This is based on the assertion that the Holy One (a Divine epithet standardly associated with *Tiferet*), exemplifies peace (*T.Z.* 3a). Moreover, the letters of the word *sukkat* can be rearranged to yield *kos t.*, namely, cup of *Tiferet*.

Another exposition based on the numerical equivalence of ninety-one follows soon after. It concerns a symbolic bird which is said to have originated from *Yesod* and hence is emblematic of the righteous. Eventually, this bird is characterized as a *malach* (i.e., angel). This celestial figure is also identified as Metatron, whose task is to elevate the "voice" of recitation of the *Shema* and the "word" of the prayer, namely, the *Amidah*. We are then informed that "voice" corresponds to *Tiferet* and "word" to *Malchut*. Finally, "he, i.e., Metatron, is a chariot for both of them in this fashion *YAHDVNHY*. Therefore *malach* [=91] yields the sum of the two names together."[19]

---

18. *T.Z.* 2b; see also *R.M.* 3:255b wherein the *gemetria* of *sukkah* is mentioned. Therein is also found a passing comment connecting *YAHDVNHY* to *Yom Kippur*.

19. *T.Z.* 2b, as well as the continuation on f. 3a. For an intricate discussion of "voice" and "word" related to both the celestial realm and *YAHDVNHY* in *R.M.*, see *Zohar* 3:228a.

There is an extended discourse in *Raaya Mehemna* section of the *Zohar* proper (hereafter *R.M.*), which is related to this material at hand. It begins with a discussion of the term *ani*, I, especially as found in Deuteronomy, Chapter 32, "I am God." *Ani* is said to refer to *ADoNaY* and, reminiscent of Gikatilla, we are told that *ADoNaY* corresponds to *hechal*. Moreover, it is related to *Gevurah* and the left side, whereas *YHVH* is said to stem from *Hesed* and the right side. "And in *Tiferet* these two Names are joined, *YAHDVNHY*" (*Zohar* 3:223a).

This is followed by an interesting analysis of the shape of the initial letter, *alef*. It is said to consist of two *yodim* divided by a *vav* (as noted in Chapter 2). This alludes to the Genesis story of the cosmic waters divided by the firmament and is stated to be represented by the mystery of *YAHDVNHY*. The first *yod* corresponds to the masculine waters and the concluding *yod* to the feminine waters. Between them are six letters (i.e., the numerical value of *vav*). Additionally, this alludes to Metatron, the six-lettered angel (*Zohar* 3:223b). Thus, in both *T.Z.* and *R.M.*, the *yichud* is associated with Metatron.

Another text from *R.M.* combines these basic elements while offering a novel interpretation of mealtime protocol as set down in *B. Berachot* 47a.

> One who breaks bread [i.e., recites the *ha-motzei* blessing in public] is not permitted to begin eating until those that are participating in the meal answer *amen*. Nor can the participants eat until the one who has broken the bread has eaten. Indeed the host breaks bread and distributes it to the participants. He does not calculate the same measure [for everyone], since it is not the custom of hosts to distribute bread evenly. To one he will give an egg size portion and to another an olive size.
>
> When they respond *amen* to the breaking of bread before the host eats, then they have joined the two measures together: the egg size and the olive size—*YAHDVNHY*. This *amen*

does not pertain to the act of eating but rather to the breaking of bread. After the two measures are joined in the *amen*, the host can eat. (*Zohar* 3:245a)

Once again, we find that *amen* (=91) is related to the unification *YAHDVNAY*, which also corresponds to 91. This time the subject matter is the breaking of bread into two distinct quantities, which are symbolically interpreted as alluding to the feminine and masculine principles. Only when they are united, by means of the proclamation "*amen*," can the bread be consumed and sustenance derived.

Returning to *T.Z.*, one finds an expansion of the liturgical function of *YAHDVNHY*. The author notes that the unification of two Divine Names takes place while standing, during the silent recitation of the *Amidah*. Therefore, "the joining of the two Names must be in silence." The four letters of *YHVH* are said to correspond to four white priestly garments, whereas the four letters of *ADoNaY* correspond to four golden garments for the queen. This discussion concludes with the assertion, "Happy is he who clothes the king and queen in the ten *Sefirot* of *Beriah*, (Creation), which are included in the name *YAHDVNHY*" (*T.Z.* 3b).

The expression "*Sefirot* of Creation" is an allusion to the kabbalistic theory of the Four (Cosmic) Worlds. The highest realm is referred to as Emanation, followed by Creation, Formation, and finally, Action. A significant statement differentiating these Four Worlds follows soon after. It is predicated upon the fact that when Ezekiel reported his vision of the Divine Chariot and the four Holy Creatures he was careful to qualify what he wrote. He continually emphasized that his characterization only resembles reality. The author of *T.Z.* writes about Ezekiel's vision.

[He saw] the image of those Creatures, but he didn't actually see the Creatures. Rather it is like a king that sends a

document with his seal and the image of the king is em-
bossed on the sealing wax. For the *Sefirot* of Emanation represent the actual image of the king. The *Sefirot* of Creation
correspond to the signet ring of the king. The *Sefirot* of
Formation represent the angels which are the Creatures,
namely the form of the seal in the wax. (*T.Z.* 4a)

From this we see that *YAHDVNHY*, which is associated
with the "*sefirot* of Creation," is like the signet ring of
the Divine king.

Another discourse in *T.Z.* that is based on numerology is connected with the word *amen*, which equals 91.
In a rather technical presentation there is the unequi-
vocal assertion that without the fear of God, even if one
has mastered the entire Mishnaic corpus, it would be
considered as if he had accomplished nothing. Moreover, the pivotal term is *emunah*, faith, which is related
to both *Binah* and *Malchut*. Their point of mediation is
Yesod, "in whom is included the two names. *Amen*
[=91]. They are *YAHDVNHY*." (*T.Z.* 5a; cf. 34b).

Whereas words whose numerical value is ninety-one
serve as the primary impetus behind many of the discussions concerning *YAHDVNHY*, another catalyst involves pairs of fours. We have already encountered this
in conjunction with the mystical significance of *tefillin*,
as well as the two sets of four garments. There is also
an interesting analysis of *Ezekiel* 1:6, which states that
each of the Creatures had four faces and four wings.
According to *T.Z.* the four faces correspond to the four
letters of *YHVH* and the four wings to *ADoNaY*. When
joined together they form the union *YAHDVNHY*, which
is also referred to as *Hashmal*. Later on we read, "Anyone who is wrapped in the cloak of commandment it
is as if he has prepared a throne for the Holy One,
blessed be He and this is *YAHDVNHY*" (*T.Z.* 25b).

Finally, many of the motifs mentioned previously
are brought together in an impressive exposition in the
18th homily. It constitutes an extended analysis of the

ability of the righteous communal leader, *tzaddik*, to have his prayer heard on high. The gates of the celestial *hechal* are opened through the recitation of the start of the *Amidah*, "*ADoNaY* open my lips." Prayer and the *yichud* merge in an imaginative interpretation of a standard rabbinic maxim. According to the Rabbis, (as discussed in Chapter 4), during certain benedictions of the *Amidah* one should bow while reciting "blessed" and straighten, when reciting *YHVH* (see *B. Berachot* 12a). In *T.Z.* we read: "Bowing in the presence of *ADoNaY* is by the *tzaddik* (the righteous one) about whom it is said, "And King Solomon shall be blessed" (1 Kings 2:45). Likewise he straightens in the presence of *YHVH*. These two should be joined in this fashion, *YAHDVNHY*" (*T.Z.* 33a).

Implicit in this discussion is the ambivalence of the term *tzaddik*, which refers simultaneously to the righteous individual and is also as an epithet for *Yesod*, the sefirotic source of *ADoNaY/Malchut*.

Another segment of this discourse begins by referring to Daniel 1:4 wherein there is mention of standing in the *hechal* (palace) of the king. This leads, once again, to the association of *hechal* and *ADoNaY* and a comment on standing during the *Amidah*, which commences with the name, *ADoNaY*. Another verse is introduced: "Then [*az*=8] you shall call out and God will answer" (Isa. 58:9). *Az* represents eight letters *YHVH EHYeH*. 'And God will answer'—He and His court. This is *YHVH ADoNaY, YAHDVNHY* corresponding to these eight letters" (*T.Z.* 33b; cf. 40a and 78b).

Thus, there are actually two distinct eight letter compilations. Eventually, we are informed that these combinations correspond to the median points of the structure of the *Sefirot*—in other words, those *Sefirot* that constitute the "middle line" which are seen as representing a balancing of the right and left side. The upper *Sefirot* are designated by the combination of *YHVH* and

EHYeH. This corresponds to "Father," *Hochmah*, and "Mother," *Binah*, and yields *YAHHVYHH*. Furthermore, the lower *Sefirot* are represented by *YAHDVNHY* (*T.Z.* 34b).

It is likely that this theory is behind a brief discussion in *R.M.* The starting point is the threefold reference to *YHVH* in the priestly blessing (Numbers 6:24–26). This evolves into an exposition on the relationship between three Divine Names: *EHYeh, YHVH,* and *ADoNaY,* (which calls to mind R. Yaakov ha-Cohen's *Prayer*). The "middle pillar" of the *Sefirot* is said to be represented by the combination *YAHDVNHY*, whereas *Malchut* is designated by a *yichud*, which commences with the letters *AY*. Unfortunately the textual transmission of this passage is faulty and various versions are offered. Of the possible readings, the only one that is readily understandable is *AYDHVNHY*, deriving from *ADoNaY* and *YHVH* (*Zohar* 3:146b).

Returning to *T.Z.*, the discourse continues by bringing together strands from previous sections concerning the celestial entity, *Hashmal*. Using the standard rabbinic etymology that *Hashmal* is a composite for periodic silence and speech,[20] mention is made of two types of prayer—seated, vocal prayer and standing, silent prayer. This fits very well with the earlier differentiation of the "voice" of the *Shema* and the "word" of the *Amidah* (*T.Z.* 34b).

An expansion of this twofold, liturgical theme is found in *R.M.* wherein the process of unification is depicted as being two-directional. *YHVH* is associated with the mouth and *ADoNaY* with the heart.

And when *YHVH* descends to the heart towards *ADoNaY* judgment is joined with mercy in the heart, which is *YAHDVNHY*. And when *ADoNaY* ascends to the mouth, namely "*ADoNaY*

---

20. *B. Hagigah* 13b; cf. *R.M.*, 3:228a.

open my lips" to meet *YHVH* in the mouth to join there the two names in one union *YAHDVNHY YAHDVNHY*, just like they are joined in the heart. (*Zohar* 3:235b)

In conclusion, we have seen that the concept of unification of Divine Names, especially *YHVH* and *AdoNaY*, was quite prevalent in Spanish *Kabbalah* in the latter half of the thirteenth century. It received its initial formulation in the writings of the "Circle of Contemplation" and eventually was adopted among others, by R. Yosef Gikatilla, the author of the *Zohar* and the author of *T.Z.* and *R.M.*

The earlier sources refer to *yichudim* in a rather limited fashion. It is only in the *T.Z.* and *R. M.* that we find elaborate discussions of this concept. In the lengthy introduction to *T.Z.*, in particular, *yichudim* function as a central motif forming the basis of many of the discourses. The creativity of *T.Z.* is evident in the way the author exploited and embellished upon the work of his predecessors. It was R. Yosef Gikatilla and his predilection for numerology that acted as a model. In *T.Z.* the numerical correspondence between *YAHDVNHY* (=91) and *sukkah, malach* and *amen* all form the basis of extended discussions. Other discourses are rooted in the number eight, corresponding to the eight letters of the *yichud*, or two sets of four, representing the two, Four-Letter Names. Additionally, there is a predominant concern with the celestial realm, especially as depicted in Ezekiel's vision and its rabbinic interpretation. Within this context the angel Metatron plays an important role. Finally, from the earliest source and onwards, these *yichudim* were used primarily to promote contemplation of the Divinity during prayer.

May we all merit participating in the ultimate unification at the End of Days.

12

CONCLUSION

The primary goal of this book has been to familiarize you with the richness and incredible diversity of traditional Jewish meditative practices. To this end, we have presented and discussed myriad texts on topics as diverse as visualizing the Divine Name, martyrdom, candle gazing, and chanting. It is my assumption that even if you do not readily connect with everything offered herein, hopefully, some of this material will resonate with each of you.

The material that we have considered has been drawn from the cornucopia of the Jewish spiritual heritage. I have always attempted to provide faithful and intelligible translations of the original texts. We have seen that the foundation of Jewish spirituality in general, and Jewish meditation in particular, is the Hebrew Scriptures; accordingly, we have focused on specific biblical figures and seminal passages. To be sure, much of our discussion concentrated on standard kabbalistic and hasidic sources, such as the *Zohar* and the writings of R. Nachman of Bratzlav.

There has also been a conscious effort to extend the scope of discourse beyond what one normally finds in a treatment of this topic. Striving for breadth, our purview has spanned more than three thousand years of sources—from the Hebrew Scriptures and the ancient philosopher Philo to the modern Israeli meditative group known as the *Hugei Argaman*. Inclusivity has likewise been an important goal. There are various constituencies that have been hitherto neglected in contemporary accounts of Jewish meditation. We have demonstrated that relevant material is also found outside of mystical writings; therefore, we frequently quoted poetry, philosophy and standard halachic works. We also began to mine the rich Sephardic heritage, by extensively citing the late nineteenth-century Baghdadi Sage, R. Yosef Hayyim.

We have likewise demonstrated that Jewish spirituality, and Jewish religious expression in general, are a dynamic and evolving phenomenon. Occasionally, one finds evidence of an openness and receptivity to external influences. While this may be problematic for some, nevertheless, in cases, such as the impact of Sufism on Jewish heart-spirituality (as presented in Chapter 10), the evidence is irrefutable.

Gender issues were also directly addressed: both the theme of feminine aspects of the Divine Being, as well as the participation of women in Jewish spirituality. Despite the admitted paucity of material pertaining to this latter topic; nevertheless, we highlighted the involvement of women in the ancient sect of the Therapeutae, as well as the personal spirituality of modern Jewish women, exemplified by the poignant diary of Etty Hillesum and the evocative poetry of Leah Goldberg.

We shall conclude by referring to the previous chapter, which was devoted to a detailed survey of texts describing the intricate meditative technique of *yichu-*

dim (unifications). Owing to the complexity of this material, it is possible to become so involved in the process that one loses sight of what is really important. This point was addressed by the twentieth-century luminary, R. Hillel Zeitlin in a paternal warning to his disciples:

> You are mistaken concerning the *yichudim*, since you still think—as many presume—that the *yichudim* are essentially a matter of concentrating and combining supernal lights, to which the letters allude. This is not truly the case. To be sure, one must undertake the proper concentrations and combinations while engaged in the *yichudim*, but it is necessary to first establish the greatness, valor and radiance of the holiness of the soul of the person who is undertaking these unifications. . . . [N]ew supernal lights will descend below, only by means of souls who have become enlightened by the light of Emanation and girded by Divine valor. These are united in holiness and purity, in order that all the residents of the world will become enlightened with the light of Wisdom, Understanding and Knowledge. (*Sifran Shel Yechidim*, 41)

R. Zeitlin's comments can likewise be applied to any of the practices that have been presented in this book. Although each of the techniques described herein has theoretical and practical aspects; nevertheless, you should not become so preoccupied with the mechanics of meditation that you neglect what is essential: striving for holiness and integrity in the service of *Ha-Shem*.

GLOSSARY

Adonay—"My Lord," a Divine epithet.

Amidah—The "Standing Prayer," also called the *Shemoneh Esreh* ("The Eighteen [Blessings]").

Ayn Sof—The "Infinite" and incomprehensible aspect of *Ha-Shem*, which transcends the *Sefirot*.

Binah—"Understanding," the third of the *Sefirot*.

Birkat Ha-Mazon—"Blessing of food," namely, grace after meals.

Devekut—"Attachment" to *Ha-Shem*.

Echad—"One."

Elohim—God.

Gematria (pl. Gematriot)—Numerology, whereby each letter of a word is considered according to its numerical significance.

Gevurah—"Power," the fifth of the *Sefirot*.

Haftorah—*Shabbat* scriptural reading from the Prophets.

Halachah—Jewish religious law.

Ha-Shem—"The Name"—a substitution for the sacred and unutterable Four-Letter Name of God.

Hasid (pl. Hasidim)—a pious individual, especially a follower of a *tzaddik*.

Hasidei Ashkenaz—"German pietists," a medieval spiritual movement.

Havdalah—"Separation," the ritual that concludes *Shabbat*.

Haver (pl. Haverim)—colleague/companion.

Hechalot—"Celestial Palaces/Temples."

Hesed—"Compassion," the fourth of the *Sefirot*.

Hitbodedut—"Self-isolation" or meditation. Social and spiritual introspection and communion with *Ha-Shem*.

Hochmah—"Wisdom," the second of the *Sefirot*.

Hod—"Majesty," the eighth of the *Sefirot*.

Kabbalah—"Received Tradition"; synonymous with Jewish mysticism.

Kabbalat Shabbat—"Receiving *Shabbat*," the prayer service that ushers in *Shabbat*.

Kavvanah (pl. Kavvanot)—Concentration upon *Ha-Shem*, while praying or performing any religious activity.

Keter—"Crown," the first or highest of the ten *Sefirot*.

Kiddush Ha-Shem—"Sanctification of the Name," or martyrdom.

Lulav—A palm branch, which is waved on *Sukkot*.

Luz—Spinal tailbone.

Maariv—The daily Evening Prayer Service.

Malchut—"Sovereignty," the tenth of the *Sefirot*—equated with the *Shechinah*.

Merkavah—The celestial "Chariot" described in Ezekiel, Chapter 1.

Mezuzah (pl. Mezuzot)—Doorpost amulet.

Midrash—Classical rabbinic biblical interpretation.

Minchah—The Afternoon Prayer Service.

Mishkan—The biblical Tabernacle.

Mishnah—The first authoritative rabbinic law code, compiled in 200 C.E. by R. Judah the Prince.

Mitzvah (pl. Mitzvot)—any of the 613 biblical commandments.

Nefesh—Soul.

Nefillat Appayim—"Prostration" prayer; see *Tachanun*.

Neshamah—Soul.

Netzach—"Victory," the seventh of the *Sefirot*.

Niggun (pl. Niggunim)—Hasidic wordless melodies.

Rosh Ha-Shanah—New Year.

Ruach—"Wind/spirit." One of the levels of the soul.

Sefirah (pl. **Sefirot**)—the ten intraDivine states or attributes that constitute the primary doctrine of the *Kabbalah.*

Shacharit—The Morning Prayer Service.

Shaddai—"Almighty," a Divine Name.

Shechinah—"The Divine In-Dwelling," usually characterized as a feminine force.

Shema—The biblical affirmation of faith that begins: "Hear, Israel." (Deuteronomy 6:4).

Shiviti—"I have placed," referring to a type of amulet/plaque.

Shulhan Aruch—The classic sixteenth-century Jewish law code compiled by R. Yosef Karo.

Siddur—The traditional Jewish prayer book.

Sukkot—Tabernacles, referring to the autumnal festival of booths.

Tachanun—"Petition"; see *Nefillat Appayim.*

Tallit (Tallis)—"Prayer shawl," on whose corners are attached the ritual fringes (*tzitzit*).

Talmud—The vast body of classical rabbinic literature, consisting of the *Mishnah* and subsequent commentaries.

Tanach—An acronym for the Hebrew Scriptures and their three parts: *Torah* (the five books of Moses), *Neviim* (Prophets), and *Ketuvim* (miscellaneous writings).

Targum—"Translation" of the Hebrew Scriptures into Aramaic.

Tashlich—"Casting," a ritual performed alongside a body of water on Rosh Ha-Shanah.

Tefillin—"Phylacteries," biblically mandated prayer objects consisting of two leather casings that contain scriptural passages and are worn on the head and arm during the daily Morning Prayer Service.

Teshuvah—"Return" or repentance.

Tiferet—"Beauty," the sixth of the *Sefirot.*

Tikkun—"Restoration."

Tikkun Hatzot—The midnight prayer vigil.

Torah—"Instruction": referring to the Five Books of Moses and by extension any authoritative Jewish teaching.

Tzaddik (pl. **Tzaddikim**)—"A righteous person," used as a designation for the charismatic leader of a hasidic group.

Tzitzit—"Fringes"; see **Tallit.**
Yeshivah—A rabbinical seminary.
Yesod—"Pillar/Foundation," the ninth of the *Sefirot.*
YHVH—The sacrosanct Four-Letter Name of God.
Yihud (pl. **Yihudim**)—"Unification," a meditative technique.
Yom Kippur—Day of Atonement.
Zemirot—"Songs," especially those sung on *Shabbat.*

Selected Bibliography

Sources in English

Bahya ibn Pakuda. *The Book of Direction to the Duties of the Heart.* Trans. Menahem Mansoor. London, 1973.

Ben-Amos, Dan, and Jerome Mintz, trans. *In Praise of the Baal Shem Tov.* New York, 1970.

Bension, Ariel. *The Zohar in Moslem and Christian Spain.* London, 1932. Repr. New York, 1974.

Bergman, Samuel. *Faith and Reason.* New York, 1961.

Bos, Gerrit. "Hayyim Vital's Practical Kabbalah and Alchemy." *Journal of Jewish Thought and Philosophy* 4 (1994).

Buber, Martin. *I and Thou.* Trans. W. Kaufman. New York, 1970.

Buxbaum, Yitzchak. *Jewish Spiritual Practices.* Northvale, NJ, 1990.

Charlesworth, James, ed. *The Old Testament Pseudepigrapha.* Garden City, NY, 1983.

The Complete ArtScroll Machzor. New York, 1990.

The Complete ArtScroll Siddur. Brooklyn, NY, 1986.

Dan, Joseph. *The Early Kabbalah.* New York, 1986.

Dov Baer of Lubavitch. *On Ecstasy*. Trans. Louis Jacobs. Chappaqua, NY, 1982–1983.

Englander, Lawrence, with Basser, Herbert. *The Mystical Study of Ruth*. Atlanta, 1993.

Fine, Lawrence. "The Contemplative Practice of Yihudim in Lurianic Kabbalah." In *Jewish Spirituality*, ed. Arthur Green, vol. 2, 64–98. New York, 1987.

Fishbane, Michael. *Judaism*. San Francisco, 1987.

Gikatilla, Joseph. *Gates of Light: Shaare Orah*. Trans. Avi Weinstein. San Francisco, 1994.

Giller, Pinchas. *The Enlightened Will Shine*. Albany, NY, 1993.

Ginzberg, Louis. *The Legends of the Jews*. Philadelphia, 1968.

Glatzer, Nahum. *The Judaic Tradition*. New York, 1969.

Gordon, Aharon David. *Selected Essays*. Trans. F. Burnce. New York, 1938.

Hillesum, Etty. *An Interrupted Life*. New York, 1983.

Idel, Moshe. *The Mystical Experience in Abraham Abulafia*. Albany, NY, 1988.

———. *Studies in Ecstatic Kabbalah*. Albany, NY, 1988.

Jacobs, Louis. *Hasidic Prayer*. New York, 1978.

———. *Jewish Mystical Testimonies*. New York, 1977.

Kaplan, Aryeh. *Meditation and the Bible*. York Beach, 1978.

———. *The Bahir*. York Beach, 1979.

———. *Meditation and Kabbalah*. York Beach, 1982.

Lewis, Samuel. *In the Garden*. New York, 1975.

Maimonides, Abraham. *The High Ways to Perfection*. Trans. S. Rosenblatt. Baltimore, 1938.

Maimonides, Moses. *Guide of the Perplexed*. Trans. S. Pines. Chicago, 1963.

Maimonides, Obadayah. *Treatise of the Pool*. Trans. P. Fenton. London, 1981.

Matt, Daniel. *Zohar: The Book of Enlightenment*. New York, 1983.

The New English Bible with the Apocrypha. New York, 1972.

Patai, Raphael. *The Hebrew Goddess*. Detroit, 1990.

Philo. Trans. F. H Colson. London, 1958.

Robinson, Ira. *Moses Cordovero's Introduction to Kabbalah: An Annotated Translation of His Or Neerav*. New York, 1994.

Schimmel, Annemarie. *Mystical Dimensions of Islam*. Chapel Hill, 1975.

Scholem, Gershom. *On the Kabbalah and Its Symbolism*. New York, 1969.

——. *Major Trends in Jewish Mysticism.* New York, 1972.

——. *Sabbatai Sevi.* Princeton, NJ, 1973.

——. *Origins of the Kabbalah.* Princeton, NJ, 1987.

——. "Der Begriff der Kawwana in der alten Kabbalah." In *MGWJ* 78 (1934). Repr. as "The Concept of Kavvanah in the Early Kabbalah." In *Studies in Jewish Thought*, ed. Alfred Jospe. Detroit, 1981.

——. *On the Mystical Shape of the Godhead.* New York, 1991.

Schrire, Theodore. *Hebrew Magic Amulets.* New York, 1982.

Sefer Ha-Razim. Trans. M. Morgan. Chicago, 1983.

Spiegel, Shalom. *The Last Trial.* New York, 1969.

Umansky, Ellen and Ashton, Dianne, eds. *Four Centuries of Jewish Women's Spirituality.* Boston, 1992.

Verman, Mark. "Panentheism and Acosmism in the Kabbalah." *Studia Mystica* 10:2 (1987).

——. "The Development of Yihudim in Spanish Kabbalah." *Jerusalem Studies in Jewish Thought* 8 (1989).

——. *The Books of Contemplation: Medieval Jewish Mystical Sources.* Albany, NY, 1992.

Weiss, Joseph. *Studies in Eastern European Jewish Mysticism.* Oxford, 1985.

Werblowsky, R. J. Zwi. *Joseph Karo: Lawyer and Mystic.* Philadelphia, 1977.

Wieder, Naftali. *Islamic Influences on the Jewish Worship.* Oxford, 1947

Wiesel, Elie. *Night.* Toronto, 1986.

Winston, David, trans. *Philo of Alexandria.* New York, 1981.

Wolfson, Elliot. "Circumcision and the Divine Name." *Jewish Quarterly Review* 78 (1987).

——. "Merkavah Traditions in Philosophical Garb." In *Proceedings of the American Academy for Jewish Research* 57 (1990/91).

Wurzberger, Walter. *Ethics of Responsibility.* Philadelphia, 1994.

Sources in Hebrew

Al Gevul Shnei Olamot. R. Hillel Zeitlin. Tel Aviv, 1965.

Ben Ish Hai. R. Yosef Hayyim. Jerusalem, 1994.

Ben Porat Yosef. R. Yaakov Yosef of Polnoyye. New York, 1976.

Daat Hochmah. R. Moshe Luzzatto. Jerusalem, 1961.

Degel Machaneh Ephraim. R. Moshe Hayyim Ephraim of Sudylkow. Israel, 1983.

Emet le-Yaakov. R. Yaakov Kamenetzky. New York, 1991.

Ha-Kabbalah be-Kitvei Rabbenu Bahya ben Asher. Ephraim Gottlieb. Jerusalem, 1970.

Ha-Shirah ha-Ivrit be-Sefarad uv-Perovans. Hayyim Schirmann. Jerusalem, 1961.

Hayyei Moharan. R. Nachman of Bratzlav. Jerusalem, 1985.

Hechalot Zutarti. Ed. Rachel Elior. Jerusalem, 1982.

Hemdat Yamim. Facsimile ed. Constantinople, 1763.

Hesed le-Avraham. R. Avraham Azulai. Lemberg [Lvov], 1863. Repr. Israel, 1968.

Hochmat ha-Nefesh. R. Eleazer b. Judah. Bnei Brak, 1987.

Hovat ha-Talmidim. R. Kalonymus Kalmish Peasetzna. Warsaw. Repr. Israel, n.d.

Iggeratov. R. Moshe b. Maimon. Leipzig, 1865.

In Di Getzelten fun Habad. M. Indritz. Chicago, 1927.

Kav ha-Yashar. R. Tzevi Hirsh Kaidanover. N.p., n.d.

Kerem Yisrael. Lubin, 1930.

Ketavim Hadashim le-Rabbenu Hayyim Vital. R. Hayyim Vital. Jerusalem, 1988.

Keter Shem Tov. R. Aharon ha-Kohen. Brooklyn, NY, 1987.

Kitvei Ramban. R. Moshe b. Nachman. Jerusalem, 1963.

KL"CH Pitchei Hochmah. R. Moshe Hayyim Luzzatto. Jerusalem, 1961.

Likkutei Moharan. R. Nachman of Bratzlav. New York, 1980.

Likkutey Yekarim. Lemberg [Lvov}, 1863.

Magen Avot. R. Shlomoh Zalman of Kopust. Berdichev, 1902.

Maggid Devarav le-Yaakov. R. Dov Baer of Mezeritch. Ed. Rivkah Shatz. Jerusalem, 1976.

Maggid Mesharim. R. Yosef Karo. Jerusalem, 1970.

Machazor Rabba. Jerusalem, n.d.

Megillat Amrafel. R. Avraham b. Eliezer Halevi. Ed. G. Scholem, *Kiryat Sefer* 7 (1930–1931).

Meirat Aynayim. R. Yitzhak of Acco. Jerusalem, 1975.

——. Ed. Amos Goldreich. Jerusalem, 1981.

Meor va-Shemesh. R. Kalonymus Kalman Epstein. Jerusalem, 1987.

Midrash Pinchas. R. Pinchas of Koretz. Tel Aviv, 1980.

Midrash Tanchuma. Jerusalem, 1970.

Mukdam u-Meuchar. Leah Goldberg. Tel Aviv, 1968.

"*Natan Adler . . .*" Rachel Elior. *Tzion* 59:1 (1994).

Nefesh ha-Hayyim. R. Hayyim of Volozhin. Bnei Brak, 1989.

Noam Elimelech. R. Elimelech of Lizhensk. Jerusalem, 1960.

Or ha-Emet. R. Dov Baer of Mezeritch. Brooklyn, NY, 1960.

Or ha-Ganuz. Martin Buber. Jerusalem, 1958.

Or ha-Ganuz [la-Tzaddikim]. R. Aharon ha-Kohen. Jerusalem, 1966.

Otzar Divrei Hachamin u-Fitgameihem. Aaron Hyman. Tel Aviv, 1972.

Pardes Rimmonim. R. Moshe Cordovero. Jerusalem, 1962.

Perakim be-Hatzlahah. Meyuchas le-Rambam. Jerusalem, 1939.

Perush ha-Torah le-Rabbenu Avraham. R. Avraham b. Maimonides. London, 1958.

Reshit Hochmah ha-Shalem. R. Eliahu de Vidas. Jerusalem, 1980.

Sefer Bahir. Jerusalem, 1975.

"*Sefer ha-Ot.*" R. Avraham Abulafia. Ed. Adolf Jellinek. In *Jubelschrift des Heinrich Graetz.* Breslau, 1887.

Sefer Haredim. R. Eleazer Azikri. Jerusalem, 1984.

Sefer ha-Semak me-Zurich. R. Yitzhak of Corbeil. Ed. R. Yitzhak Rozenberg. Jerusalem, 1973.

Sefer Hasidim. Ed. J. Wistinetzki. Berlin, 1891.

Sefer ha-Yashar. Jerusalem, 1967.

Shaarei Orah. R. Yosef Gikatilla. Ed. Yosef Ben Shlomoh. Jerusalem, 1981.

Shaar ha-Gilgulim. R. Hayyim Vital. Jerusalem, 1981.

Shaar le-Sodot ha-Hitbonenut. Jerusalem, 1981.

"*Shirat ha-Rav.*" Avraham Habermann. *Sinai* 17 (1945).

Shirim Nivcharim. R. Yehudah Halevi. Jerusalem, 1950.

Shivhei ha-Besht. Ed. Avraham Rubinstein. Jerusalem, 1991.

Shnei Luhot ha-Brit. R. Yeshayahu Horowitz. Israel, n.d.

Shoshan Sodot. Koretz, 1784.

Shulhan Aruch ha-Ari. R. Yizhak Luria. Munkacs, 1940.

Sichot ha-Ran. R. Nachman of Bratzlav. Bnei Brak, n.d.

Siddur Rinnat Yisrael. Jerusalem, 1982.

Sidrei de-Shimusha Rabba. Ed. Gershom Scholem. Tarbitz 16 (1945).

Sifran Shel Yechidim. R. Hillel Zeitlin. Jerusalem, 1979.

"Sulam ha-Aliyah. Perek Tet." R. Yehudah al-Botini. Ed. Gershom Scholem. *Kiryat Sefer* 22 (1945).

"Sulam ha-Aliyah. Perek Yod." R. Yehudah al-Botini. In *Kitvei Yad ba-Kabbalah*, ed. Gershom Scholem. Jerusalem, 1930.

Taamei ha-Minhagim. R. Avraham Sperling. Jerusalem, n.d.

Tefillah le-Moshe. R. Hirsh of Zidaczow. Lemberg [Lvov], 1856.

Tekstim be-Torah ha-Elohut. Ed. Yosef Dan. Jerusalem, 1977.

Torat ha-Maggid. Maggid of Mezeritch. Ed. Yisrael Klafholtz. Bnei Brak, 1976.

Torat Moshe. R. Moshe Alshech. Israel, 1970.

Tzeror ha-Mor. R. Avraham Saba. Brooklyn, NY, 1961.

Tzevvaot Ve-Hanhagot. Ed. R. Yaakov Weintraub. Bnei Brak, 1987.

Zemirot Shabbat. Jerusalem, 1985.

CREDITS

The author gratefully acknowledges permission to reprint from the following sources:

Philo of Alexandria, by David Winston. Copyright © 1981 David Winston. Used by permission of Paulist Press.

In the Garden, by Samuel L. Lewis. Copyright © 1975 the Lama Foundation. Used by permission of the Sufi Islamia Ruhaniat Society.

Portions of chapters 5, 6, 8, 9, and 10 were revised from essays by Mark Verman that originally appeared in *Four Worlds Journal* 1, 2, 3 (1984–1985). Copyright © 1984–1985 *Four Worlds Journal*. Used by permission.

A portion of chapter 9 was revised from an essay by Mark Verman that originally appeared in *Studia Mystica* 8:3 (1985). Copyright © 1985 The Foundation, California State University, Sacramento. Used by permission.

Chapter 11 was revised from an essay by Mark Verman that originally appeared in *Jerusalem Studies*

INDEX

About the Author

Mark Verman is currently a visiting professor and director of Judaic Studies at Carleton College. He received rabbinical ordination in 1974 from Rabbi Gedalyah Felder, *z"l*. His academic degrees include a masters degree in medieval studies from the University of Toronto and a doctorate from Harvard University, specializing in kabbalistic literature. Among his publications are *The Books of Contemplation: Medieval Jewish Mystical Sources* and some fifty journal articles and reviews, including the entry on Jewish meditation for *The Oxford Dictionary of the Jewish Religion*. Since 1980 he has taught courses and workshops throughout the country in Jewish mysticism and meditation. Dr. Verman and his wife, Dr. Shulamit H. Adler, reside in Minneapolis.